Balkan Yearbook of European and International Law

Volume 2024

The Balkan Yearbook of European and International Law publishes peer-reviewed scholarly articles, notes, comments and book reviews on private and public European and International Law. The yearbook contains summaries and analyses of recent decisions by national and international courts and arbitral or other tribunals. The yearbook has one section with a special hot topic or focus as well as sections about European and international law in each volume. Moreover, it presents book reviews to recent publications from the region or with a major impact for the region. The yearbook focuses on recent developments of European and International Law and presents a forum for scholarly discourse on European and International Law from the perspective of the region of South-East Europe. However, the publication is not exclusive in that regard: contributions from the perspective of the wider world are also strongly encouraged and welcomed.

Zlatan Meskić • Ivana Kunda • Enis Omerović
Dušan V. Popović
Editors

Balkan Yearbook of European and International Law 2024

Springer

Editors
Zlatan Meskić
College of Law
Prince Sultan University
Riyadh, Saudi Arabia

Ivana Kunda
Faculty of Law
University of Rijeka
Rijeka, Croatia

Enis Omerović
Faculty of Law
University of Zenica
Zenica, Bosnia and Herzegovina

Dušan V. Popović
Faculty of Law
University of Belgrade
Belgrade, Serbia

ISSN 2524-8715 ISSN 2524-8723 (electronic)
Balkan Yearbook of European and International Law
ISBN 978-3-031-89954-6 ISBN 978-3-031-89952-2 (eBook)
https://doi.org/10.1007/978-3-031-89952-2

This Springer imprint is published by the registered company Springer Nature Switzerland AG
The registered company address is: Gewerbestrasse 11, 6330 Cham, Switzerland

Preface

This Yearbook's special section on *Sustainability and Law* aims to explore the evolving legal frameworks that can drive positive change toward sustainability and resilience. Once a term primarily confined to environmental discourse, sustainability has now become a global priority that impacts all facets of governance, economics, and society. The law, including domestic legislation, international treaties and soft law instruments as well as national and international case law, may play a crucial role in shaping policies that balance environmental, social, and economic considerations. Through the lens of fairness and justice, law can incentivize the transition to more sustainable models of production, consumption, and living. It can establish accountability mechanisms that ensure governments, businesses, and individuals act in alignment with long-term sustainability goals. This volume brings together perspectives primarily focused on the UN 2030 Agenda, in particular the Sustainable Development Goals (SDGs). While SDG 16 is probably most directly related to law because it is focused on the prevention and reduction of violence, the promotion of the rule of law, access to justice, the provision of effective public services, etc., other SDGs are also relevant, given that law is not only the framework for addressing immediate legal issues but also a powerful tool for shaping broader societal outcomes. Law influences how resources are allocated, how economic opportunities are distributed, and how environmental protection is enforced. For example, SDG 13 (Climate Action) requires strong legal frameworks to ensure environmental regulations are met, while SDG 5 (Gender Equality) necessitates laws that safeguard the rights of women and girls in all spheres of life. Likewise, SDG 9 (Industry, Innovation, and Infrastructure) highlights the need for legal structures that support innovation, technological advancement, and the equitable development of infrastructure. In this way, law plays a cross-cutting role, providing the necessary legal instruments, policies, and structures to advance the entire 2030 Agenda and achieve the SDGs in a balanced and integrated manner. Two papers were accepted for publication in this section, each addressing some of these key issues. The first paper in this collection analyzes the correlation between climate change and the rule of law, with a focus on SDGs 13 (Climate Action) and 16. The second paper examines SDGs in the context of International Investment Law, with particular attention to SDGs 3 (Good Health and Well-being) and 9 (Industry, Innovation, and Infrastructure).

The two permanent sections on *European Law* and *International Law* focus on recent developments in these dynamic and rapidly evolving areas, aiming to serve as a forum for scholarly discourse on these topics from a South-East European perspective. The legal systems of Southeast Europe have been in transition for over three decades and have reached various stages in different segments of transition. Following the profound political and economic changes of the early 1990s, these countries embarked on their own paths of development, sharing not only a common legal history but also continuous influences from European and international law. The impact of EU law on regional developments is particularly strong across all national legal systems in Southeast Europe. However, the extent of this influence varies, depending largely on each country's progress toward EU membership. Additionally, legal obligations under international law continue to present ongoing challenges for these countries.

The two papers in the International Law section explore significant issues such as individual criminal responsibility for autonomous weapon systems from an international law perspective, as well as developments and tendencies in case law in Slovenia and Lithuania regarding the matter of maintenance from a comparative law viewpoint. The European Law section offers insight into a diverse range of topics, including the discussion related to the EU Succession Regulation and the CJEU Judgment C-21/22, the account of the representations and warranties in M&A transactions under Bosnian law, and the analysis of novelties regarding the changes in the liability regime for internet intermediaries with respect to the user-uploaded content under the new provisions of Digital Services Act (DSA) and the Copyright in the Digital Single Market Directive (CDSMD).

Riyadh, Saudi Arabia — Zlatan Meškić
Rijeka, Croatia — Ivana Kunda
Belgrade, Serbia — Dušan V. Popović
Zenica, Bosnia and Herzegovina — Enis Omerović

Contents

Part I
Special Topic: Sustainability and Law

Combining SDGs 13 and 16: Addressing Climate Change Through the Rule of Law—Lessons from the European Court of Human Rights and the Constitutional Court of Serbia

Bojana Čučković

1 Introduction

Of the seventeen United Nations Sustainable Development Goals (SDGs) that were adopted by world leaders in 2015,[1] there are two goals that stand out for a number of reasons.

SDG 13 on climate action and SDG 16 on justice and strong institutions are both new to the UN agenda and were not recognized as global issues in 2000 when the eight Millennium Development Goals, the predecessors of the SDGs, were drafted and adopted.[2] Although the UN Millennium Declaration recognized the rule of law and its strengthening as one of the means to achieve the Millennium Development Goals,[3] the rule of law, access to justice and strong institutions have not been perceived as a global threat to the extent that they have been made a goal in their own right. On the contrary, 15 years later, climate change was given its place as a separate Goal 13 due to its qualification as an issue of global concern, while the rule

[1] Transforming our World: the 2030 Agenda for Sustainable Development, 25 September 2015, UN General Assembly Resolution, A/RES/70/1.

[2] United Nations Millennium Declaration, 8 September 2000, UN General Assembly Resolution, A/RES/55/2. For the process of drafting and adopting the MDGs and SDGs and their overall assessment, see Nanda (2016), pp. 390–407; Craciunean (2015), pp. 202–211; Diaz and Castor (2016), pp. 9–48; Fernandez (2016), pp. 49–82; Gellers and Cheatham (2019), p. 277; Lopez-Carlos et al. (2020), pp. 217–219.

[3] United Nations Millennium Declaration, 18 September 2000, UN General Assembly Resolution A/RES/55/2, pp. 3, 6, 8.

B. Čučković (✉)
University of Belgrade, Faculty of Law, Belgrade, Serbia
e-mail: cuckovic@ius.bg.ac.rs

Z. Meskić et al. (eds.), *Balkan Yearbook of European and International Law 2024*,
Balkan Yearbook of European and International Law 2024,
https://doi.org/10.1007/978-3-031-89952-2_1

of law was explicitly integrated into SDG 16 through a specific target 16.3, which emphasizes the relevance of "the rule of law at both the national and international levels and ensuring equal access to justice for all".[4] And while all the SDGs inevitably intersect, the level of achievement of SDGs 13 and 16, more than any other specific goal, will have important consequences for the success or failure of all the others.[5] SDG 5 on gender equality can serve as an example. As climate change disproportionately affects men and women, and in particular certain vulnerable groups of women, inadequate climate action will further deepen gender inequality,[6] while without access to justice and strong institutions, the preventive and remedial potential to address gender inequality will be limited. Furthermore, and most importantly for the topic of this chapter, SDGs 13 and 16 appear to be interlinked in multiple ways and to a greater extent than any other two sustainable development goals. Viewed as separate goals, SDG 13 has come under criticism for its lack of clear added value.[7] However, when used transversally with SDG 16 and its target 16.3, the added value becomes much more visible, thus potentiating SDG 16 to "enable transformative, more inclusive, equitable and effective climate action" based on the rule of law.[8]

There can be both positive and negative outcomes from the interaction between climate action and the rule of law. The rule of law can be used as a tool to strengthen climate action and to mitigate climate change, i.e. to limit both the causes and the consequences of climate change. Surprisingly, however, the rule of law can also be used to limit efforts to tackle climate change, even to serve the GHG reduction goals of other states to the detriment of a state's own climate action and environmental protection. Last but not least, failing to act on climate change will undoubtedly be catastrophic for the rule of law and may even threaten its very existence.[9]

The interaction between SDGs 13 and 16, and the respective link between climate change and the rule of law, is analysed through recent decisions of two judicial bodies—the European Court of Human Rights (ECtHR, the Court)[10] and the

---

[4] A/RES/70/1, p. 25.

[5] Some authors make pessimistic predictions that "the Sustainable Development Goals will most likely not be achieved" due to the challenges posed by climate change. Voigt (2020), p. 52. Similarly, Ladan claims that "failure to address climate change effectively will compromise the ability of countries to achieve many of the SDGs". Ladan (2018), p. 47.

[6] Čučković (2023), pp. 134–135.

[7] Kim (2016), p. 18.

[8] IDLO (2021), p. 6. Gill and Ramachandran go a step further, interpreting target 16.3 as the placement of "the judiciary as an enabler to promote the environmental rule of law and ensure equal access to justice for all". Gill and Ramachandran (2021), pp. 229–230. On the other hand, the SDG targets, in particular target 16.3 have been criticized for their language, which is "too vague to be of much use". Knox (2015), p. 529.

[9] Buser (2023), p. 595; Voigt (2020), pp. 50–51; Babie and Wawryk (2021), pp. 365–367; Carević and Novokmet (2021), p. 594; Sulyok (2024), pp. 4–5; Vásquez Torreblanca (2024), p. 85.

[10] European Court of Human Rights, Case of Verein Klimaseniorinnen Schweiz and Others v. Switzerland, Application No. 53600/20, Judgment (GC) of 9 April 2024, ECtHR website.

Constitutional Court of Serbia (CCS).[11] Curiously, both courts advanced the rule of law argument in cases that directly (ECtHR) and indirectly (CCS) addressed states' climate (in)action, albeit in contradictory ways. The contrasting approaches of the two courts will be used to assess the main hypothesis of the chapter, namely that crises of global proportions challenge the very concept of the rule of law and many of its elements, and that the rule of law can be both used and abused in the face of climate change as the most challenging problem of our time.

After the introduction (Sect. 1), the second part of the chapter will serve to briefly outline the abstract concepts of climate change and the rule of law, and to identify those elements of the rule of law that appear to be crucial for assessing the chances of successful climate action (Sect. 2). Based on the above-mentioned jurisprudence, the central part of the chapter will analyse the threefold link between the rule of law and climate action (Sect. 3). The rule of law will be examined from the perspective of its positive effects on climate action (Sect. 3.1), both as a tool for shaping and enhancing climate action within existing legal institutions and categories (Sect. 3.1.1) and through their innovative interpretation and understanding (Sect. 3.1.2). However, the rule of law will also be analysed in terms of its potential either to constrain progressive climate action (Sect. 3.2) or to be misused to serve the climate goals of other states to the detriment of the state's own climate action (Sect. 3.3). The final part of the chapter offers concluding remarks (Sect. 4).

2 Setting the Scene: Climate Change and the Rule of Law Within and Beyond Borders—Essential Elements for Assessing the Prospects of a Promising Climate Action

The latest synthesis report on climate change, prepared and published by the Intergovernmental Panel on Climate Change (IPCC), warns the international community that the current pace and scale of climate action is not sufficient to adequately address the causes and consequences of climate change. In particular, it stresses that the Paris Agreement's goal of "holding the increase in the global average temperature to well below 2 °C above pre-industrial levels and pursuing efforts to limit the temperature increase to 1.5 °C"[12] would likely not be met, not only because of the significant "gaps between global ambitions and the sum of declared national ambitions", but also "gaps between declared national ambitions and current implementation for all aspects of climate action", including mitigation and adaptation.[13]

As an issue of global concern, whose causes and consequences transcend national borders and affect present and future generations, climate change challenges the

[11] Constitutional Court of Serbia, IUo-39/2022, Decision of 11 July 2024, Official Gazette of the Republic of Serbia 59/2024.

[12] Art. 2(1)(a) of the Paris Agreement, U.N. Doc. FCCC/CP/2015/L.9/Rev/1 (Dec. 12, 2015).

[13] IPCC (2023), p. 57.

ability of law to regulate it,[14] both at the national and international levels. In doing so, it challenges the concepts of the rule of law in general and the international rule of law in particular. As Meguro rightly points out, the unprecedented challenges that climate change poses to existing legal orders go far beyond specific complex legal issues such as causality and identifying those legally responsible for climate change.[15] Rather, the question is to what extent the rule of law is capable of translating legally defined commitments into actual action, how far its role should extend in this regard, and whether there are, or should be, limits to the rule of law in addressing climate change as the most pressing issue in the global arena.

Without attempting to define the abstract and vague concepts of the rule of law and the international rule of law, this part of the chapter will attempt, on the basis of the existing literature and the relevant international instruments, to define their contours and to identify certain undisputed elements of the rule of law, both at the national and international levels, which will serve in the next part of the chapter to answer the questions posed in the previous paragraph.

Writers seem to agree that the rule of law is a highly contested principle and a difficult concept to define.[16] Legal theorists identify various characteristics that the law should meet in order to achieve its main purpose of constraining those who govern and the arbitrary use of the power they possess.[17] Thin and thick visions of the rule of law have been distinguished according to whether it is limited to criteria of the quality of rules and the processes of their enactment, or whether it also encompasses substantive issues of equality, accountability and human rights, as well as considerations of the values to which it aspires in a particular moment and place.[18] Furthermore, while authors claim that national and international rule of law cannot be equated due to their different legal natures,[19] there are also suggestions in the literature that there are common criteria for the rule of law at both levels.[20]

In order to avoid dilemmas raised by legal philosophers that go beyond the scope and purpose of this chapter, but also because the chapter discusses the rule of law in the context of target 16.3 of the UN SDGs, the elements of the concept will be determined on the basis of UN and other international instruments. These elements will also be used to assess the capacity of the international climate change regime, broadly understood, to regulate states' climate action. The United Nations defines the rule of law as "a principle of governance in which all persons, institutions and

[14] Mai (2024), p. 16.

[15] Meguro (2020), p. 933.

[16] Carlarne (2020), p. 14.

[17] Postema's recent work distinguishes between three main principles of law's rule: sovereignty, equality and fidelity. The idea of law's sovereignty is further perceived by the author through three subprinciples of exclusivity, legality and reflexivity. Postema (2022), pp. 51–77.

[18] Buser (2023), pp. 597–599; Carlarne (2020), pp. 14–16; Babie and Wawryk (2021), pp. 375–379; Keith (2015), p. 408; De Sadeleer (2024), pp. 3–14.

[19] Hurd (2014), pp. 39–40; Hurd (2015), pp. 366–367, 394.

[20] Postema (2022), pp. 307–331.

entities, public and private, including the State itself, are accountable to laws that are publicly promulgated, equally enforced and independently adjudicated, and which are consistent with international human rights norms and standards".[21] The principle also requires "measures to ensure adherence to the principles of supremacy of law, equality before the law, accountability to the law, fairness in the application of the law, separation of powers, participation in decision-making, legal certainty, avoidance of arbitrariness and procedural and legal transparency".[22] The Council of Europe's Commission for Democracy through Law has provided a more comprehensive and somewhat differently organised checklist of rule of law requirements, organised around five criteria: legality, legal certainty, prevention of abuse of power, equality before the law and access to justice.[23]

The rule of law deficit in the context of climate change is best perceived through some of the requirements mentioned above. However, the same rule of law principles have an under-exploited potential to mitigate the causes and consequences of climate change. Philippe Sands, the leading international lawyer specialising in environmental issues, asserts that "the rule of law implies the idea that human activity that has impacts on our climate system is subject to certain limitations in our rules of positive law".[24] At the level of international law, such anthropogenic impacts on the climate system are also subject to limits that states accept through their international obligations. The question, then, is not whether there is a rule of law on climate change, but what it means in practice and to what extent it is capable of achieving meaningful results.

These questions can be examined at two different levels: the role of the international rule of law in addressing the consequences of climate change beyond borders, i.e. in relations between states, and its role within borders, i.e. in relations between the state and individuals within its jurisdiction.[25]

Beyond borders, the international rule of law has the potential to limit the causes and consequences of climate change, albeit to a limited extent. When international climate law is briefly scanned through the common rule of law principles of legal bindingness/clarity, universality/equality, standing/justiciability/accountability and human rights, the results are as follows.

---

[21] Report of the UN Secretary General The rule of law and transitional justice in conflict and post-conflict societies, S/2004/616, 23 August 2004, par. 6.

[22] *Ibid.* The same definition has been recently endorsed by Ms Edite Estrela, Rapporteur of the Council of Europe Committee on Social Affairs, Health and Sustainable Development, in her Report on Climate Crisis and the Rule of Law, Doc. 15353, 26 August 2021, par. 5. Similar elements of the rule of law, although structured differently, have been outlined by non governmental organizations. For the World Justice Project's definition see Rivkin et al. (2015), pp. 150–151. The UN definition of the rule of law has also been acknowledged by the doctrine and even qualified as "common values of the international community". Carević and Novokmet (2021), p. 604.

[23] European Commission for Democracy through Law (2016), pp. 11–28.

[24] Rule of law and climate change, interview with Philippe Sands, QC and Tom Burke, co-founder and chair of E3G, 30 Jun 2021, https://www.e3g.org/news/lcaw-rule-of-law-and-climate/.

[25] Čučković (2024), p. 460.

The vast majority of states have agreed to be bound by international climate change treaties (United Nations Framework Convention on Climate Change[26] and the Paris Agreement), thereby accepting obligations to mitigate and adapt to the consequences of climate change. However, the obligations set out in these treaties are rather abstract, imprecise and leave ample room for evasion, while there are no effective or binding mechanisms to monitor the compliance of states parties with the obligations they have chosen to undertake. These two features of the international climate change regime are sufficient to illustrate the limits of the international rule of law to achieve its purpose of constraining the power of states and opening up the exercise of state power to scrutiny and control, as well as of ensuring confidence that every State party to the said climate regime will play its part. This is all the more important when we consider that the impact of climate change varies greatly from one country to another and that some countries, such as small island states, are far more vulnerable than others.

However, other international legal mechanisms available outside the climate change treaty regime have recently been used to further elaborate on the international legal obligations of states to ensure the protection of the climate system and to define the legal consequences for states that fail to comply with these obligations, thus complementing the universal climate change regime. The International Tribunal for the Law of the Sea issued an advisory opinion on 24 May 2024,[27] while advisory proceedings are still pending before two other international courts—the International Court of Justice[28] and the Inter-American Court of Human Rights.[29]

These developments show that alternative avenues are being explored to bring climate issues before international judicial bodies, with important implications for the clarity and precision of international climate treaties and other sources of international law relevant to climate change, as well as for the inter-state obligations of states, thereby contributing to the strengthening of rule of law principles beyond borders. They also confirm the tendency to make international climate law as coherent as possible, to integrate it as much as possible into general rules and principles of international law, and to combine and complement international obligations of a universal nature with those specific to particular subcommunities and regions.

On the other hand, and as an example of the latter remark, the international rule of law has been engaged to address climate change harms within borders, i.e. intrastate

[26] United Nations Framework Convention on Climate Change, United Nations Treaty Series, Vol. 1771, p. 107.

[27] International Tribunal for the Law of the Sea (2024) Advisory Opinion upon Request Submitted by the Commission of Small Island States on Climate Change and International Law, 21 May 2024, ITLOS website.

[28] International Court of Justice, Obligations of States in Respect of Climate Change, Request for Advisory Opinion, 12 April 2023, ICJ website.

[29] Inter-American Court of Human Rights, Request for an advisory opinion on the Climate Emergency and Human Rights submitted by the Republic of Colombia and the Republic of Chile, 9 January 2023, IACtHR website.

matters between states and individuals. National climate change litigation has been on the agenda in several states for a number of years,[30] relying on international rules of law with varying degrees of success,[31] while recently the European Court of Human Rights issued its first ever judgment on climate change. The judgment is an important development for climate change law in a number of respects, as will be thoroughly analyzed in the next section of the chapter. However, the 'within borders' or 'intrastate' aspect of the international rule of law deserves three remarks at this point.

Firstly, although the conclusions of the ECtHR, as will be explained, are undoubtedly significant and can be described as a breakthrough in the international settlement of climate change disputes, their scope is limited to the regional European Convention system, leaving all those outside this system without such a level of legal protection. It remains to be seen whether the standing of the ECtHR will influence other international, regional and national courts to follow the same or similar path, thus making the protection of the law available to a wider public. However, reaching universality is surely out of the question.

Secondly, the fact that international mechanisms are available to individuals if they are not satisfied with the decisions of national authorities also confirms the existence of an international rule of law within borders, at least for states parties to specific, most significantly human rights, legal regimes. If an international court or body finds that the state within its borders has failed to act in accordance with its international obligations, the state will be obliged to remedy the consequences of its acts or omissions in the case of an international court decision, or at least to consider acting in accordance with the decision in the case of an international quasi-judicial body. In this way, international law not only serves as a corrective mechanism with respect to the national legal system, but also, through its mechanisms, has means to govern those who govern by national law, an important element of the rule of law.

Third, and most importantly, the ECtHR's recent active engagement in climate cases has brought the issue of climate change into the context of human rights, thus using the potential of human rights as an element of the thick concept of the rule of law to correct, complement and reinforce states' climate action.

3 The Threefold Link Between the Rule of Law and Climate Action

Recent cases of the ECtHR and the CCS, which directly or indirectly relate to the obligations of states with regard to climate change, provide valuable insights and ample space for an analysis of the current state of the rule of law, both beyond and

[30] Buser (2023), pp. 605–612; Maed and Maxwell (2022), pp. 617–648; Peel and Osofsky (2020), pp. 21–38; Tintor (2021), pp. 250–257.

[31] Preston (2021), pp. 1–32.

within borders. The long-awaited and first ever climate-related judgment of an international court, the ECtHR Grand Chamber judgment in Verein Klimaseniorinnen Schweiz v. Switzerland, delivered in April 2024, explicitly referred to the rule of law in the context of climate change. However, Judge Eicke did the same in his partly concurring and partly dissenting opinion, albeit in the opposite way.

From the outset, in the discussion of preliminary issues, the Court used the rule of law as an argument for its involvement in a case that raised unprecedented issues with which the Court had never before had to deal. While recognising that judicial intervention, including its own, cannot replace the action which must be taken by the legislative and executive branches of government, the Court emphasised that "democracy cannot be reduced to the will of the majority of the electorate and elected representatives, in disregard of the requirements of the rule of law".[32] This is why it sees it as the task of the judiciary, both at national and international level, "to ensure the necessary oversight of compliance with legal requirements", whereas its own task is "to also determine the proportionality of general measures adopted by the domestic legislature".[33] On the other hand, Judge Eicke, in his opinion, stated that "proceedings before the Court are much more likely to distract the Contracting Parties and slow down the necessary processes" and that "any delay or failure in the implementation of the judgment is only likely to undermine the need for urgent action and, potentially, the rule of law".[34] The Constitutional Court of Serbia also referred to the rule of law as the basis for its decision that the Government Decree on the Termination of the Decree on the Establishment of the Spatial Plan of the Special Purpose Area for the Implementation of the "Jadar" Project for the Extraction and Processing of Jadarite Minerals[35] was not in accordance with the Constitution and the law. As will be explained in the following sections of this chapter, although the CCS case does not appear to be directly related to climate change, its consequences for the realisation of the controversial mining project by Rio Tinto will undoubtedly have important negative repercussions for Serbia's climate action and its environment, but also some desirable ones for the climate action of other European states.

This section of the chapter will therefore examine the role of the rule of law in the context of global warming. It will assess the reach of the rule of law as a tool in efforts to mitigate the causes and consequences of climate change, as suggested by the European Court of Human Rights (Sect. 3.1). However, the rule of law will be examined from the perspective of whether it is being overstretched in the context of climate change, to the detriment of its authority and credibility, as argued by Judge Eicke (Sect. 3.2). It will also be examined from the perspective of whether it is being

---

[32] ECtHR, Case of Verein Klimaseniorinnen Schweiz and Others v. Switzerland, par. 412.

[33] *Ibid.*

[34] Partly Concurring Partly Dissenting Opinion of Judge Eicke, par. 15.

[35] Decree on the Termination of the Decree on the Establishment of the Spatial Plan of the Special Purpose Area for the Implementation of the "Jadar" Project for the Extraction and Processing of Jadarite Minerals, Official Gazette of the Republic of Serbia No. 8/22.

used to serve the climate policies of other states, to the detriment of the state's own international climate commitments and environmental protection, as appears to be the case with the decision of the CCS (Sect. 3.3).

3.1 The Rule of Law as a Tool to Foster Climate Action: Lessons from the ECtHR

The rule of law is often seen as "an essential tool for limiting climate change".[36] This is not to say that the rule of law is not called into question by the unprecedented nature of climate change, and that there may not be legal conundrums and gaps that do not always fit within existing legal categories, but require creative legal reasoning and innovative legal arguments to the extent that they go beyond established legal standards.

In Verein Klimaseniorinnen Schweiz v. Switzerland four elderly women and an association consisting of elder women concerned about the adverse effects of global warming on their health and well-being, submitted an application before the ECtHR against Switzerland for its failure to take sufficient action to mitigate the consequences of climate change.

The period leading up to the judgment, and doubts about the ECtHR's willingness and ability to deal with the legal challenges presented by the complex issue of climate change, attest to the fact that the outcome seemed uncertain and could easily have been different.[37] However, the ECtHR Grand Chamber judgment in the Swiss case is an excellent example of applying the rule of law elements to their current full capacity. Using both existing legal standards and, at times, going beyond them, the ECtHR succeeded in improving the clarity and precision of rather abstract and loose international climate change obligations, in overcoming the seemingly insurmountable obstacle of victim status, in holding Switzerland accountable for its failure to meet its international climate change obligations, and, most importantly, in establishing human rights as the most important and useful benchmark for evaluating states' climate change actions. Thus, the rule of law elements of clarity, standing/justiciability, accountability and human rights, which had previously been identified as the most problematic in the international climate change regime, were actually used to help strengthen states' climate change actions.

Acknowledging at the outset that climate change has significant characteristics that are different from other environmental problems,[38] the Court stressed its intention to situate the climate change issue within its existing environmental standards (Sect. 3.1.1). However, it also noted at the outset that existing standards

[36] Carlarne (2020), p. 13.

[37] Heri (2022), pp. 3–4; Rocha and Sampaio (2023), pp. 279–289.

[38] ECtHR, Case of Verein Klimaseniorinnen Schweiz and Others v. Switzerland, par. 416–421.

and categories can only "offer guidance up to a point",[39] beyond which creative legal reasoning becomes essential in order for the rule of law to achieve meaningful results and overcome climate change challenges (Sect. 3.1.2).

3.1.1 Strengthening Climate Action Through Existing Legal Categories and Standards: Using the Rule of Law Elements of Human Rights, Clarity and Accountability

At the very beginning, the ECtHR had to establish climate change as a human rights issue, link it to the European Convention on Human Rights (ECHR, Convention)[40] and establish that climate change has an impact on the enjoyment of human rights guaranteed by the Convention. To do so, the ECtHR decided to apply its usual approach in regular environmental cases and to take into account "the scientific, political and judicial recognition of a link between the adverse effects of climate change and the enjoyment of (various aspects of) human rights".[41] It has not itself undertaken the difficult task of establishing the impact of global warming and climate change on the enjoyment of human rights, but has chosen to rely on the reports of other international bodies, such as the IPCC, and has found it a "fact that there are sufficiently reliable indications that anthropogenic climate change exists, that it poses a serious current and future threat to the enjoyment of human rights guaranteed under the Convention, that States are aware of it and capable of taking measures to effectively address it, that the relevant risks are projected to be lower if the rise in temperature is limited to 1.5 °C above pre-industrial levels and if action is taken urgently, and that current global mitigation efforts are not sufficient to meet the latter target".[42]

By applying its standard approach of interpreting the Convention in the light of contemporary conditions and in accordance with developments in international law,[43] the ECtHR made its important contribution to the rule of law deficit of the international climate regime and provided clarity on the content of states' climate change obligations.[44] In addition to relying on its environmental standards developed under Articles 2 and 8 of the Convention,[45] it identified states' positive climate action obligations by interpreting the rights to life and private life in line with the

---

[39] *Ibid.*, par. 414.

[40] Council of Europe, European Convention for the Protection of Human Rights and Fundamental Freedoms, as amended by Protocols Nos. 11 and 14, ETS 5, 4 November 1950.

[41] ECtHR, Case of Verein Klimaseniorinnen Schweiz and Others v. Switzerland, par. 434.

[42] *Ibid.*, par. 436.

[43] *Ibid.*, par. 455–456.

[44] This has been identified by some authors as the most important role for international adjudication. Bodansky (2017), p. 712.

[45] Čučković (2018), pp. 254–266, 272–286; ECtHR, Case of Verein Klimaseniorinnen Schweiz and Others v. Switzerland, par. 538–540.

UNFCCC and the Paris Agreement.[46] In order to ensure that individuals enjoy effective protection against serious adverse effects on their life, health, well-being and quality of life resulting from the impacts and risks caused by climate change, the ECtHR drew up a checklist of obligations under the general "primary duty to adopt, and effectively apply in practice, regulations and measures capable of mitigating the existing and potentially irreversible, future effects of climate change".[47] The main Paris Agreement commitment to mitigate climate change has been clarified to include the obligation to adopt general measures setting a target time frame for achieving carbon neutrality, to adopt intermediate greenhouse gas emission reduction targets, to provide evidence of compliance with greenhouse gas emission reduction targets, to update targets with due diligence and on the basis of the best available evidence, and to act in a timely and appropriate manner when implementing relevant legislation and measures.[48] In addition, the second pillar of the Paris Agreement—the obligation to adapt to climate change—has been interpreted by the ECtHR as an obligation to adopt and effectively implement adaptation measures, consistent with the general structure of positive obligations of States in the wider environmental context, including the obligation to establish the relevant legislative and administrative framework to provide effective protection and to effectively apply that framework in practice.[49] Most importantly, the procedural aspects of Article 8 have been transposed to the climate change context, thereby extending the scope of States' climate change actions to include relevant procedural safeguards. States' decision-making processes in the context of climate change must therefore comply with two additional procedural obligations: to make available to the public, and in particular to those who may be affected by climate change regulations and measures, or the lack thereof, information held by public authorities and relevant studies, and to allow the public to participate in decision-making processes relating to climate change measures, or the lack thereof.[50] Although the contribution of the ECtHR in this respect has been assessed as modest, since "the Court does not require all that much from states",[51] it must be stressed that the added value lies in the inclusion of mitigation and adaptation obligations of States within the scope of the right to life and the right to private life. In doing so, the Court has enabled the development of these duties through the concept of positive obligations of States, an approach that has been used to constantly and continuously develop the obligations of States in other areas, most notably environmental protection. On the one hand, the Court has never before "gone through the trouble of spelling out in such detail what specific measures a state ought to adopt".[52] On the other hand, the

---

[46] *Ibid.*, 546.

[47] *Ibid.*, par. 545.

[48] *Ibid.*, par. 550.

[49] *Ibid.*, par. 552.

[50] *Ibid.*, par. 554.

[51] Milanović (2024).

[52] Pedersen (2024).

list is not exhaustive, so the Court left the door open for future cases to further specify and develop states' positive climate obligations.

Finally, the principle of common but differentiated responsibilities, one of the guiding principles of the international climate regime,[53] has fortunately not been interpreted by the ECtHR as a shield against the responsibility of states for climate inaction. Given that the global levels and impacts of greenhouse gas emissions come from multiple sources and multiple actors, and given that not all of these actors contribute to climate change in the same way and to the same extent, the principle of common but differentiated responsibilities was seen as a potential obstacle to determining each state's share of responsibility for climate change and, consequently, for the protection of human rights. Despite the Swiss Government's attempt to use it to avoid accountability for its inadequate climate action, the ECtHR interpreted the principle to mean that "each State has its own share of responsibilities to take measures to tackle climate change and that the taking of those measures is determined by the State's own capabilities rather than by any specific action (or omission) of any other State".[54] Again, the ECtHR drew on its existing standards and jurisprudence to strengthen climate action by providing the rule of law element of accountability.[55] It stressed that in order for the state's responsibility to be engaged, it is important that "reasonable measures which domestic authorities failed to take could have had a real prospect of altering the outcome or mitigating the harm", which, in the context of climate change, "should be understood in the light of Article 3(3) of the UNFCCC according to which States should take measures to anticipate, prevent or minimize the causes of climate change and mitigate its adverse effects".[56]

Although referring to the International Court of Justice and the International Tribunal for the Law of the Sea, Sands distinguished four factors in assessing the prospects of international tribunals contributing to strengthening state action on climate change: the role of international tribunals in establishing scientific facts, the role in determining the scope and precise content of the rules to be applied, the ability to actively engage with the issues presented, and the question of standing.[57] For its part, the ECtHR has managed to resolve satisfactorily all the challenging issues identified by the doctrine. While it solved the first two problems by relying on its existing environmental standards, it arrived at the solution to the last problem through a creative legal argument.

[53] Čučković (2019), pp. 63–72.

[54] ECtHR, Case of Verein Klimaseniorinnen Schweiz and Others v. Switzerland, par. 442.

[55] *Ibid.*, par. 443.

[56] *Ibid.*, par. 444.

[57] Sands (2016), p. 27.

3.1.2 Contributing to Climate Action Through Innovative Legal Reasoning: Overcoming the Victim Status Obstacle and Introducing the Rights of Future Generations

The most challenging ECHR issue that has arisen in the context of climate change is that of standing, i.e. the admissibility requirement of victim status.[58] Again, the respondent government sought to prevent the ECtHR from deciding the case by arguing that the applicants, neither the four individuals nor the environmental association, were directly and specifically affected by climate change.[59] However, since *actio popularis* is not an option before the ECtHR, the Court has had to find a way to allow applications about harms that affect everyone, such as climate change, and avoid taking this obstacle to its extreme "that the more people that are impacted by environmental harm, the less likelihood there is of anyone being able to impugn the harmful activity before a tribunal".[60]

Since neither the individual applicants nor the environmental association were covered by the general principles of victim status/*locus standi* developed by the ECtHR in its case-law,[61] the ECtHR had to think creatively but pragmatically in the specific circumstances of climate change and find a solution that would open the Court's door to climate inaction claims while closing it to countless individuals, almost anyone, who might be affected by climate change. The ECtHR thus chose to adhere to its classic requirements for victim status with regard to individual applicants, but to set new standards and interpret the Convention creatively with regard to associations.

The result of such an approach is that it will be virtually impossible for individual claimants to meet the criteria for victim status in the specific circumstances of climate change. Faced with the state's climate inaction, the individual will still be required to show that "he or she was personally and directly affected by the impugned failures", more precisely that he or she was "subject to a high intensity of exposure to the adverse effects of climate change" and that there was "pressing need to ensure the applicant's individual protection, owing to the absence or inadequacy of any reasonable measures to reduce harm".[62] The applicant's personal circumstances, in particular the nature of their vulnerability, will be decisive.[63] In the specific circumstances of the four individual applicants, the ECtHR did not consider that these strict criteria had been met. Although the elderly women who brought the case before the Court claimed that they faced numerous difficulties during the heatwaves as a direct consequence of climate change and that there were effects on their health, the ECtHR found that this was not done "with a degree of intensity

---

[58] Schmid (2022).

[59] ECtHR, Case of Verein Klimaseniorinnen Schweiz and Others v. Switzerland, par. 340–345.

[60] Pedersen (2023).

[61] ECtHR, Case of Verein Klimaseniorinnen Schweiz and Others v. Switzerland, par. 460–477.

[62] *Ibid.*, par. 487.

[63] *Ibid.*, par. 488.

giving rise to a pressing need to ensure their individual protection, not least given the high threshold which necessarily applies", and that their medical condition was not critical to the extent that it could not be alleviated by the adaptation measures already available in Switzerland.[64]

On the contrary, by invoking the Aarhus Convention[65] and conducting its own inquiry,[66] the ECtHR has enabled environmental associations to fill this gap in the rule of law and, given the specificities of climate change, has explicitly recognised the standing of associations in cases involving climate change issues.

The ECtHR thus departed from its established practice and excluded associations in the particular context of climate change from "showing that those on whose behalf the case has been brought would themselves have met the victim-status requirement for individuals in the climate change context" as set out in the relevant paragraphs of the judgment and as outlined in the previous paragraph of this article.[67] Instead, as the Court found, associations need only meet three simple conditions: they must be established in accordance with the law of the relevant jurisdiction; they must be able to demonstrate that they are pursuing their statutory objectives of protecting human rights from the threats posed by climate change; and they must be considered qualified and representative to act on behalf of those affected by climate change.[68]

While discussing the issue of standing, but also in other contexts, the ECtHR has introduced another novelty—the relevance of considering future harm and the rights of future generations. Indeed, in explaining its reasons for recognising the *locus standi* of associations in climate cases, the Court emphasised that "States should take adequate action notably through suitable general measures to secure not only the Convention rights of individuals who are currently affected by climate change, but also those individuals within their jurisdiction whose enjoyment of Convention rights may be severely and irreversibly affected in the future in the absence of timely action".[69] These considerations should be linked to the Court's preliminary discussion that "the damaging effects of climate change raise an issue of intergenerational burden-sharing"[70] and its subsequent confirmation that "while the legal obligations arising for States under the Convention extend to those individuals currently alive who, at a given time, fall within the jurisdiction of a given Contracting Party, it is clear that future generations are likely to bear an increasingly severe burden of the consequences of present failures and omissions to combat climate change".[71] Taken together, they seem to lead to four possible conclusions. First, the ECtHR decided to

---

[64] *Ibid.*, par. 533.

[65] Convention on Access to Information, Public Participation in Decision-Making and Access to Justice in Environmental Matters, United Nations Treaty Series, Vol. 2161, p. 447.

[66] ECtHR, Case of Verein Klimaseniorinnen Schweiz and Others v. Switzerland, par. 490–494.

[67] *Ibid.*, par. 502.

[68] *Ibid.*

[69] *Ibid.*, par. 499.

[70] *Ibid.*, par. 410.

[71] *Ibid.*, par. 420.

introduce the concept of the rights of future generations and the international environmental law principle of intergenerational equity into its reasoning. Second, it did not consider the moment ripe enough to draw specific implications for states' climate change obligations, responsibilities and consequences thereof. Third, it used the rights of future generations as an additional argument to justify its position that there must be a possibility of judicial review of decision-making processes because "short-term interests and concerns may come to prevail over (...) pressing needs for sustainable policy-making".[72] Fourthly, it can be expected that the future climate change jurisprudence of the ECtHR will bring new developments based on intergenerational equity, possibly going further than the Court's well-established standards and "reinterpreting rule of law obligations in order to protect future generations against arbitrary treatment by present-day decision-makers", and thus aligning itself with the reasoning of certain national courts that have successfully engaged in "intergenerational interpretation of rule of law pillars".[73]

The two examples of the ECtHR's contribution to strengthening national action on climate change demonstrate that, when faced with issues of global concern, the role of international courts is not limited to interpreting and applying the law to the specific facts of a case, but also to progressively developing the law and "informing the developments of an international public consciousness" on such issues.[74] According to some authors, radical measures may prevail over incremental ones that are deemed insufficient to achieve the intended goals of sustainability transformations,[75] because in times of crisis, such as the climate crisis, meaningful results cannot be achieved through regular legal avenues. Instead, as Mai concludes, "in crisis, the imperative is to change – to come up with something new".[76] However, the opinion is not unique in this regard, with arguments based on the rule of law in general, and some of its elements in particular, being used to limit its role in advancing climate action.

3.2 The Rule of Law Is Overstretched in the Context of Climate Change: Is Judge Eicke's Argument Valid?

Following up on Judge Eicke's argument that the ECtHR's involvement in states' climate action is likely to have the opposite effect of slowing it down, because

[72] *Ibid.*

[73] Sulyok (2024), pp. 2, 9. For a similar position on the role of the judiciary in reinterpreting the rule of law to include considerations based on intergenerational equity, see: Vásquez Torreblanca (2024), p. 85.

[74] Sands (2016), pp. 25–26.

[75] Gill and Ramachandran (2021), p. 234.

[76] Mai (2024), p. 21.

delaying or failing to implement the judgment will undermine the rule of law,[77] this part of the chapter will analyse the second possible link between climate action and the rule of law and attempt to answer the question of whether the rule of law can and/or should be used as a tool to limit states' climate action. In other words, does climate change stretch the rule of law to the point of compromising its authority, and are there limits to how the rule of law can be used to address the causes and consequences of climate change?

The element of the rule of law most frequently used to put constraints on applying other elements of the concept in order to strengthen states' climate action through climate litigation is the separation of powers.[78] However, due to the ECtHR's clear position on this issue,[79] it seems that we are now well past this argument and that the separation of powers cannot be used to limit the review of states' climate (in)action by national and international courts. Although there are features of the climate change regime which, as explained above, make the rule of law deficit quite obvious, this does not mean that state action on climate change is purely a matter of politics. The adoption and entry into force of international climate change treaties and related national legislation has transformed climate policy into law, allowing international and national courts to review states' actions and inactions in accordance with their respective jurisdictions. The argument regarding the lack of clarity and precision of climate treaties and laws, and the resulting policy choices made by states to achieve proclaimed GHG emission reduction targets, has also been rejected by the ECtHR. The Court clearly stated that "where complaints raised before the Court relate to State policy with respect to an issue affecting the Convention rights of an individual or group of individuals, this subject matter is no longer merely an issue of politics or policy but also a matter of law having a bearing on the interpretation and application of the Convention".[80]

Therefore, the question is no longer whether the judiciary, both national and international, should review states' climate action or lack thereof, but whether there are limits to how far the courts can go with their findings and legal reasoning, i.e. does the creativity of the courts put pressure on the rule of law while at the same time achieving the exact opposite with respect to states' climate action—limiting it rather than fostering it?

Judge Eicke's position was supported by legal doctrine even before the Swiss climate case was decided. It has been suggested that "legally dubious and overly ambitious findings by national judges about the content of international climate law could frustrate governments and lead them to withdraw or limit obligations through national reform".[81] At the level of international law and international adjudication, this could include the possible withdrawal of states from international climate

[77] Partly Concurring Partly Dissenting Opinion of Judge Eicke, par. 15.

[78] Burgers (2020), pp. 57–58.

[79] ECtHR, Case of Verein Klimaseniorinnen Schweiz and Others v. Switzerland, par. 412–413.

[80] *Ibid.*, par. 450.

[81] Buser (2023), p. 595.

treaties. However, such moves, however likely or unlikely,[82] will have no impact on states' climate commitments under international human rights regimes, in particular the European Convention on Human Rights system, which have recently emerged as "the predominant standard according to which climate policy and international climate law are to be assessed".[83] First, the various international human rights systems have long traditions of state participation and have been able to withstand other crises, challenges and creative legal reasoning without states withdrawing from them.[84] Second, focusing on the ECHR system, the fact that the respondent state is not a party to the specific international treaty has never been an obstacle for the ECtHR to use it as a basis for interpreting the positive human rights obligations of the state. Third, it is questionable whether the ECtHR's approach can be described as legally dubious and overly ambitious. Indeed, it is not clear what the relevant threshold is for assessing the dubiousness and ambition of legal reasoning. The only possible criterion is the rule of law and its elements, which means that judicial findings in the pursuit of promoting climate action by states should only remain within the rule of law and not go beyond it. As explained in the previous section, the ECtHR has stayed within the contours of the rule of law, both in incorporating climate change into its established standards and in tailoring new standards to the specific characteristics of climate change.

Judge Eicke's intervention raises another question, which is a follow-up to the previous considerations. Namely, should the ECtHR be guided by external factors when interpreting and applying legal rules to climate (in)action, both by adapting them to existing standards and by developing new ones? For example, should the ECtHR take into account the ability of the respondent state to implement the judgment and the potential impact of the judgment on other states and the wider public? Judicial prudence and realism are welcome and sensible because "radical changes can be reactive, resisted and trigger organizational crisis thereby creating discontinuity".[85] However, the only threshold against which this should be measured is again the rule of law. Sticking firmly to the pillars of the rule of law and not going beyond them is the only guarantee that the undesirable outcomes of a judgement dealing with challenging and complex issues of climate (in)action by states will not turn into something that would limit and discourage climate mitigation and adaptation measures by states. The reactions of both Switzerland and other Council of Europe member states are instructive in this regard. The Swiss Government took almost 5 months after the ECtHR ruling to respond, indicating that it did not want its response to be hasty and ill-considered.

---

[82] Five months after the ECtHR ruling against Switzerland, the Swiss government has not announced its withdrawal from the international climate treaties.

[83] Buser (2023), p. 606.

[84] Switzerland's reaction is also instructive in this respect, since, as will be explained, its Federal Council has emphasised its commitment to the ECHR system despite the undesirable outcome of the ECtHR proceedings.

[85] Gill and Ramachandran (2021), p. 234.

In its response to the ECtHR ruling of 28 August,[86] the Federal Council contested the ECtHR's position on the legal standing of environmental associations, while at the same time stating that the Court's conclusion that Switzerland did not meet its climate policy requirements did not take into account certain legislative measures introduced to achieve the country's climate target. At the same time, Switzerland stressed its continued commitment to the Council of Europe and its ECHR system. Switzerland's response can be described as cautious and balanced. On the one hand, it contested the aspect of the ECtHR's judgement that does not require any kind of implementation by the respondent state. On the other hand, and more importantly, the Federal Council began to argue that Switzerland was complying with the climate policy requirements of the ECtHR ruling and that its current climate measures, including the legislative measures not considered by the Court, were in line with its human rights obligations. At least for the moment, it appears that Switzerland does not dispute that it has to take climate action to meet its ECHR obligations, but that the Court's conclusion is based on incomplete data about its climate legislation and measures. It remains to be seen how this position will be further explained and argued before the Committee of Ministers once the process of implementing the judgment begins, but also what the position will be of other Council of Europe member states who now face the realistic prospect of finding themselves in Switzerland's position once environmental associations begin to benefit from the ECtHR's position on their standing.

In cases involving new and complex legal issues such as climate change, adhering to an overly simplified and formal thin understanding of the rule of law would not contribute to the current state of the climate system and the climate (in)action of states. On the contrary, in such cases the rule of law must be applied in its thick model and go beyond purely formalistic and procedural aspects.[87] The recent decision of the Serbian Constitutional Court can serve as an example of bad practice and the problematic consequences that the application of the thin rule of law concept can have on climate action.

3.3 The Rule of Law as a Justification for Serving the GHG Reduction Targets of Other States to the Detriment of a State's Own Climate Protection Measures: The Curious Decision of the Constitutional Court of Serbia

Rio Tinto, one of the world's largest mining companies, has been actively involved in the exploration of lithium and borate deposits in western Serbia. Although the

[86]The Portal of the Swiss Government: Federal Council clarifies its position on the ECHR ruling on climate protection, 28 August 2024, Bern, https://www.admin.ch/gov/de/start/dokumentation/medienmitteilungen.msg-id-102244.html.

[87]Vaughan (2022), pp. 5–6; Babie and Wawryk (2021), p. 380.

deposits were discovered 20 years ago, the so-called Jadar project, named after the river that flows through the region and which bears the name of the mineral composed of lithium and borate, only became a hot topic in Serbia a few years ago when it became clear that the project would soon move from the exploration phase to the exploitation phase. Concerned about the project's negative environmental impact, local residents opposed the project and were subsequently joined by environmental and other associations, leading to widespread public protests in both the capital and many other cities in Serbia.

Faced with such massive opposition at a rather sensitive political moment, with elections approaching, the Serbian government decided to terminate in 2022 the Decree on the Establishment of the Spatial Plan of the Special Purpose Area for the Realization of the Project for the Exploitation and Processing of the Jadarite Mineral "Jadar", previously adopted in 2020.[88] The then Serbian Prime Minister even explicitly stated that the Government "fulfilled all the demands of the environmental protests and put an end to Rio Tinto in Serbia".[89] However, as soon as the public calmed down and the elections were over, the Constitutional Court of Serbia issued a decision on the incompatibility of the Decree on the Termination of the Decree on the Establishment of the Spatial Plan of the Special Purpose Area for the Realization of the Project for the Exploitation and Processing of the Jadarite Mineral "Jadar" with the Constitution and the law, thus paving the way for the Government to issue a new Decree in 2024 on the application of the original Decree from 2020.[90]

The CCS concluded that "the contested Decree was not adopted in a manner consistent with the provision of Article 3 of the Constitution and the provisions of the Law on Government and the Law on Environmental Impact Assessment".[91] It stated that the Government exceeded the limits of its competence by adopting the contested Decree, because it invoked the negative opinion of the interested public as "the sole and exclusive reason for its adoption", something that "can only be

[88] Decree on the Establishment of the Spatial Plan of the Special Purpose Area for the Realization of the Project for the Exploitation and Processing of the Jadarite Mineral "Jadar", Official Gazette of the Republic of Serbia 26/2020. The Decree on the Termination of the Decree from 2020 is published in the Official Gazette of Serbia 8/22.

[89] RTS, Brnabić: Ukinuta uredba Vlade o prostornom planu projekta Jadar, stavljena tačka na Rio Tinto, 20 January 2022, https://www.rts.rs/lat/vesti/politika/4672418/brnabic-ukinuta-uredba-vlade-o-prostornom-planu-projekta-jadar-i-vise-ne-postoji.html.

[90] Decree on the Application of the Decree on the Establishment of the Spatial Plan of the Special Purpose Area for the Realization of the Project for the Exploitation and Processing of the Jadarite Mineral "Jadar", Official Gazette of the Republic of Serbia No. 60/2024.

[91] Constitutional Court of Serbia, IUo-39/2022, section V. The invoked Article 3 of the Constitution provides that "the rule of law is the fundamental premise of the Constitution and rests on inalienable human rights". In paragraph 2 the same provision stipulates that the rule of law is to be "achieved through free and direct elections, constitutional guarantees of human and minority rights, separation of powers, independent judicial authority and obedience of the authorities to the Constitution and the law". Constitution of the Republic of Serbia, Official Gazette Nos. 98/2006 and 115/2021.

evaluated in the procedure and in the manner prescribed by the Law on Environmental Impact Assessment".[92]

Article 3 of the Constitution, which enshrines the rule of law as a fundamental premise, was therefore the main provision under which the CCS terminated the controversial Decree from 2022. Such a basis for the CCS's decision, together with its prosaic reliance on the reasons for the cancellation of the decree, is rather surprising, unsubstantiated and disregards other provisions of the supreme legal instrument guaranteeing fundamental human rights, whose guardian the CCS is supposed to be. Firstly, the rule of law argument should not have been used by the CCS in a case of such importance, the outcome of which is of interest not only to the mining company that initiated the proceedings, but to the entire population of Serbia. Second, invoking the rule of law in such an abstract way and without clear legal arguments can only lead to the conclusion that the CCS lacked valid arguments to substantiate its conclusion. The CCS's position is contained in a single paragraph, whereas the rest of the decision consists of summarizing the provisions of the legislation that it found pertinent. Its conclusion is all the more questionable given the complexity of the concept of the rule of law. Thirdly, the CCS does not dispute the authority of the government to revoke the decree it issued, but claims that the government exceeded its authority by basing its reasons for revoking the decree on environmental protests, which the CCS claims is contrary to the rule of law. However, two points need to be made here. On the one hand, didn't the CCS, by dealing with the reasons for the government's decision to repeal the decree, actually interfere with "the right and duty of the Government to establish and conduct policy" and "to decide on the further implementation of the specific project", something it explicitly stated in the decision that it should not do, while at the same time disregarding whether the government's act was "in accordance with the Constitution and the law", something that is the essence of the rule of law?[93] On the other hand, the CCS uses the rule of law as its main argument for overturning the government's decree, while at the same time circumventing it in the present proceedings. As can be seen from the opinions of the two judges, the Court decided to disregard its usual procedures and to issue the decision without carrying out the preliminary procedure and without taking a decision on the initiation of the procedure. Instead, the CCS skipped the preparatory phase and immediately issued a decision declaring the unconstitutionality and illegality of the contested decree.[94] Fourth, the challenged procedural approach of the CCS not to conduct the preliminary procedure curiously coincides with the timing of the CCS decision. The decision was issued on 11 July 2024, just 5 days before the government adopted the new decree on the application of the original decree from 2020, and conveniently in time for the signing of the Memorandum of Understanding between the European Union and the Republic of

---

[92] CCS, IUo-39/2022, section V.

[93] *Ibid.*

[94] Consenting Separate Opinion of Judge Tamás Korhecz, par. 2; Dissenting Opinion of Judge Milan Škulić, par. 3.

Serbia on a Strategic Partnership on Sustainable Raw Materials, Battery Value Chains and Electric Vehicles on 19 July 2024.

And this is precisely what seems to be the most problematic aspect of the CCS decision in the context of this chapter. The CCS decision does not directly address Serbia's climate change policies. However, by invoking the rule of law argument and enabling the government to adopt the new Decree in 2024, the CCS enabled the following chain of events and the continuation of a controversial lithium mining and processing project that will have serious negative impacts on Serbia's environment.[95] In the context of national climate change policies, the CCS decision essentially secured the future exploitation of the lithium deposits found in the Jadar area, which "have the potential to meet up to 90% of Europe's current lithium requirements"[96] needed to meet the European Union's climate target of net zero CO2 emissions by 2050. At the same time, the CCS decision may have pushed Serbia further away from meeting its own climate commitments. As Bogojević eloquently put it, others' net-zero strategy comes "at an environmental cost (as well as other costs)" even if not in their own backyard.[97] While helping other countries to meet their climate targets, Serbia will be pushed away from its own greenhouse gas reduction goals. As certified by scientists, the Jadar project will cause "land degradation and soil erosion that correspond to the term 'desertification' and represent a direct negation of the principles of the Rio conventions", including the UNFCCC, thus undermining "the United Nations Sustainable Development Goals and the accepted Agenda 2030".[98] Specifically, "the 204 hectares of forest in Serbia planned to be removed due to the project Jadar would store about 56 kt of carbon" while the total annual CO2 emissions from the project are estimated to be between 428 and 522 CO2eq/kt per year. Thus, by implementing the Jadar project, Serbia would increase its greenhouse gas emissions instead of reducing them in line with its international climate change commitments.

By limiting its deliberations to procedural issues, the CCS appears to have interpreted Article 3 of the Constitution in its thin, formal and procedural version. It chose to ignore other elements of the rule of law that go beyond purely procedural issues, most importantly human rights. Although the CCS outlines in detail numerous provisions of relevant legislation, in particular the Law on Environmental Impact Assessment, at no point in its ruling does the CCS invoke the constitutional provision on the right to a healthy environment and the consequent responsibility of the Republic of Serbia to protect the environment. This fundamental human right was only recognized by Judge Škulić in his dissenting opinion, when he stated that "any assessment by the competent authorities regarding the balanced achievement of those legitimate goals, both the one related to the realization of vital economic interests and the one related to the realization of the citizens' right to a healthy

[95] Đorđević et al. (2024), pp. 2–3.

[96] Đorđević et al. (2024), p. 2.

[97] Bogojević (2022).

[98] Đorđević et al. (2024), p. 2.

environment, should in a democratic legal state, which is characterized by the rule of law, to be implemented in a legal and constitutionally valid procedure."[99] According to Article 3 of the Constitution, the rule of law is based on inalienable human rights. The CCS should at least have had the professional propriety not to use the rule of law as its main argument, to apply the standard procedure and to make the effort to find other arguments to support the decision it deemed appropriate.

4 Conclusion

The recent developments outlined with regard to the international climate change regime and related litigation before international courts seem to offer three main conclusions, which at the same time answer the question of the role of the rule of law in the international climate change regime.

First, the international rule of law is indeed an indispensable tool in efforts to limit the causes and consequences of climate change. Despite the obvious limitations of both the international climate change regime and international law in general, the recent recourse to various mechanisms available at the international level has begun to yield important results in developing clearer and more precise obligations of states with respect to climate change and their accountability.

Second, these developments highlight the dual role of the international rule of law in addressing climate change. It serves to limit the causes and consequences of climate change both in horizontal relations between states and in vertical relations between states and individuals. As international human rights law pierces the veil of various areas of national law, including environmental law and more specifically climate change law, further internalisation of international standards and the consequent internationalisation of national law and practice can be expected.

Last but not least, these developments should not be seen as putting undue pressure on the rule of law with the risk of undermining it, as suggested by British Judge Eicke in his opinion. Although overly ambitious statements by national and international judges on the content of international climate law could indeed lead governments to react in an undesirable way or to disregard judgments of international and national courts, this argument simply does not seem valid.

The benefits of strengthening and clarifying the obligations of states in a legal regime characterised by imprecision and loose commitments clearly outweigh the mere possibility that one or more governments might react in a specific way because they are not satisfied with a court decision. The potential spill-over effect of these developments, both on national legal systems and on other international regional systems, thus extending their effects to a larger number of States, outweighs the negative aspect of the risk that a dissatisfied defendant State might decide not to implement a court judgment or to disregard its international obligations.

[99] Dissenting Opinion of Judge Milan Škulić, par. 7.

In other words, there is no such thing as too much pressure on the international rule of law to address the causes and consequences of climate change. Faced with the adverse consequences of climate change for both present and future generations, the law simply does not have the luxury of not making full use of its principles, resources and mechanisms. Otherwise, climate change may threaten not only the existence of the rule of law, but our very existence.

References

Babie P, Wawryk A (2021) Climate change, the rule of law, and market-based schemes to encourage renewable energy and energy efficiency. Mich State Int Law Rev 29(3):362–412

Bodansky D (2017) The role of the International Court of Justice in addressing climate change: some preliminary reflections. Arizona State Law J 49:689–712

Bogojević S (2022) The race for lithium and the rule of law. https://www.ucl.ac.uk/law-environment/blog-climate-change-and-rule-law/race-lithium-and-rule-law

Burgers L (2020) Should judges make climate change law? Transnatl Environ Law 9(1):55–76

Buser A (2023) National climate change litigation and the international rule of law. Leiden J Int Law 36:593–615

Carević M, Novokmet R (2021) Challenges for the contemporary International Legal Framework and the rule of law: is the international community doing its best for the protection of climate migrants? Zbornik Pravnog fakulteta Sveučilišta u Rijeci 42(3):591–610

Carlarne C (2020) Climate change, human rights, and the rule of law. UCLA J Int Law For Aff 25: 11–40

Craciunean M (2015) Looking at the Millennium Development Goals and the sustainable development goals through an all human rights lens. Acta Universitatis Lucian Blaga 1:202–211

Čučković B (2018) Protection of the environment in international human rights law [Zaštita životne sredine u međunarodnom pravu ljudskih prava]. University of Belgrade Faculty of Law, Belgrade

Čučković B (2019) From equality towards equity and differentiated responsibilities – a contemporary international environmental law perspective. Ann Faculty Law Belgrade 3:59–76

Čučković B (2023) Screening international environmental law through gender lenses: already gender-sensitive, still not gender-responsive? In: Krstić I, Evola M, Ribes Moreno I (eds) Legal issues of international law from a gender perspective. Springer, pp 133–152

Čučković B (2024) International rule of law: the law's rule beyond and within borders. In: Jin-Sook Y (ed) The rule of law, justice and the future of democracy - the 31st World Congress of the International Association for Philosophy of Law and Social Philosophy. IVR 2024 Organizing Committee, Seoul, p 460

de Sadeleer N (2024) The rule of law: a core premise for the effectiveness of international environmental law. Eur J Risk Regul. https://doi.org/10.1017/err.2024.16

Diaz B, Castor M (2016) Sustainable development goals: an unpredictable and fragmented principle. Anuario Espanol de Derecho Internacional 32:9–48

Đorđević D, Tadić J, Grgur B, Ristić R, Sakan S, Brezjanović J, Stevanović V, Šolaja B (2024) The influence of exploration activities of a potential lithium mine to the environment in Western Serbia. Sci Rep 14:1–9

European Commission for Democracy through Law (2016) Rule of law checklist. CDL-AD(2016) 007, Strasbourg, 18 March 2016

Fernandez L (2016) Sustainable development goals and changes of international law. Anuario Espanol de Derecho Internacional 32:49–82

Gellers JH, Cheatham TJ (2019) Sustainable development goals and environmental justice: realization through disaggregation. Wisconsin Int Law J 36(2):276–297
Gill G, Ramachandran G (2021) Sustainability transformations, environmental rule of law and the Indian judiciary: connecting the dots through climate change litigation. Environ Law Rev 23(3): 228–247
Heri C (2022) Climate change before the European Court of Human Rights: capturing risk, ill-treatment and vulnerability. Eur J Int Law 20(20):1–27
Hurd I (2014) The international rule of law: law and the limits of politics. Ethics Int Aff 28(1):39–51
Hurd I (2015) The international rule of law and the domestic analogy. Glob Constitut 4(3):365–395
Intergovernmental Panel on Climate Change (2023) Climate change 2023: synthesis report. Contribution of Working Groups I, II and III to the Sixth Assessment Report, Geneva
International Development Law Organization (2021) Climate justice: a rule of law approach for transformative climate action, Rome
Keith K (2015) The international rule of law. Leiden J Int Law 28:403–417
Kim RE (2016) The nexus between international law and the sustainable development goals. Rev Eur Comp Int Environ Law 25(1):15–26
Knox JH (2015) Human rights, environmental protection, and the sustainable development goals. Washington Int Law J 24(3):517–536
Ladan MT (2018) Achieving sustainable development goals through effective domestic laws and policies on environment and climate change. Environ Policy Law 48(1):42–63
Lopez-Carlos A, Dahl A, Groff M (2020) Global governance and the emergence of global institutions for the 21st century. Cambridge University Press, Cambridge
Maed S, Maxwell L (2022) Climate change litigation: national courts as agents of international law development. In: Sobenes E, Mead S, Samson B (eds) The environment through the lens of international courts and tribunals. T.M.C. Asser Press, The Hague, pp 617–648
Mai L (2024) Navigating transformations: climate change and international law. Leiden J Int Law. https://doi.org/10.1017/S0922156524000062
Meguro M (2020) Litigating climate change through international law: obligations strategy and rights strategy. Leiden J Int Law 33:933–951
Milanović M (2024) A quick take on the European Court's climate change judgments. https://www.ejiltalk.org/a-quick-take-on-the-european-courts-climate-change-judgments/
Nanda VP (2016) The journey from the Millennium Development Goals to the sustainable development goals. Denver J Int Law Policy 44(3):389–412
Pedersen O (2023) Climate change hearings and the ECtHR Round II. https://www.ejiltalk.org/climate-change-hearings-and-the-ecthr-round-ii/
Pedersen O (2024) Climate change and the ECHR: the results are in. https://www.ejiltalk.org/climate-change-and-the-echr-the-results-are-in/
Peel J, Osofsky H (2020) Climate change litigation. Annu Rev Law Soc Sci 16:21–38
Postema G (2022) Law's rule: the nature, value and viability of the rule of law. Oxford University Press
Preston B (2021) The influence of the Paris Agreement on climate litigation: legal obligations and norms (part I). J Environ Law 33(1):1–32
Rivkin DW, Lamb SJ, Leslie NK (2015) The future of Investor-State Dispute Settlement in the energy sector: engaging with climate change, human rights and the rule of law. J World Energy Law 8(2):130–153
Rocha A, Sampaio R (2023) Climate change before the European and Inter-American Courts of Human Rights: comparing possible avenues before human rights bodies. Rev Eur Comp Int Environ Law 32(2):279–289
Sands P (2016) Climate change and the rule of law: adjudicating the future in international law. J Environ Law 28(1):19–36
Schmid E (2022) Victim status before the ECtHR in cases of alleged omissions: the Swiss climate case. https://www.ejiltalk.org/victim-status-before-the-ecthr-in-cases-of-alleged-omissions-the-swiss-climate-case/

Sulyok K (2024) Transforming the rule of law in environmental and climate litigation: prohibiting the arbitrary treatment of future generations. Transnatl Environ Law. https://doi.org/10.1017/S2047102524000116

Tintor L (2021) Značaj slučaja Urgenda za razvoj klimatskih parnica na području Evrope. Strani pravni život 65(2):249–265

Vásquez Torreblanca IA (2024) The environmental rule of law, intergenerational equity and climate litigation in Latin America. Catolica Law Rev 8(1):83–108

Vaughan S (2022) Climate change and the rule of law(yers): what thinner and thicker accounts might require of those in practice. UCL Res Paper Ser 11:1–9

Voigt C (2020) Climate change, the critical decade and the rule of law. Aust Yearb Int Law 37:50–64

Sustainable Development Goal and International Investment Law: Toward a Normative Justification of Human Rights Approach

Astle and Narem V. N. S. S. Usha Amulya

1 Introduction

Foreign Direct Investment is an essential engine for any transformative economy. It serves as an accelerating force in emerging economies, providing a nexus of capital, industrial modernization, and technology, resulting in a surge in productivity and sustainable growth. International investments boost human capital development and create a synchronous financial infrastructure and sustainability.[1] The United Nations Sustainable Development Agenda has 17 goals for people and for the planet. SDG Goal 9, which is 'Industry Innovation and Infrastructure', is in kosher with the foreign direct investment (FDI), which eventually emphasizes other socio-economic goals such as SDG 1 'No Poverty, SDG 2 'Zero Hunger', SDG 3 'Good Health and well-being', and SDG 6 'Clean Water and Sanitation'. The prism of public international law may examine the potential impact and the impact assessments on how a state complies with international rules and obligations in treaty law, customary law, or contractual agreements. These obligations arise under the multilateral and bilateral treaties from an environmental and human rights perspective. For instance, the International Covenant on Economic, Social and Cultural Rights (ICESCR) and the Paris Agreement of 2015 create a framework for the states to secure their economic development and growth but not dilute environmental sustainability and human rights. Under the United Nations Guiding Principles on Business and Human Rights (UNGP), the United Nations has also established a foundation on businesses and their responsibility to adhere to human rights values and address the adverse impact

[1] Borensztein et al. (1998).

Astle (✉) · N. V. N. S. S. Usha Amulya
GITAM - Deemed to be University, School of Law, Visakhapatnam, India

School of Law, GITAM (Deemed to be University), Visakhapatnam, India

Z. Meskić et al. (eds.), *Balkan Yearbook of European and International Law 2024*, Balkan Yearbook of European and International Law 2024,
https://doi.org/10.1007/978-3-031-89952-2_2

on exigency in case of any breach.[2] Compliance is not limited to the treaties between nations but also includes private multinational companies' adherence to corporate social responsibility (CSR) activities and sustainability. In foreign direct investment (FDI), these multinational companies (MNCs) shape the significant economic landscape for both host and home countries and also contribute to the emerging economy. However, it's important to assess and monitor compliance with legal standards by these MNCs. The imperative of economic development shall be in accordance with the emerging legal landscape, prioritizing human rights and sustainable practices.[3]

The burgeoning need to address the asymmetric international law is because of the adverse impact of foreign investments, mostly in developing nations, as the law seeks to indemnify the investors and settle their rights, but at what cost? Unstructured sustainable development, asymmetric legal landscape by host nation, and other social and environmental issues. The urgent need is to align the goals of the United Nations Sustainable Development (2030 agenda) with the required public international law. It will secure a nation's economic growth, environmental stewardship, and social equity.[4] Scholars often critique the legal landscape in international investment agreements (IIAs), arguing that the imbalance between human rights and foreign investment agreements' obligations results in the local public bearing the brunt of adverse impacts (stakeholders). The centre of the discussion is also on the effectiveness of Corporate Social Responsibility (CSR) and the lack of its enforceability. The discourse is the alignment of foreign investment and their protection under the aegis of human rights laws and the sustainability agenda of the United Nations by 2030. The due diligence of human rights and investment agreements shall go hand in hand while protecting the interests of the host nation's multinational companies (MNCs). The twofold approach to the protection of the rights of foreign investors in the host nation and the strict implementation of human rights aligned with the sustainable agenda at the time of project execution shall be of paramount importance. In case of any dispute, the substantial settlement method in bilateral and multilateral treaties would be an international arbitration mechanism on investment. The nation applying coherence in implementing the obligation for international investment agreements under multilateral or bilateral treaties will create a legal landscape for the way forward of foreign investment dispute settlement mechanisms.

The available literature on the issue of sustainability, environmental concerns, and CSR activities are abundant, but the burgeoning need is its implementation. As the investment laws are soft laws and international law is weak law,[5] the Bilateral International Treaty (BIT) under UNCTAD through policy will ensure adherence. The human rights concern as notably hypothesized by the author, being a genesis and CSR and sustainability being a sub genesis. However, the human rights concern

[2]Ruggie (2011), pp. 224–253.

[3]Ballor and Yildirim (2020), pp. 573–586.

[4]Ellis and Edmonds (2023), pp. 251–271.

[5]Patel and Parakh (2022), p. 196.

as an ' obligation' through translation public policy have been conceptualized in three-pointers, adding the arbitral awards in invoking basics of fundamental rights, CSR article under BIT and UNDRIP and international institutions role for indigenous people rights in foreign investment. The effectiveness and efficiency of IIAs, ICSID, and ISDS have been evaluated to assess the intrinsic proposition of human rights concerns through Transnational orders in foreign investment.

2 Corporate Social Responsibility Clause 'IN' International Investment Treaties: Panacea for Sustainable Growth, Human Rights—Environmental Issues and Investor Accountability

The concept of CSR and Investment laws, Little attention; The concept of CSR 'in' Investment treaties has got its prominence for aligning it with human rights. The concept of CSR is panacea as, its significance in the realm of environment, human rights, labour legislation and various other policies cannot be denied, but, Social responsibility, including corporate social responsibility (CSR),[6] is identified as a weak link as the clause has been criticized for needing more effective implementation. This has resulted in fragile investors' accountability.[7] The transcending translation investment requires a modified clause of CSR in concurrence with 'environmental obligation and human rights'.[8] This ensures significant changes to be in accordance with the Organisation for Economic Cooperation and Development (OECD) and United Nations Guiding Principles on Business and Human Rights. The investors will be envisaged to be accountable for the local population, and the redressal mechanism shall be arbitration in the home state and host state, subject to arbitration claims.

International law through the lenses of foreign investment and human rights do share the *'odi Et Amo'* relationship; the love-hate aspects and the nuances can be understood with the sequential derivation of investment laws and human rights issues dealt with through an arbitral award. The decision in *Phoenix Action Ltd v The Czech Republic,*[9] ICSID, the tribunal holds it true that no party shall be granted an arbitration award by investing without ensuring human rights principles, as of investment made ignoring torture, slavery, genocide, human trafficking and other

[6]Bowen (1953).

[7]Mbiyavanga (2017), pp. 132–150.

[8]Bueno et al. (2023), pp. 179–216.

[9]Phoenix Action, Ltd. v. The Czech Republic, ICSID Case No. ARB/06/5.

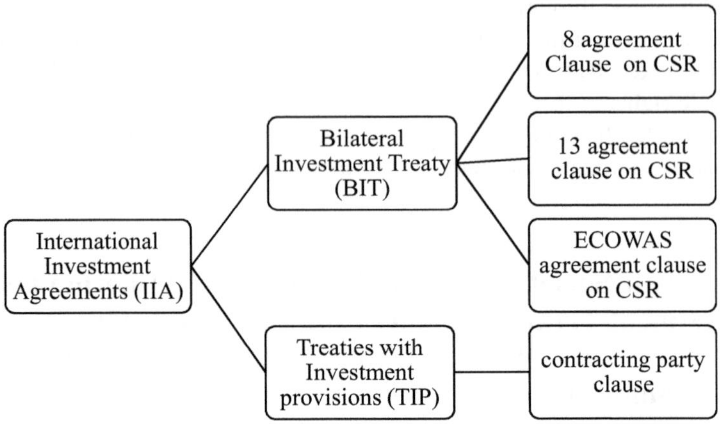

Fig. 1 Classification of agreement and sub classification based on social activities

human right violation.[10] So, a factual analysis of an investment shall be made relying on the BIT agreement, including human rights issues in investment.[11]

The foreign investors are duty bearers to the people, and a mechanism has been provided in the domestic court of the home state and host state. Human rights and foreign investment are aligned. Rather, it is seen that an investment that has to follow social responsibility is a cardinal principle of human rights. Hence, the International investment agreements (IIA), in the agreement's clauses between the treaty's parties, include the business model that advocates human rights and environmental concerns.[12] However, the critique often concerns the 'tokenistic' aspect of the clauses invoking human rights under IIA.[13] Despite the model and laws, the asymmetry between the rights and responsibilities of investors is not soothed but gets exacerbated.[14] Though there are ample obligations on the investors from the host state to be by the state's labour laws, it is to ensure not the labour law principles but to restrict the investors from taking any economic gain by plummeting the local environment and labour standards. The figure represents the type of IIA's and special focus on sub-classification of BIT based on social responsibility agreement clauses, as can be seen in Fig. 1.

There is a debate on whether the social responsibility by foreign investors is responsibility or obligation.[15] The identified IIA clauses have been categorised based on the conduct of social responsibility, which are

[10] Ibid, *See* paragraph 78.

[11] For a detailed study on approaches to human rights and investment laws *see*, Kriebaum (2018).

[12] Emphasis added.

[13] See the Report on Human rights-compatible International Investment Agreements (IIAs), (2021), A/76/238. Available at https://documents.un.org/doc/undoc/gen/n21/208/09/pdf/n2120809.pdf.

[14] Ibid see para 20.

[15] Bueno et al. (2023), pp. 179–216.

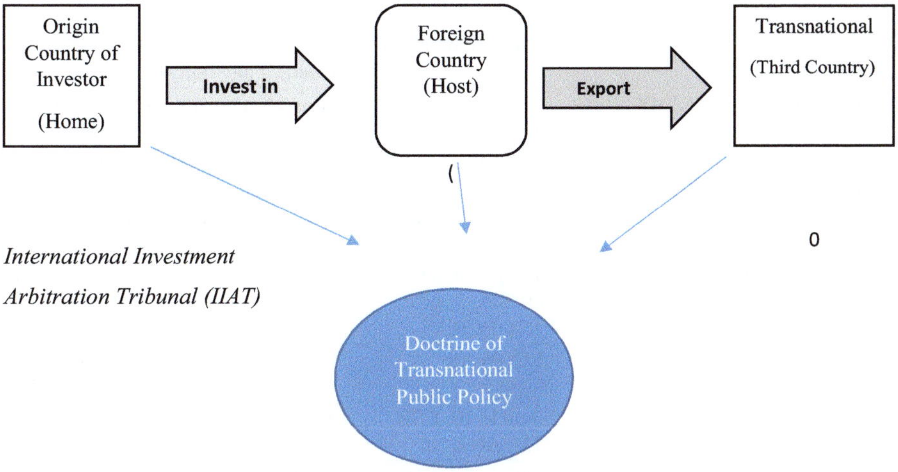

Human Rights in Transnational Orders as an "**Obligation**" (See the discussion in CSR and Investment treaties)	Principles of Fundamental Human Rights (Approach)
	Corporate Responsibility (Both Social and Environmental) - Approach -Social - Labour condition, equality Environmental - Water pollution, Greenhouse gases etc
	Rights of Indigeneous People

Fig. 2 The investment arbitration and human right approach through the lens of transnational policy

(a) 8 clause agreement, as where the investors obligation is very limited to tax and corruption (e.g., see Fig. 2—India–Taiwan BIT, the CSR part is reproduced here)

> Investors and their enterprises operating within each territory shall endeavour to voluntarily incorporate internationally recognized standards of corporate social responsibility in their practices and internal policies, such as statements of principle that have been endorsed or are supported by the authorities of the territories. These principles may address issues such as labour, the environment, human rights, community relations and anti-corruption.[16]

[16] India–Taiwan BIT (2018), Article 12.

Table 1 A table of treaties to decipher the obligation in different clauses BIT

Parties to Treaty	CSR arrangement clauses	Conduct and obligation
1. India–Taiwan BIT, 2018	8 agreement clauses Article 12 CSR activity	No such human rights clause only on adherence to host country laws for corruption and taxation
2. Brazil-India BIT of 2020	Article 12, 13 agreement clauses, OECD	No reference to standard code of conduct though specific in its 'obligation'
3. Brazil Mozambique CFIA in 2015	13 agreement clauses, Article 10 OECD	No reference to model business code though specific CSR activities
4. Morocco–Nigeria BIT of 2016	ECOWAS	Inclusion of Human rights in CSR activities
5. Canada–Honduras FTA 2013	Article 10, CSR, 13 agreement	Sustainable investment approach
6. EFTA–India TEPA (2024)	*TIP agreement,* Article 11.7 Clause (a), CSR	Trade and Economic Partnership Agreement (Norway, Switzerland with republic of India)
7. Bahrain–Hong Kong, China SAR BIT (2024)	Signed (Not in Force)	Document yet to
8. Indo-Pacific Economic Framework for Prosperity Agreement Relating to a Fair Economy	ILO Standards, Anti-corruption and taxes, Article 14	Lack of clauses related to environmental issues and human right concerns.

The list in brief has dealt with most recent IIAs and sequentially deriving other treaties based on CSR clauses [See more at UNCTAD navigator, BIT (Home page), Treaties between countries, can be accessed at https://investmentpolicy.unctad.org/international-investment-agreements]

(b) 13 clause agreement, where there is wide scope of the social activities creating responsibility on the investors but unable to meet up the international business conduct model (e.g., refer to Brazil-India BIT, 2020)
(c) ECOWAS, *Economic community of West African States*, this is comprehensive and an effective model which has significant human rights values in the treaty (see Table 1—Morocco v Nigeria BIT 2016)

Though the human right aspect is still under the obsolete when it comes to foreign investment obligation under BIT and its implementation. Although the recent BIT between EU - Kyrgyzstan EPCA (2024), showed the existence of human rights under article 5, the clause is reproduced for reference,

EU - Kyrgyzstan EPCA (2024[17])
"Article 5

Human rights and fundamental freedoms

[17] EU - Kyrgyzstan EPCA (2024).

The Parties shall cooperate in the promotion and protection of human rights and fundamental freedoms, and enhance dialogue and cooperation with the aim of:

(a) ensuring the respect for human rights, the principle of non-discrimination and the rights of persons belonging to minorities and vulnerable groups;
(b) ensuring the protection of fundamental freedoms, including freedom of expression, freedom of assembly and of association; freedom of the media and freedom of religion;
(c) promoting economic, social and cultural rights;
(d) promoting gender equality, promoting, protecting and fulfilling girls' and women's rights, including by ensuring their active participation in private and public spheres;
(e) strengthening national human-rights-related institutions, including through their participation in the decision-making processes;
(f) strengthening cooperation within the United Nations human rights bodies and Special Procedures of the Human Rights Council, including a proper follow-up of their recommendations in accordance with national legislation of the Parties."[18]

The remedy on the violation has also been procured through an arbitral award; in the case of *Bear Creek Mining Corporation (claimant)*[19] under the investment treaty of *Canada Peru Free Trade Agreement,*[20] with applicable law to ICSID arbitration rule, the company was in the sector of hydrocarbons and mining and faced damage due to some negligent part in violation by the host country, the arbitral award was in favour of the investors and was indemnified with 5% of compound interest from order date till the full reimbursement made to the claimant. Also, 75% of the cost of arbitration and compound interest on the amount of damage, which was USD 18,237,592, has to be paid to the claimant. This reflects the rationality in bipartite agreements under foreign investment, ensuring safety for the investors and compliance with human rights.[21] The investment treaties and human rights discussion overlook the important aspect of equivocal roles; it's equally important for the host state to protect the investors and to get protected from investors' investments. Fair and equitable treatment, in recent times, the new theory in BIT, which includes the human rights clause, has evolved; the recent Kazakhstan and EU BIT (2024)[22] have shown a glimpse of the interrelation of human rights and investment laws. The legal lenses have also been designed to ensure the streamlining of the redressal mechanism by providing an appropriate framework; usually and mostly, it is an

[18] Ibid Article 5.

[19] ICSID Arbitration, case ref, ARB/14/2, para 154–165.

[20] Canada Peru Free Trade Agreement (2009).

[21] *Ibid*, ICSID arbitral decision ARB/14/2.

[22] See 16, paragraph 74.

arbitral award that is most significant and effective and generally is of three types for arbitral award enforcement

(a) New York Convention (1958)
(b) Panama Convention (1975)
(c) ICSID settles international disputes between state and private players, state and state, and others.

The decision of Bernhard von Pezold v Zimbabwe[23] stated that whenever there is a contrast between the BIT and human rights, not all the time discussion would be on human rights as BIT doesn't incorporate the universe of human rights; it is subjected to regulatory and investment related aspects as well. At times, these denials may result in adverse impact on activism in the intersectional study of Human rights and Investment treaties. Ideally, the submission of human rights and investment treaties are subject to due diligence and designing a model as per international investment standards,[24] keeping business models in consonance as BITs are not always subject to international humanitarian laws. The CSR standards are often termed "soft law"; as argued, it is more aspirational than practical.[25] It alleviates the business model and is efficient in terms of human rights and environmental impacts. Although domestic laws have legal theories for CSR, their international application still finds a way to fit in through international institutions and other agencies.[26] The key concerns are the absence of control and execution mechanisms, which are soft laws and not core legal bindings. Though, as in the decision of Pezold v Zimbabwe,[27] it is essential to keep investment in check, creating a universe of human rights and investment treaties and an integral part of the international legal framework is equally important.[28] The semantic and taxonomy study submits the rooting of CSR in human rights.

[23] Bernhard von Pezold and Others v. Republic of Zimbabwe, ICSID Case No. ARB/10/15.

[24] Emphasis added.

[25] Banerjee (2008), pp. 51–78.

[26] *Ibid,* see pp. 54–58.

[27] Supra 22.

[28] See, generally the argument is on creating a policy or treaty by the home state to secure the state's national labour, environmental laws, but the wordings have to be clear in the treaty (BIT), the choice of jurisdiction, states liability is equally important and integral part, so arbitral award should have legal framework in the treaty itself by ensuring the human rights aspect, for further reading refer, Paulsson (1995).

3 Normative Justification of Human Rights: An Integrative Approach

In practice, matters pertaining to investment law has seldom taken the interpretation route of International Human Rights law. Furthermore, this perception has been accentuated by the nature of human rights law being treated as a separate segment from the international investment law. In few cases, where International Human Rights were given attention to, focus had been on the human rights of the investors and seldom on human rights for protection of public interest. This has resulted from the legal dilemmas faced by the host state with regards to the investor as to balancing the obligations of the investors whilst upholding its commitments to human rights. Moreover, host states are driven by protection of investor's commercial interests as they contribute to nation development which sometimes, is at loggerheads with sustainable development. of particular concern is the awards given through arbitrations that could strain the limited economic resources of the host state, if it especially happens to be a developing country. It is at this juncture, that it is notable to observe that whilst investor's rights are enforced, obligations are oftentimes bypassed by the veil of separate corporate legal personality. Nevertheless, it is to be noted that there are no intrinsic conflicts between application of International Human Rights law in investment conflicts, in as much as the cause of the rise of conflicts being that of an element of lack of reconciliation between the two branches of law. This has been apparent, for instance, with the rise of the welfare state vis-a-vis privatization of public services, a conflict accentuated by the role of investors in the host state's public sector.[29]

Prior, there has been a view that non-economic laws like that of human rights ought not to be included in interpretation of investment disputes. Nevertheless, this has been negated by the contention that merits of the case can validate the application of International Human Rights law and systematic integration approach. Treaty arbitration in investment law is driven by a choice of law approach,[30] based on the merits of the case. It is at this point, that human rights law can be interpreted, provided that it has not been explicitly excluded by the parties. Despite such an interpretative reading, it might be construed that it could forego any such rigid application due to the non-binding nature of the international norms.[31]

The test of proportionality that measures the harm caused to investor versus harm cause to public interest, had become a sort of yardstick with an objective to uphold human rights,

The concept of systematic integration has been given effect by virtue of the Article 31(3)(c) of the Vienna Convention on the Law of Treaties. Based on the presumptions, viewed both positively and negatively, Human Rights could be given

[29] Yang Gao (2021), pp. 1–12.

[30] Santacroce (2019), pp. 136–155.

[31] Supra 30, at 23, *see generally*, Yang Gao (2021), pp. 1–12.

effect in Investment Disputes. Irrespective of the choice of law, viewed positively, the parties could have intended that general principles of law or customary law be applicable if the issue has not been sufficiently addressed by the choice of law, treaty by the parties. On the basis of later, it could be viewed by the parties, as irrespective of choice of law, the parties ought not have intended to act inconsistent with obligations of the broad ambit of international law, which includes international human rights as well.[32] Therefore, there should be a systematic integration between economic rights as well as social rights. This has to commence from the pre-investment stage itself, wherein the host state and the investor's rights & obligations in respect of human rights ought to be conveyed through a human rights audit. This will ensure that the legitimate expectations are set in terms of both the investor as well as the host state. A Harmonious interpretation ought to be given to give effect to both Investment law & Human rights law, whilst obliging by the choice of law in arbitral awards.[33] Whereas Harmonious interpretation seeks interpretations of both these laws, Prioritisation is concerned about justification in normative superiority in giving effect to these laws.[34]

In *Tulip vs Turkey*,[35] when parties are disputing the applicability of Human Rights Law in interpretation of Article 52 (1) (d) of the International Centre for Settlement of Investment Disputes Convention, Article 31(3)(c) of the Vienna Convention on the law of the treaties has been given effect to include all International Law sources as are relevant to the parties.[36] Interpretation and due regard have been given to human rights in investment treaty in *Urbaser vs Argentina*.[37] It has to be observed that the courts did give effect to International Human Rights law in several cases of Investment disputes, as can be seen in the cases of *Mondev International Ltd v United States of America*,[38] *Técnicas Medioambientales Tecmed, SA v United Mexican States*.[39] Nevertheless, there were instances when the court refused to apply Human Rights law into International Investment Disputes and did not consider the contention that there were interdependent, as can be seen in the case of *Border Timbers Limited and Others v. Zimbabwe* and in *Suez, Sociedad General de Aguas de Barcelona, S.A. and Vivendi Universal, S.A. v. Argentine Republic*[40] which decided in the favour of investor as the respondent failed to state the doctrine of necessity in application of human rights law in the case concerning water dispute. Similar line of decision has been taken in the case of *EDF International S.A., SAUR*

[32] Santacroce (2019), pp. 136–155.

[33] Simma (2011), pp. 573–596.

[34] Fahner and Happold (2019), pp. 741–759.

[35] Para 86–87, ICSID Case No. ARB/11/28 annulment proceeding.

[36] Mclachlan (2005), pp. 279–320.

[37] Para 1193–1212, ICSID Case No. ARB/07/26.

[38] Para 108, ICSID Case No. ARB (AF)/00/2.

[39] Para 141, ICSID Case No. ARB(AF)/99/2.

[40] ICSID Case No. ARB/03/19.

International S.A. and León Participaciones Argentinas S.A. v. Argentine Republic,[41] *Siemens A.G. v. The Argentine Republic.*[42]

In interpreting fair & equitable treatment in investment disputes and in interpreting the international responsibility, the court relied on *Azurix Corp v The Argentine Republic.*[43] Human rights of Third parties to investment dispute has been upheld in the case of *Joseph Houben v. Republic of Burundi*.[44] Furthermore, the UN Committee on Human rights have given interpretation to the compliance of ICCPR in International Investment Disputes in the case of *Hesham Talaat M. Al-Warraq v Indonesia.*[45] In this case, the court held that the obligations in investment law as regards the investors extends to giving effect to human rights compliance as well.[46] In *Philip Morris Brands Sàrl, Philip Morris Products S.A. and Abal Hermanos S.A. v. Oriental Republic of Uruguay,*[47] where Phillip sought to make a case for his company, was decided against his favour and in favour of the state by giving effect to interpretation of human rights into investment law dispute.

4 Cultural Rights & Indigenous Rights

Investments are needed for the economic development of any nation. Nevertheless, this has to be achieved without compromising the future generation's needs, forming a conceptual framework for sustainable development. At this juncture, it is the responsibility of the state to ensure that the development that is pursued, without affecting the cultural and human rights of the indigenous people. At this juncture, the protection given by United Nations Declaration on the Rights of Indigenous People[48] (UNDRIP), 2007, International Labour Organisation convention concerning Indigenous and Tribal Peoples in independent countries, 1989 has to be interpreted in consonance with economic laws. Article 15 of the Indigenous and Tribal People's convention, 1989,[49] states that consultation of the people concerned to the lands in which natural resources are based, shall be consulted to ascertain as to whether their interests would be affected by such exploitation or exploration.

---

[41] ICSID Case No. ARB/03/23.

[42] ICSID Case No. ARB/02/8.

[43] Para 149, ICSID Case No. ARB/01/12.

[44] ICSID Case No. ARB/13/7.

[45] Final Award dated 15 December 2014, https://www.italaw.com/sites/default/files/case-documents/italaw4164.pdf.

[46] Newcombe and Marcoux (2015), pp. 525–533.

[47] Para 45, ICSID Case No. ARB/10/7, *see generally,* Feria-Tinta (2017), pp. 601–630.

[48] Cinelli (2016), pp. 711–744.

[49] Article 15 of the Indigenous and Tribal People's convention, 1989 also states that such people whose lands on which natural resources are situate, shall be given the right to not merely conservation of those resources but in the use and management as well.

In the case of *Bernhard von Pezold and Others v Zimbabwe and Border Timbers Ltd and Others v Zimbabwe,*[50] in adjudicating the arbitration pertaining to land belonging to indigenous communities in relation to ancestral lands, in relation to lands affected by investor's rights. This potentially addresses indigenous communities living in the areas where foreign investments are made. Natural resources are often located in places where indigenous people live as they often end up bearing the disproportionate effects of environmental impacts and that of their livelihood. In the case of *Álvarez y Marín Corporación and others v. Panama,*[51] investments were situated in the lands of indigenous communities in panama, in *Ngabe Bugle,* where they sought to develop eco-tourist project. Similar ratio was held in the case of *Bear Creek Mining Corporation vs Republic of Peru,*[52] it has been viewed that the rights inherent in Indigenous people are not lesser than that of the rights vested in an investor. It is in recognition of their distinctive contributions that promote cultural diversity of humankind. where mining operations were located in place which is place of habitation of indigenous people in Bolivia, it was held in *South American Silver Ltd. vs The Plurinational State of Bolivia,*[53] that protection of the rights of indigenous communities would imply the protection of human rights in investment disputes. Therefore, the cultural entitlements form a part of human rights of the indigenous communities. In *Sawhoyamaxa Indigenous Community v. Paraguay,*[54] it was held that in exploration of investment, ancestral lands of indigenous tribes. Furthermore, the consent of the indigenous tribes has to be taken to give effect to right to self-determination. This provides a linkage between cultural rights as well as human rights. effect to right to self-determination.[55] This provides a linkage between cultural rights as well as human rights

5 International Institutions and Rights of Indigenous People 'Population' in Foreign Investment

The population living in a certain geographical area has been identified as a distinct group referred to as indigenous peoples or indigenous populations.[56] United Nations Declaration on the Rights of Indigenous Peoples (UNDRIP), a resolution adopted by the general assembly on 13th September 2007 on recommendations of the Human Rights Council, is a prime and most important document for safeguarding the

---

[50] Para 21–23, ICSID Case No. ARB/10/15.

[51] ICSID Case No. ARB/15/14.

[52] Para 36, ICSID Case No. ARB/14/21.

[53] Para 561, para 634, PCA Case No. 2013-15.

[54] Para 248, IACtHR (ser. C) No. 146, 2009.

[55] Vadi (2014), p. 241.

[56] World Health Organization. Indigenous Populations, https://www.who.int/topics/health_services_indigenous/en/.

Table 2 Cases pertaining to indigenous people's issues

	Arbitral case name ISDS	Indigenous people issue	Arbitral award
01	Glamis Gold Ltd v. USA	NAFTA, Mining and Hydrocarbon sector *Native American tribe*	In favour of state and arbitral cost
02	Grand River Enterprises Six Nations, Ltd., Et Al. v. United States of America	Manufacturing industry, NAFTA *Native American Tribe*	State favour, NDP
03	Bear Creek Mining Corp. v. Republic of Peru	ICSID, Mining and Quarrying reimburse Claimant 75% of its arbitration costs, plus compound interest. *Aymara Population*	Columbia centre for Sustainable investment as amicus curiae
04	Álvarez y Marín Corporación v. Republic of Panama	Netherlands–Panama BIT (2000) and Central America-Panama Real State *Comarca Bugle indigenous*	In favour of state
05	Pac Rim Cayman LLC v. Republic of El Salvador	ICSID, CAFTA Mining Industry *Inhabitants of Cabana*	ICSID granted an award of US $8 million to the Government of El Salvador to cover its legal fees and costs

interest of Indigenous people. International organizations like the United Nations Conference on Trade and Development (UNCTAD), International Investment agreements (IIAs), Bilateral Investment Treaties (BITs), and dispute mechanisms by ISDS. United Nations Conference on Trade and Development has passed the Investment Policy Framework for Sustainable Development (IPFSD).[57]

The disputes related to human rights concerns and investor profitability have recently increased, and investor-state dispute settlement ISDS frames policy for the investment laws.[58] Institutions like the Permanent court of arbitration (PCA) and the International Centre for Settlement of Investment Dispute (ICSID). The ISDS is seen as a threat to the state's ability to protect public health in foreign investment cases.[59] The literature on environmental rights, sustainability, and investment laws is in abundance, but the protection of indigenous people and their rights to foreign investment is mainly through the United Nations resolutions or arbitral cases.[60] The section would decipher the arbitral award related to Indigenous people. A few cases of different segment have been taken for example to understand the interrelation of indigenous community and the arbitral award (see Table 2).

[57] See for the documents UNCTAD, Permanent forum on indigenous issues.

[58] Wang et al. (2021), p. 7798.

[59] Spiegel et al. (2020), p. 2362.

[60] Ibid.

The diverse range of cases where the ICSID and other international agencies enforced the indigenous people's rights is a sub-genesis under human rights concerns as 'obligation' argued in the chapter. The strengthening of investment social responsibility could be achieved by

(a) Ensuring Free, Prior, informed consent (FPIC),[61] which is a tool where Consent from the indigenous populations is undertaken related to land, water, social, and other issues. This will significantly be a more deserving and meaningful form of association and engagement opportunity with indigenous people.
(b) Guiding Principles for Business and Human Rights by the United Nations is an attempt for businesses to adapt to both the foundational and operational principles of CSR.[62]

International instruments like UNDRIP, ICSID, FPIC[63] and International investment arbitration tribunal (IIAT) and (ILO convention 169) are key players to enforce transnational order and ultimately inclusion of human right concerns. ILO 169 is an international standard for indigenous people rights and does not exclude Indigenous and Tribal Populations Convention and Recommendation, 1957. The stakeholders (Indigenous population) shall decide their well-being and priority based on their standards; investors shall incorporate social responsibility, as it is their belief, faith, and their motherland that the investors are going to occupy. Free and informed Consent shall strictly be adhered to for significant changes. In the case of Bear Creek v Peru, the dissenting judge, Philippe Sands (on ILO 169), stated it to be important, and without its effect, the model would lose legal significance. Also, the consensus on the indigenous community should be taken into Consent and consideration before projects are undertaken by private international investors. Most importantly, the quest to ensure the rights of Indigenous people has been inscribed in international institutions and arbitration tribunals through Transnational public policy, which shall potentially be impactful and of the way forward for Indigenous people's rights.[64]

[61] See Columbian Centre for Sustainable Investment, Government Briefing on FPIC, https://ccsi.columbia.edu/content/government-briefing-incorporating-free-prior-and-informed-consent-fpic-investment-approval.

[62] Buxton and Wilson (2013).

[63] Abbreviations: United Nations Declaration on the Rights of Indigenous Peoples, International Centre for Settlement of Investment Disputes respectively.

[64] Marcoux (2020), pp. 809–846.

6 Transnational Policies to Secure Human Rights via Investment Arbitration

The transnational (or international) aspect of the investment law is to ensure reliance on the treaties and contracting parties.[65] A transnational approach would dismay the irrationality of enforcement of human rights concerns (if any) arising from the host country's investors.[66] Transnational public policy would significantly assure the socio-environmental aspect by providing legal framework by referring to it through fundamental values and international consensus and would prioritize the international treaty laws rather than the domestic legal framework.[67] The transnational (or international) aspect of the investment law is to ensure reliance on the treaties and contracting parties. A transnational approach would dismay the human rights concerns (if any) arising from the host country's investors. Transnational public policy would significantly assure the legal framework by referring to it through fundamental values and international consensus and would prioritize the international treaty laws rather than the domestic legal framework.

Investment law, from the lens of an international perspective, is primarily for the protection of the investors and the state. In case of any dispute, the tribunal would set up a mechanism for dispute settlement.[68] The authors, political scientists, and jurists showed concerns about the application of a tribunal for integrating human rights issues. In order to alleviate the precarious situation of enforcement and adjudication, the intellectual community has agreed to propose the transnational order in the form of public policy. The doctrine of Transnational public policy is effective for the procurement of claims and for settling disputes in a more effective way both in (a) contractual investment arbitration[69] (b) Treaty-based arbitration.

In *World Duty Free v Kenya,*[70] where the contracting parties were not states, but state and investors and the claimant submitted that the Kenyan government had failed to adhere to contractual obligations and disposed of the property by illegal means, the formula has to be more efficient with the application of public policy under transnational public order.[71] The primary question is, though most scholars, jurists, and political scientists have accepted the narrative to include the human rights enforcement through the arbitration tribunal, there's a section that also believes transnational public policy is inefficient to align it with human rights. So,

---

[65] Bueno et al. (2023), pp. 179–216.

[66] Ibid, Bueno and Vastardis (2023).

[67] See for defining Transnational order, refer Paulsso, Idea of Arbitration (2013) also see *Dolores Bentolila (2017)* Arbitrators as Lawmakers. Kluwer law, (2006), the reference has been made for definition from Kluwer laws, though literature of public policy and international law could append the existing knowledge see e.g. International Arbitration and Public policy, Juris Net 2006.

[68] Sornarajah (2003), pp. 1–20.

[69] See Dumberry (2012).

[70] World Duty Free Co. Ltd. v. Republic of Kenya, ICSID Case No. ARB/00/7.

[71] Ibid, para 157.

the question persists whether human rights could be invoked by an international arbitration tribunal through transnational public policy or not? The discussion is twofold; adhering to foreign investment is the most significant way, through public policy, as the human rights and CSR activities under investment are considered as soft law,[72] so providing strength to it would be a tough decision. Also, the normative approach of human rights with transnational public policy would conceptualize obligations to investors, which is an intrinsic part of public policy. The scholars also claimed to append the inclusion not only by policy but also by recognized international institutions.

The arbitration tribunal has admitted the norms in various arbitral disputes to decipher the advances in human rights issues dealt with by a transnational public policy. As in the *Plasma Consortium Ltd v Republic of Bulgaria,*[73] the tribunal referred to the notion of public policy and alienated the legal theory. In fact, in *Inceysa v El Salvador,*[74] the investment tribunal addressed the issue of illegal acts and their proper enforcement. This decision is also an exception to the award where considerate amount was bestowed to human norms. In *Union Fenosa Gas, S.A v Arab Republic of Egypt,*[75] the tribunal evaluated the impact of international public policy on the investor's rights. The deliberate use of illegal ways (fraud, forgery, others) and enforcing the right arising from it shall be inadmissible as being in contravention to public policy, as dealt with in the case of *Churchill Mining v Indonesia.*[76]

The Bilateral investment treaty (BIT) or the contractual agreement between the investors and state is subject to IIA, the discourse of intersectional study of human right in BIT is through the prism of IIAs and UNCTAD and imperative effectiveness on human rights concerns;[77] the argument advanced where the scholars agreeing to keep international agencies and arbitration tribunals to have an intrinsic proposition and integration of human right issues. The most accepted form and tested method is applying the 'Doctrine of Transnational Public Policy,' which in turn would make the arbitral award in accordance with the human rights and CSR concerns. The integration of human rights concerns and CSR in BIT clauses through mandatory IIAs is an increasingly most accepted approach, this will create an imperative notion and will scrutinize the lacunae in the document.

The aim is to advocate human rights Transnational order as an obligation on the investors and state (see Fig. 2). The approach would be principles of fundamental human rights, such as slavery, human trafficking, etc., through a public policy; secondly, CSR activities, both social and environmental aspects; and finally, the

[72] See, Supra 26.

[73] ICSID Case No. ARB/03/24, Expert opinion 8th Feb 2005.

[74] Inceysa Vallisoletana S.L. v. Republic of El Salvador, Award, 2nd August 2006, pp. 2–7.

[75] Unión Fenosa Gas, S.A. v. Arab Republic of Egypt, ICSID Case No. ARB/14/4.

[76] Churchill Mining PLC and Planet Mining Pty Ltd v. Republic of Indonesia, ICSID Case No. ARB/12/14 and 12/40, pp. 24–27.

[77] Yan (2020).

rights of Indigenous people or local people where the investment infrastructure is being submitted. The implementation would be through transnational policy as the core human right values shall not be compromised. In *Urbaser v Argentina,*[78] the tribunal raised the issue of basic rights to be followed and by illegal means the rights shall not be enforced. In *Biwater Gauff (Tanzania) Ltd. v. United Republic of Tanzania,*[79] the tribunal enunciated on human right concerns, though not human rights in specific but the social aspect in investment treaties.

The CSR and international investment have been discussed above with referring to different cases and we advocated for the CSR activities as mandatory part of any BIT and ensuring inclusion of human rights.

7 Final Consideration

The surge in the literature related to environmental jurisprudence has sparked widespread discussion on the intrinsic inclusion of human rights concerns in foreign investment agreements. To enforce CSR principles and human rights concerns as obligations, many scholarly attempts have been made. However, it left a few pragmatic questions that need to be addressed. How shall the execution of CSR in accordance with the highest standards be achieved, or how does the model put investors into the sling of consent-based investment, ensuring human rights under the aegis of environmental and social responsibility and Indigenous people's responsibility? The question is whether the international institute would ensure the effectiveness of the United Nations resolutions like UNDRIP and whether they would work in consonance with arbitration tribunals. The chapter presents key consideration in order to address these concerns:

1. Both Investors and host states shall incorporate *Free, Prior, and Informed Consent* (FPIC); in Foreign Investment Policy though this is a state (host) subject, getting the trust of the Indigenous people shall be of utmost importance for foreign investors.
2. There exists an asymmetry of rights and obligations of foreign and foreign investors in the host state. International agencies like OECD, ICSID, IIAs, ISDS and UNCTAD shall ensure an effective Integration of CSR activities with certainty and mandatorily enforceable, as many of the treaties do have CSR activities but need to be more certain in their execution, unlike the country's domestic laws related to CSR.
3. The findings of the chapter extrapolate the nature of investment disputes and its disputable contentions given by the parties representing investors in applicability of human rights law. An integrated approach has to be taken in giving effect to

[78] ICSID Case No. ARB/05/22, procedure order no 1, para 3–9.

[79] ICSID Case No. ARB/07/26, Award, 8th December 2016.

> conventions and treaties pertaining to human rights whilst giving effect to international investment disputes. Sustainable development involves consideration of environmental as well as cultural rights of the indigenous communities. Developmental projects ought to take the consent of the indigenous community and the state should realise that in consideration of the ownership of resources, it acts as a trustee and not an absolute owner, whilst granting investment projects. This has to be integrally interpreted into the ambit of cultural rights, as consideration of human rights. It is advisable to carry out environmental impact assessment as well as human rights audit prior to investor agreements to initiate compliance measures as obligations of the investors while interpreting the rights of the investors.

The juxtaposition of human rights concerns and CSR in investment treaty seems to be effective but its implementation lacks the enforcement. The argument advanced and the chapter summarising the key challenges and also suggesting a model for consideration, which is Transnational public policy doctrine, where the arbitration tribunals and international agencies shall incorporate the impact by assessment of the BIT and the indigenous population consent. Both Investors and state interest shall be of utmost importance, as investors invest for benefits, so limited but strengthen CSR shall be binding on them and state responsibility is to go welfare and be accountable to their people and resources shall use the suggested approach and most importantly the legal theorem, the legal landscape should be strong and shall be derived from strong international agencies creating a model being in consonance with highest standards or minimum standards (where required) by the authorities (usually United Nations). Application of the Shewhart cycle shall be used, which shall be the primary tool or the first step for problem-solving, as the integration is across different agencies, where the planning and act for incremental changes is required for facilitating the investor's proper and state.

8 Conclusion

The rapid technological change and unprecedented COVID-19 pandemic have resulted in a transformative legal approach across the sector. Foreign Investment theory and human rights are no exception. International investment agreements were earlier criticized for being a soft law (as also referred to in a few scholarly articles), so the effectiveness was fragile, and indeed, the aspect of social responsibility was at the novice stage. The article comprehended many different investment treaties in the Bilateral Investment Treaty (BIT) segment, and the finding was that there has now been a paradigm shift as the documents (investor-state or state-state) do contain CSR. However, the language is inefficient for its execution as there's no certainty, so the chapter primarily argued for subdividing clauses of CSR into 8 clauses, 13 clauses, and others based on effectivity. The human rights in this chapter were hypothesized to be the genesis of CSR; indigenous rights are an intrinsic part of human rights concerns. The legal landscape was from the lenses of arbitral awards and their decision by ICSID. With respect to the mechanism of enforcement, the liability of investors was ensured in the host state by injecting the doctrine of Transnational public policy and not law alone to strengthen these international agencies like ILO, UNHR, ISDS and International Tribunal for arbitration decisions, where the rights were not settled if it was arising from the exploitation of human rights (as slavery, forced labour, etc.). So, Human Rights intrinsically have a nexus with investment.

The approach for implementation of transnational order and ultimately settling has been taken in three stages, principles of (basic) human rights such as slavery, forced labour etc., secondly, Corporate social responsibility clause, which have been discussed in the above-mentioned para. Finally, the rights of Indigenous people, where many legislations, such as UNDRIP, IPFSD, free, prior, informed consent (FPIC) were addressed and advocated to implement for ensuring the utmost welfare to the Indigenous people, which shall be applicable for both states and investors. Cases on arbitral awards, the types of indigenous tribes involved, and the final result were referred to for assessment of paradigm shift in the policy. Private international investors, though for any business profitability, are realistic but suggest strict interpretation in these three avenues.

With the accentuating investor disputes in the Era of globalization, it becomes pertinent to understand and analyze the underlying issues that are seldom addressed. Of particular significance is the rights as well as obligations of the investors not merely as defined in investors agreements or in interpretation of economic laws but also adherence to non-economic laws which form the basis for sustainable development. These includes an integrated and harmonious interpretation of human rights in consonance with investment agreements and the choice of law by parties. Furthermore, the ambit of human rights extend to cultural rights of indigenous communities who are the inhabitants in habitats where natural resources are abundant and form part of their cultural heritage in ancestral lands. This involves giving effect to their consent in carrying out investment projects as well as with respect to the tapestry of their culture that are inherent in their socio-economic fabric of life.

References

Ballor GA, Yildirim AB (2020) Multinational corporations and the politics of international trade in multidisciplinary perspective. Bus Polit, 573–586. https://www.cambridge.org/core/services/aop-cambridge-core/content/view/5698D9A182A7CF72445BC184678ED8D2/S1469356920000142a.pdf/multinational-corporations-and-the-politics-of-international-trade-in-multidisciplinary-perspective.pdf

Banerjee SB (2008) Corporate social responsibility: the good, the bad and the ugly. Crit Sociol 34(1):51–78. https://doi.org/10.1177/0896920507084623

Borensztein E, De Gregorio J, Lee J-W (1998) How does foreign direct investment affect economic growth? J Int Econ:115–135. https://olemiss.edu/courses/inst310/BorenszteinDeGLee98.pdf

Bowen H (1953) Social responsibilities of businessman, business & economics. University of Iowa Press

Bueno N, Vastardis AY, Djeuga IN (2023) Investor human rights and environmental obligations: the need to redesign corporate social responsibility clauses. J World Invest Trade 24(2): 179–216. https://doi.org/10.1163/22119000-12340278

Buxton A, Wilson E (2013) FPIC and the extractive industries: a guide to applying the spirit of free, prior and informed consent in industrial projects. International Institute for Environment and Development. ISBN: 9781843699095

Cinelli C (2016) Foreign investment, indigenous peoples and sustainable development: the Inter-American Court of Human Rights case-law. Nijhoff International Investment Law Series, 711–744. https://doi.org/10.1163/9789004311473_026

Dolores Bentolila (2017) Arbitrators as Lawmakers. Kluwer Law (2006)

Dumberry P (2012) International investment contracts. International investment law: sources of rights and obligations. Brill/Nijhoff, Leiden, 215–244

Ellis J, Edmonds D (2023) Coming to terms with the SDGs: a perspective from legal scholarship. Leiden J Int Law 36(2):251–271. https://www.cambridge.org/core/services/aop-cambridge-core/content/view/13AAB02C2284501192852C59B1AB1845/S0922156522000838a.pdf/coming-to-terms-with-the-sdgs-a-perspective-from-legal-scholarship.pdf

EU - Kyrgyzstan EPCA (2024) UNCTAD documents. https://www.eeas.europa.eu/sites/default/files/documents/2024/Kyrgyz-Rep-EPCA%20%28003%29.pdf

Fahner JH, Happold M (2019) The human rights defence in international investment arbitration: exploring the limits of systemic integration. Int Comp Law Q 68(3):741–759. https://doi.org/10.1017/S0020589319000241

Feria-Tinta M (2017) Like oil and water? Human rights in investment arbitration in the wake of Philip Morris v. Uruguay. J Int Arbitr 4:601–630. https://kluwerlawonline.com/journalarticle/Journal+of+International+Arbitration/34.4/JOIA2017029

India–Taiwan BIT (2018) Article 12. https://dea.gov.in/sites/default/files/BIA%20between%20ITA%20and%20TECC.pdf

Ursula Kriebaum (2018) Human rights and international investment arbitration. Edward Elgar, ISBN 9781782549116

Marcoux JM (2020) Transnational public policy as a vehicle to impose human rights obligations in international investment arbitration. J World Invest Trade 21(6):809–846

Mbiyavanga S (2017) Combatting corruption through International Investment Treaty law. J Anti-Corruption Law 1(2):132–150. https://doi.org/10.14426/jacl.v1i.1257

Mclachlan C (2005) The principle of systemic integration and article 31(3)(C) of the Vienna Convention. Int Comp Law Q 54(2):279–320. https://doi.org/10.1093/iclq/lei001

Newcombe A, Marcoux J-M (2015) Hesham Talaat M. Al-Warraq v Republic of Indonesia imposing international obligations on foreign investors. ICSID Rev 30(3):525–532. https://doi.org/10.1093/icsidreview/siv033

Patel A, Parakh A (2022) International law as a weak law issue. Int J Law Manag Hum 3:196. https://ijlmh.com/paper/international-law-as-a-weak-law/

Paulsson J (1995) Arbitration without privity. ICSID Rev For Invest Law J 10(2):232–257. https://doi.org/10.1093/icsidreview/10.2.232

Phoenix Action, Ltd. v. The Czech Republic, ICSID Case No. ARB/06/5

Report on Human rights-compatible International Investment Agreements (IIAs) (2021) A/76/238. https://documents.un.org/doc/undoc/gen/n21/208/09/pdf/n2120809.pdf

Ruggie J (2011) Report of the special representative of the secretary-general on the issue of human rights and transnational corporations and other business enterprises: Guiding principles on business and human rights: implementing the United Nations ‘protect, respect and remedy’ framework. Netherlands Q Hum Rights, 224–253. https://digitallibrary.un.org/record/705860?ln=en&v=pdf

Santacroce FG (2019) The applicability of human rights law in international investment disputes. ICSID Rev For Invest Law J 34(1):136–155. https://doi.org/10.1093/icsidreview/siz005

Simma B (2011) Foreign investment arbitration: a place for human rights? Int Comp Law Q 60(3): 573–596. https://doi.org/10.1017/S0020589311000224

Sornarajah M (2003) The clash of globalizations and the international law on foreign investment: the Simon Reisman lecture in international trade policy. Can For Policy J 10(2):1–20. https://doi.org/10.1080/11926422.2003.9673321

Spiegel SJ, Thomas S, O'Neill K, Brondgeest C, Thomas J, Beltran J et al (2020) Visual storytelling, intergenerational environmental justice and indigenous sovereignty: exploring images and stories amid a contested oil pipeline project. Int J Environ Res Public Health 17(7):2362. https://doi.org/10.3390/ijerph17072362

UNCTAD navigator, BIT (Home page), Treaties between countries. https://investmentpolicy.unctad.org/international-investment-agreements

Vadi V (2014) International investment law and arbitration. Cambridge University Press, p 241. ISBN: 978-1-107-038486

Wang C, Ning J, Zhang X (2021) International investment and indigenous peoples' environment: a survey of ISDS cases from 2000 to 2020. Int J Environ Res Public Health 18(15):7798. https://doi.org/10.3390/ijerph18157798

Yan Y (2020) Anti-corruption provisions in international investment agreements: investor obligations, sustainability considerations, and symmetric balance. J Int Econ Law 23(4):989–1013. https://doi.org/10.1093/jiel/jgaa026

Raymond Yang Gao (2021) Bridging separate worlds—application of human rights law in Investment Treaty Arbitration. Northwest J Int Law Bus 42(1):1–12. https://scholarlycommons.law.northwestern.edu/njilb/vol42/iss1/1

Part II
International Law

Ensuring Child Support: Tendencies in Caselaw on Maintenance in Slovenia and Lithuania

Neža Pogorelčnik Vogrinc and Agnė Limantė

1 Introduction

In Europe, the prevalence of single-parent households varies significantly across different countries. As of 2020, approximately 14% of households with children in the European Union were single-parent households, representing about 4% of total households. After Sweden, Denmark and Estonia, Lithuania (25%) ranked among the countries with the highest percentage of single-parent households in Europe. Slovenia, on the other hand, had a lower proportion of single-parent households compared to Lithuania, with the recorded share being 9%.[1] However, even with such relatively positive numbers, almost 1 in 10 children lived with a single parent.[2]

Child maintenance plays a crucial role in supporting children living in single-parent households. Single parenthood is gendered, and a very high proportion of single-parent households are headed by women.[3] Single mothers often struggle with three major challenges: insufficient resources, limited employment opportunities,

[1] Eurostat (2021).

[2] Single parenthood can be defined as a situation in which a child is raised by only one parent or one parent at a time. It can occur after separation, divorce, or the death of one of the parents. European Parliament. Directorate General for Internal Policies of the Union (2014), p. 11.

[3] In the EU, the proportion of lone mothers has decreased only slightly from 82.74% to 81.35% between 2013 and 2020. Lanza-León and Cantarero-Prieto (2024), p. 1. See also European Parliament. Directorate General for Internal Policies of the Union (2014), p. 14.

N. Pogorelčnik Vogrinc (✉)
University of Ljubljana, Faculty of Law, Ljubljana, Slovenia
e-mail: neza.pogorelcnik@pf.uni-lj.si

A. Limantė
Law Institute, Lithuanian Centre for Social Sciences, Vilnius, Lithuania
e-mail: agne.limante@teise.org

Z. Meskić et al. (eds.), *Balkan Yearbook of European and International Law 2024*,
Balkan Yearbook of European and International Law 2024,
https://doi.org/10.1007/978-3-031-89952-2_3

and ineffective policies.[4,5] Therefore, financial child support from the parent living separately, is often an important help for a single mother in her efforts to ensure the living standard of the child.[6] From the other perspective, when fathers pay child support, they are also making statements about fatherhood, gender, power,[7] but also about shared parental responsibilities, and their commitment to their children's well-being.

When a child lives with both parents, both are presumed to cover the child's needs, and maintenance questions rarely arise. However, in the case of divorce or separation of a child's parents, or in situations where the child never lived with (one or both) parents, maintenance becomes one of the primary issues that courts and parents address when settling parental responsibilities. In many countries, including Lithuania and Slovenia maintenance payments are typically established either through mutual agreement between the parents or, if such an agreement is not possible, by a court order.[8]

Set-up of maintenance schemes differs substantially between countries, due to underlying structures, legislation, and organization of welfare distribution,[9] though certain tendencies can be noted in countries belonging to the same region or sharing similar history. Taking a comparative perspective, this paper examines legal regulation and case law[10] pertaining to child maintenance payments in Slovenia and Lithuania.[11] The selection of Slovenia and Lithuania as the focal points for the paper is motivated by a desire to explore the diversity in legal systems within Europe and to identify common trends in child maintenance practices. Both countries are members of the European Union, however geographically located in different regions, the countries had developed their family law rules without cross-influence. Moreover, as noted above, the share of single-parent households in the country differs. The authors of the paper seek to establish, how close are the principles of establishment of child maintenance payments in the two countries and whether there are some best practices to be learned from.

The paper starts with the explanation of the concept of child maintenance, with a brief presentation and comparison of the legal rules in the two European countries analysed. Then, through an analysis of case law and its trends, the main criteria for

---

[4]Nieuwenhuis (2021), p. 563.

[5]Moreover, the studies indicate a positive correlation between single-parent households and the risk of poverty. Antonelli et al. (2024), pp. 1–15; Calegari et al. (2024), pp. 481–498.

[6]Hakovirta and Jokela (2019), pp. 264, 268.

[7]See in this regard, e.g., Natalier and Hewitt (2010), p. 490.

[8]E-Justice portal information. European E-Justice Portal - Family Maintenance (2024).

[9]Fernqvist et al. (2023), p. 2.

[10]Where national court decisions are cited, the parts cited have been translated by the authors of the chapter.

[11]The so-called EU Maintenance Regulation does not regulate how the amount of maintenance is determined, which is left to national laws. Council Regulation (EC) No 4/2009 of 18 December 2008 on jurisdiction, applicable law, recognition and enforcement of decisions and cooperation in matters relating to maintenance obligations. OJ L 7, 10.1.2009, pp. 1–79.

determining the amount of maintenance will be presented. This will highlight the similarities between the two systems, on the one hand, and the differences, on the other. The authors seek to underline the strengths and weaknesses of each of the different regimes and explain the reasons why and how each arrangement evolved. By scrutinising the legal frameworks and practices of both countries, the authors aim to offer a comprehensive understanding of the rules governing parents' financial responsibilities towards children and how these regulations are implemented in practice. An extensive analysis of case law—inaccessible to most non-native readers due to language barrier—seeks to offer insights into the judicial interpretations and precedents that shape the application of child maintenance laws in these jurisdictions.

2 The Concept of the Child Maintenance Duty

Child maintenance policy is not just about money, it also raises fundamental questions about social values and fairness.[12] The concept of child maintenance first of all revolves around the legal and moral obligation of both parents to support their children financially.[13] The non-custodial parent[14] is seen as having a moral responsibility to help cover both the financial costs (e.g., food and lodging) and the non-financial costs (e.g., impact on the custodial parent's career due to increased childcare responsibilities) of the residential parent.[15]

As a legal definition, child maintenance involves the consistent provision of financial support, which is expected to be regularly[16] paid by a non-resident parent to the so-called residential parent, contributing to the financial cost of raising a

[12] Skinner et al. (2012), p. 338.

[13] While the obligation of parents to support their children is essentially based on the family relationship, some emphasize also its elements of a civil law obligation (e.g., the debtor may default on payment). However, unlike a typical civil law obligation, maintenance has certain specific features. For example, the creditor and the debtor are predetermined and cannot be changed, and the maintenance debt cannot be set off. See Gabrilo (1996), p. 126.

[14] In general, the terms "non-custodial parent" and "non-residential parent" are used interchangeably in this paper, though they can carry slightly different connotations. The term "non-custodial parent" focuses on the legal custody arrangement, where the parent does not have physical custody of the child (where the child lives), but may still share legal custody (decision-making authority) and have visitation rights. The term "non-residential parent" is more specifically related to where the child resides. A non-residential parent is one with whom the child does not primarily live, but it does not necessarily imply anything about legal custody.

[15] European Parliament. Directorate General for Internal Policies of the Union (2014), p. 16.

[16] Typically, the preferred form of child maintenance is periodic monthly payments. In some jurisdictions, including Lithuania, child maintenance may also be awarded as a lump sum payment or awarding of certain property to the child. However, this practice is rather exceptional and is usually applied only when the parent has no regular income.

child.[17] It is intended to cover the child's essential needs, ensuring their well-being by contributing to necessities such as housing, food, clothing, health care, education, and daily expenses. The aim of the legal duty to pay child maintenance is thus to ensure a stable and supportive environment for the child, at the same time emphasising the financial responsibility of both parents in taking care of the child's needs and overall welfare.

In Lithuania and Slovenia, child maintenance is a constitutional obligation of parents (see Article 38(6) of the Constitution of the Republic of Lithuania[18] and Article 54 of the Constitution of the Republic of Slovenia[19]). The Supreme Court of Lithuania has held that the obligation to take care of a child, to educate and maintain him/her, and to create normal conditions of living environment, arises from the inherent obligation of parents to be responsible for the situation of their children until they reach adulthood. Parents cannot thus refuse to fulfil their obligation to maintain a child up to the age of majority or to transfer this duty to other persons, including the parent with whom the child lives. Therefore, though the financial situation of parents is an important factor in determining the amount of maintenance, even if the child's parents have no income or assets, their obligation to provide maintenance to a child does not disappear.[20] Furthermore, under Article 3.195 of the Civil Code of

[17] Hakovirta and Jokela (2019), p. 259.

[18] In Lithuania, two main sources of the family law are the Constitution of the Republic of Lithuania and the Civil Code (LTCC). While the Constitution set the main principles, the LTCC regulates family law in detail. LTCC is divided into six books, one from which—Book Three—is entirely dedicated to family law matters. The provisions of the Book Three define the general principles of the legal regulation of family relations and govern the grounds and procedures of entering into marriage, validity and dissolution of marriage, property and non-property personal rights of spouses, establishment of maternity and paternity, mutual rights and responsibilities between children, parents and other family members. It also sets the basic provisions on adoption, guardianship, curatorship and on the procedures of registering acts of civil status.

[19] Article 54 of the Constitution of the Republic of Slovenia determines the following: "Parents have the right and duty to maintain, educate, and raise their children. This right and duty may be revoked or restricted only for such reasons as are provided by law in order to protect the child's interests. Children born out of wedlock have the same rights as children born within it." However, this is only a definition of rights and obligations at a principled level. Parental obligations in Slovenia are defined in more detail in the SLFC, which applies from 15 April 2019 and which replaced the Marriage and Family Relations Act (*Official Gazette* SRS, no. 15-644/1976), which had been previously in force for more than 40 years. The Constitutional Court of the Republic of Slovenia has in the past dealt with the above-mentioned provisions for several times. A clear overview of its relevant decisions can be found in Trefalt and Jager Agius (2014), p. 29 and the following.

[20] In Anglo-Saxon countries, the state enforces family obligations between parents and children. In contrast, Nordic and some Central European countries follow a different approach, where the state guarantees at least part of the child maintenance if the responsible parent is unable or fails to make the payments (Hakovirta and Jokela 2019, p. 259). Under Article 3.204 LTCC, if minors do not receive maintenance from father/mother over 1 month, maintenance is paid by the state (99 EUR in 2024). A state that has granted maintenance to minor children then has a right of recourse to recover child support payments from the child's parents or other relatives.

Lithuania[21] (LTCC) and Article 184 of the Slovenian Family Code[22] (SLFC), the obligation of child maintenance remains even if the child is separated from the parents or their parental authority is restricted, except in cases where the child is adopted. In Lithuania, the responsibility for avoiding maintaining a child is also foreseen in the Criminal Code.[23,24] The same in Slovenia, where the sentence for failure to pay maintenance, despite being able to do so, is imprisonment for up to 1 year, and up to 3 years if the person entitled to maintenance is or could be at risk because of that (Article 194 of the Criminal Code[25]). The importance of maintenance is also reflected in the fact that the SLFC specifically provides that renunciation of the right to maintenance by the child shall have no legal effect (Article 188). However, it is true that the beneficiary can *de facto* achieve the same effect by simply not filing a maintenance claim.[26]

Child maintenance can be seen as part of parental duties.[27] In Lithuanian law, the concept of parental duties includes the duties of care and protection, bringing up and educating children, taking care of their wellbeing, maintenance of children and keeping contacts with them, as well as the right to determine child's name, family name, place of residence, and also covers child's legal representation and administration of his/her property.[28] The legal regulation of parental obligations in Slovenia is comparable; the laws partly use different terminology, but are very similar in substance.[29] Maintenance is the only aspect of parental responsibility that is limited by the parents' ability to earn and afford, while their financial situation does not and

[21] Civil Code of the Republic of Lithuania. *Official Gazette,* 2000, No. 74 with subsequent amendments.

[22] *Official Gazette* RS, no. 15/17 with subsequent amendments. The terminology used in writing the Slovenian part of this article was that of the unofficial translation of the Family Code, which is published on the website https://pisrs.si/aktualno/zakonodaja-v-anglescini (accessed 15 September 2024).

[23] Criminal Code of the Republic of Lithuania. *Official Gazette*, 2000, No. 89-2741, with later amendments.

[24] For a more extensive analysis see Žalnieriūnas and Girdenis (2013).

[25] *Official Gazette* RS, no. 55/08 with subsequent amendments.

[26] Ahlin Doljak et al. (2024), p. 563.

[27] The obligation to provide maintenance arises for persons registered as the child's parents. In the case of a child born to a married couple, the spouses are registered as the parents, and in the case of a child born to unmarried persons, paternity is established by a couple's joint declaration or by a court decision (Art. 3.140 LTCC). The rule is the same is Slovenia (see Articles 113 and 114 SLFC).

[28] On child rights in family cases in Lithuania, see Kudinavičiūtė-Michailovienė and Uusen-Nacke (2022).

[29] Thus, Article 137 SLFC provides the following parental obligations: (1) Parents shall be obliged to care for the life and health of their children, providing safety, basic care, upbringing and supervision. (2) Parents shall be obliged to provide their children with conditions for healthy growth, balanced personal development and independent life and work. (3) Parents shall maintain their children in accordance with the provisions of this Code. (4) Parents shall, within their powers, provide for the schooling and professional education of their children according to their capacities, talents and wishes.

should not have an impact on the implementation of the other segments of parental responsibility.[30]

As in most European states, the laws of Lithuania and Slovenia[31] establish the obligation of parents to maintain their children until they reach the age of majority (18 years). Moreover, legal regulation in both countries includes the duty of parents in certain cases support their healthy adult children.[32] But whereas a minor child receives the right to maintenance by birth, an adult child must fulfil additional requirements in order to be entitled to such maintenance.[33] In this regard, Article 3.192[1] LTCC provides that parents should support their children until the age of 24 if they continue their high school education, are seeking professional qualification or university degree (only in case of first professional qualification and university degree) and need financial support.[34] In Slovenia, the obligation to provide maintenance for a child in secondary or higher education continues until the child turns 26, but only applies until the first completion of secondary education, short-cycle higher education, or an undergraduate/single master's program. This obligation is conditional on the child being a full-time student,[35] not employed, and not registered as seeking employment (Article 183 SLFC).[36]

It should be noted, however, that the concept of maintenance of minor children and the concept of maintenance of adult children (who are in full-time education and in need of support) are fundamentally different, which also results in differences in regulation. Firstly, an adult child has full legal capacity and therefore applies to the court for maintenance himself/herself.[37] Secondly, in both countries, compared to the criteria for the award of maintenance to a minor child, additional criteria have been established for the maintenance of an adult child (e.g. age limit; seeking professional qualification). Moreover, there are certain other differences, for instance, in case of adult child maintenance in Slovenia, both parties can choose the method of maintenance. While the rule is that parents maintain minor children

[30]Novak et al. (2019), p. 415.

[31]See Article 183 SLFC.

[32]While most countries base their definition of a child on Article 1 of the Convention on the Rights of the Child, which defines a child generally as a person who has not yet reached the age of 18, the concept of a child, as regards maintenance, is extended, exceptionally, to a child who has reached the age of majority (Rijavec 2019, p. 69). See also Končina Peternel (2019), pp. 93–98.

[33]Ahlin Doljak et al. (2024), p. 544.

[34]For a detailed analysis of this duty see Kudinavičiūtė-Michailovienė and Šimkienė (2018). See also Kudinavičiūtė-Michailovienė and Vėgelienė (2012), pp. 221–224.

[35]This term should not be interpreted literally. For a more detailed presentation of the situations in which case law considers that such condition is met, see Ahlin Doljak et al. (2024), pp. 544–546.

[36]For more on that see Weber (2019), pp. 10–11.

[37]While the Slovenian Non-contentious Civil Procedure Act (*Official Gazette* RS, no. 16/19) (SNCPA) emphasises the principle of investigation in disputes concerning children (Article 7), case law applies this principle with great restraint in the procedure for deciding on the maintenance of an adult child. This is probably because the SNCPA itself imposes the application of the principle in order to protect the rights and legal interests of children, but at the same time it implies that a child shall be a person under age of 18 (Article 6(3)) (Burkelc 2023, p. 11).

within the household,[38] they can make other arrangements with adult children. Parents can choose how to support their adult child: they can take (keep) the child into their household and provide maintenance there or pay her/him monthly maintenance (Article 194(2) SLFC). However, an adult child whose parents want to support him or her in their own household, may, for certain reasons, ask for monthly monetary maintenance to be set and paid while not living in the household with his or her parents (e.g. to attend school in a distant place).[39] In such an event, the adult child and the parent shall conclude an agreement (in the form of an enforceable notarial deed) on the maintenance to be paid by the parents (Article 193 SLFC).[40]

3 Criteria for Establishing Child Maintenance Amounts

The methodology for establishing child maintenance allowances differs across various countries (for example, the percentage-of-income system, the system of balancing needs and potential, the system of expense distribution, and others).[41] While it was possible to draw strong parallels between the Slovenian and Lithuanian legal systems when comparing the general rules, a notable difference emerges when it comes to the mechanism of determining the appropriate maintenance for a minor child.

Under Lithuanian law, the amount of maintenance must be proportional to the needs of the children and the financial situation of their parents, and to ensure the conditions necessary for the child to develop (LTCC 3.192(2)). Therefore, the courts, when awarding maintenance, have to evaluate two main aspects: (1) the needs of a specific child; and (2) the financial situation of the parent from whom the maintenance is claimed.[42] In general, in Lithuania, a reference criterion for awarding maintenance to a child to meet his or her essential needs is the minimum monthly salary minus state child support (to be divided by two as both parents have a duty to maintain their child; this amounts to 305 EUR in 2024). Such reference amount in

---

[38] Parents shall maintain children in their household, unless this is contrary to the best interests of the child. If a parent does not maintain a minor child in their household (because of the separation, divorce with child's other parent or any other reason), they shall contribute to their maintenance with a monthly maintenance payment. See Articles 183(5) and 194 SLFC.

[39] Novak (2017), p. 141.

[40] The reason is that all maintenance agreements between adults are concluded before a notary. Weber (2018), p. 23.

[41] Kudinavičiūtė-Michailovienė and Vėgelienė (2012), p. 212.

[42] In case of several children from different partners, the amount of maintenance for each child also depends on the other parent's ability to provide maintenance. For example, in one case, the father had two children from different mothers. One of them owned an apartment where she lived with the child, while the other was renting the apartment. This justified a departure from the principle of equal maintenance for all children and different maintenance amounts awarded to children. LT Supreme Court, ruling of 5 April 2011, No. 3K-3-154/2011.

practice means that the parent seeking child maintenance is not obliged to provide detailed evidence to justify expenditure on the child not exceeding the minimum monthly salary. However, a parent who seeks to prove that the child's needs are above or below the minimum monthly salary has the burden of substantiation (e.g., bills regarding child-related expenditure are usually provided by a parent seeking to have a higher amount of maintenance to be awarded). It has to be highlighted, though, that this criterion is only indicative and is applied in the light of the particular circumstances of the case.[43] Moreover, the obligation of both parents to provide maintenance for their children does not always mean, as discussed below, that each parent must provide maintenance at the same level: the concrete amount to be awarded may vary depending on a number of factual circumstances, such as the place of residence of the minor child (as the residential parent is considered to be taking more child-care duties) and the financial situation of parents.

Though child's needs and the financial situation of the parents are the main criteria[44] analysed to establish maintenance,[45] the way child maintenance is determined is slightly different in Slovenia. In Slovenia, SLFC contains the principle of proportionality, which states that spouses shall contribute to the subsistence of the family in proportion to their capacities (Article 61 SLFC). This is also the general rule for sharing the burden of maintaining a child between parents.[46] Differently from Lithuania, there is no reference amount of maintenance that a child can expect, but it is calculated in each specific case. As will be discussed in more detail later in this paper, a rough calculation is made firstly of the needs of the individual child and secondly of the material and financial resources of both parents (Article 189 SLFC). Although both parents are responsible for maintenance of their child, this does not mean that they automatically share the cost of maintenance in half. The ratio of the division of maintenance between the parents is determined according to their financial situation.

3.1 *The Needs of the Child*

One of the most important factors in calculating the amount of maintenance in both the Slovenian and Lithuanian systems is the needs of the individual child. However, child needs might be understood in various ways. What is the necessary amount of financial support for a child's living expenses? Should a child have the right to benefit from their parents' wealth, or is the purpose of child support solely to ensure

[43] LT Supreme Court, ruling of 9 February 2010, No. 3K-3-71/2010.

[44] Strobelj (2020), p. 67.

[45] These are standard criteria in many EU states. See, e.g. on the Netherlands, Curry-Sumner and Montanus (2012), p. 307.

[46] Novak et al. (2019), p. 172.

a basic level of subsistence for the child? Does the age of the child matter? There are many questions that national case law has to answer when deciding on child support.

As regards the criterion of the child's needs, in Lithuania, legal doctrine divides them into general (e.g. food, clothes) and individual (dependent on child capabilities and wishes).[47] The Supreme Court of Lithuania has recognised that the child's needs for food, clothing, housing, health, education, recreation, leisure, cultural and other education must be met by parents. The child must also be provided with the material means, in accordance with his or her abilities and wishes, to participate in various additional activities, sports and cultural events, to attend theatres, concerts, and children's holiday camps, and to acquire the necessary means for the child to develop his or her abilities.[48] Similar requirements can be found in Slovenia, where the SLFC (Article 189) states that the amount of maintenance shall be calculated with regard to the needs of the beneficiary, the maintenance allowance must ensure "the conditions necessary for the child's development",[49] and that the courts shall, in assessing maintenance, consider the best interests of the child, so that maintenance adequately provides for their good physical and mental development. Maintenance shall cover the costs of the child's basic needs, in particular the costs of accommodation, food, clothes, footwear, care, schooling, education, leisure, free time and other needs.[50] However, the statutory provisions set only general criteria, and it is then up to the courts to decide how to apply them when determining maintenance for a particular child. In both countries, when deciding on the amount of child maintenance in a particular case, account must be taken of the child's reasonable needs, which are determined by his or her abilities, aptitudes and inclinations. Overall, there is a tendency to preserve for the child the standard of living he or she had before the parents' split up.[51]

In Slovenia, the cost of maintenance in court proceedings is calculated according to the approximate costs for each child's specific needs in a month.[52] All the costs of accommodation, clothing and footwear, schooling, personal accident insurance, extra-curricular activities, leisure time, hygiene, cosmetics, mobile phone, summer holidays, pocket money and whatever else is relevant for the individual child are considered. Expenses known in advance (e.g. monthly childcare costs, monthly language course costs) are taken into account at that amount, while other expenses (e.g. food, clothing) are taken into account at a flat rate according to the age of the child.[53] Thus, for example, such a calculation for a concrete 2.5 year old child made

---

[47] Kudinavičiūtė-Michailovienė and Vėgelienė (2012), p. 213.

[48] LT Supreme Court, ruling of 10 November 2009, No. 3K-3-495/2009.

[49] Article 183(1) SLFC.

[50] Article 190 SLFC. See also Pavec (2006), pp. VI–VII.

[51] The same in Slovenia. See for example Ljubljana Higher Court, ruling of 21 February 2018, No. Cp 314/2018.

[52] Ljubljana Higher Court, ruling of 21 February 2018, No. IV Cp 314/2018.

[53] For example, the court found that the cost of internet in the apartment was not necessary for a 3-year-old child (Ljubljana Higher Court, ruling of 19 January 2017, No. IV Cp 3078/2016).

by Ljubljana Higher Court in 2022, looked like this: private care costs (350 EUR), housing costs (43 EUR), food (120 EUR plus 12 EUR for supplements), clothing and footwear (95 EUR), hygiene products and nappies (90 EUR) and entertainment (70 EUR).[54] Therefore, in Slovenia, the amount of maintenance largely depends on the child's age. This applies both to under-age children (where the cost of daycare ceases when the child starts school, and the cost of extracurricular activities and school trips starts anew) and to children of full age. Such process of identifying the needs of each child and then determining the amount needed to cover each need is not simple, and the introduction of a reference amount, as known in Lithuania, could, therefore, potentially simplify the process in Slovenia as well.

In both countries, the amount of maintenance may be increased in case of additional childcare costs (child illness, injury, medical nursing or permanent care). For instance, in Lithuania, if necessary, the court may also award reimbursement for future medical treatment of the child costs (Article 3.201 LTCC). If the additional costs are incurred at the decision of one parent (e.g. one parent decided that odontological treatment was needed for the child), he or she is entitled to have the other parent reimburse for a proportion of those costs in proportion to his or her financial situation, provided that the need for the additional childcare was objective, that the manner and means chosen to meet that need were necessary and appropriate, and that the amount of the costs incurred is reasonable.[55] In Slovenia, the case law reveals that the same applies if the child needs special (self-funded) therapies of any kind. In one of the cases, the cost of these was €1000 per month, which the court added to the other costs when calculating maintenance, despite the father's objections. The court noted that the father had sufficient maintenance capacity to contribute his share of the self-funded therapies which benefited his son.[56]

Moreover, maintenance costs could be higher where the child has certain abilities and had access to activities or educational institutions before the parents' split-up that should possibly have to be preserved.[57] These are considered to be individual (specific) needs of the child, and thus, their coverage should be commensurate with the parent's financial situation.[58] For example, in one case in Lithuania, the Supreme Court found that the parties' daughter attended sports classes with the consent of both parents, and that both parties were in favour of this activity, so the mere fact that the parents' marriage was dissolved cannot lead to the abandonment of such activities.[59] In Slovenia, in one of the cases the court awarded the cost of dance lessons for a minor girl, despite the father's objections. The court took into account the girl's top results, the fact that she trained 4–6 times a week, her recognised status

[54] Ljubljana Higher Court, ruling of 23 May 2018, No. IV Cp 1012/2022.

[55] LT Supreme Court, ruling of 29 June 2016, No. 3K-7-231-969/2016.

[56] Ljubljana Higher Court, ruling of 6 March 2019, No. IV Cp 50/2019.

[57] LT Supreme Court, ruling of 22 June 2016, No. 3K-3-330-378/2016.

[58] Kudinavičiūtė-Michailovienė and Vėgelienė (2012), pp. 213–214; Sagatys (2005), p. 124.

[59] LT Supreme Court, ruling of 28 December 2017, No. e3K-3-480-378/2017. See also LT Supreme Court, ruling of 2 December 2020, No. e3K-3-495-1075/2020.

as a promising athlete, and the fact that she competed in national and international competitions, all of which entailed additional, higher costs. The court noted that these costs were not really necessary for her life, but that the coverage of such extra needs depended on the ability of the maintenance debtors.[60]

Another question worth a closer look is how child move to another country to live impacts maintenance amount. In 2017, the Supreme Court of Lithuania was asked to establish whether the fact that the child moved to live abroad means that the maintenance amount should be higher.[61] In the present case, the courts found that the mother had decided to move with a minor son to live in the United Kingdom where the standard of living was much higher than in Lithuania. The father gave his consent to the removal of the son only for a temporary period of time.[62] The mother claimed, however, that since the child lives abroad, the amount of maintenance to be awarded should be higher than in cases where a child lives in Lithuania. The Supreme Court did not agree. It confirmed its earlier case law stating that when a child, on the initiative of one of the parents, leaves to live in a foreign country with a higher standard of living than that of Lithuania, the parent of the child remaining in Lithuania should not be obliged to assume the increased expenses for the child's needs.

3.2 The Financial Situation of the Parents

3.2.1 Financial Capacity of Each Parent

Countries exhibit varying practices in assessing the financial situation of parents for the purpose of child maintenance. Some jurisdictions evaluate solely the financial situation of the non-residential parent, while others consider the income of both parents. The rules for calculating the maintenance amounts also vary between countries from rigid formula to (mostly) discretion.[63] The financial capacity of the maintenance debtor sets an upper limit on child maintenance payments. In this regard, similar to assessing the child's needs, the financial capacity is a relative concept, allowing the judge to consider the individual's overall circumstances on a case-by-case basis.[64]

The rationale behind consideration of the financial capacity of the child's parents when determining child maintenance is to a large extent similar in Slovenia and Lithuania. Both countries take into account the actual income, earning capacity,

[60] Ljubljana Higher Court, ruling of 11 January 2018, No. IV Cp 2379/2017.

[61] LT Supreme Court, ruling of 30 June 2017, No. e3K-3-288-378/2017.

[62] For a child's relocation abroad with the residential parent, the written consent of the other parent is required. See on this Sagatys and Intė (2017), pp. 92–93.

[63] Hakovirta and Jokela (2019), p. 260.

[64] Curry-Sumner and Montanus (2012), p. 310.

property owned and living standard of the parents. However, Slovenian courts, in many cases, engage in a more detailed calculation as to both parents' income. While Lithuanian courts identify the income of the parents, the property owned, and the living standard, there is no tendency to use this calculation to set clear proportion of the maintenance contributions (%-%).

In Slovenia, firstly, each parent's earning capacity is determined. In this respect, the courts emphasise that such capacity should be assessed broadly,[65] taking into account parents' general earning capacity, i.e. their ability to work and earn an income (professional qualifications and employment prospects), and not only their actual income.[66] Therefore, what matters primarily is not how much a parent earns, but how much she/he could earn.[67] One could note that decisions regarding employment, such as one parent choosing to stay at home or pursuing a particular career path (including low paid), are considered to be private matters while the parents are still living together. However, upon separation, the situation shifts, and the courts assume a more active role in assessing each parent's financial capability.[68] Therefore, analysis of the financial situation of the parent focuses on the parents' earning capacity rather than their employment choices, ensuring that the children's needs are prioritized and adequately met. It is, therefore, the parent's responsibility to be active and to seek and take advantage of all opportunities to earn an income.[69] This approach is clearly reflected in the case law. For instance, in a case where the mother was a lawyer employed in a law firm, and had no alleged health or other problems that would have prevented her from earning, the court considered that she had the potential to earn an income of 1300 EUR, even though she herself claimed to earn less.[70] In another case where the father (an entrepreneur) earned around 1700 EUR a month, but his income fell to 700 EUR during the pandemic, the court concluded that, given the circumstances (his level of education and the absence of health obstacles to earning an income), he was capable of earning between 1400 EUR and 1500 EUR a month.[71]

[65] In Slovenia, when calculating the debtor's financial standing, the court does not make a precise mathematical calculation. It does not analyse the debtor's financial transactions, inflows or earnings in detail, but merely makes an approximate estimate of their value (see for example Ljubljana Higher Court, ruling of 22 March 2023, No. I Cp 1676/2022). Thus, the court does not usually appoint an expert in economics for this type of calculation.

[66] SL Supreme Court, ruling of 17 March 1994, No. II Ips 171/94, Ljubljana Higher Court, ruling of 19 January 2017, No. IV Cp 3078/2016, Ljubljana Higher Court, ruling of 8 March 2018, No. IV Cp 354/2018, Ljubljana Higher Court, ruling of 15 December 2015, No. IV Cp 3184/2015.

[67] Ljubljana Higher Court, ruling of 11 December 2019, No. IV Cp 1996/2019, Ljubljana Higher Court, ruling of 8 March 2018, No. IV Cp 182/2018.

[68] Moseley Clark (1999), p. 167.

[69] Ljubljana Higher Court, ruling of 8 March 2018, No. IV Cp 182/2018.

[70] Ljubljana Higher Court, ruling of 31 August 2021, No. IV Cp 1285/2021.

[71] Ljubljana Higher Court, ruling of 19 October 2021, No. IV Cp 1475/2021. However, although it is considered that a parent must make use of all his or her earning capacity, in another case the court ruled that it is not necessary for the father to work in the afternoons in addition to his regular job. See Ljubljana Higher Court, ruling of 3 September 2021, No. IV Cp 1044/2021.

In addition to the basic salary, when calculating the parent's income, the court also takes into account overtime pay and any additional income, such as subsistence and dividends,[72] the fact that the parent has enough money to lend out,[73] parent's ownership of several properties and the fact that he/she owns a vacant property that he/she does not rent out (and therefore does not take advantage of income-generating opportunities).[74] Therefore, it is important not only what income the parties report but also their general earning capacity, wealth, and even lifestyle.[75] Thus, for instance, in one of the cases the fact that the mother had larger income than 1000 EUR a month was ruled to be reflected in her lifestyle, since she rented a large house with a monthly rent of 800 EUR, and she had just paid off a loan of 13,650 EUR.[76] Similarly, in another case, the father claimed to earn a living by occasionally mowing the grass and walking the dogs. The court ruled that his lifestyle revealed that he had more money at his disposal, as he spent holidays on a speedboat, visited European capitals and hired a festival hall for his wedding.[77]

Moreover, it is established case law in Slovenia that a reduction in income (even significant[78]) due to a change of job does not mean a change in circumstances that would justify paying less maintenance (as it is seen by courts as a self-inflicted reduction of income).[79] In the same vein, a loss of a job (and therefore income) does not affect the ability to pay maintenance if the parent is generally able to work;[80] the same applies even if the parent has been unemployed for several years.[81] A similar approach was taken in a case where the mother did not work until the child was 4 years old but cared for the child at home while she was generally capable of working. The court ruled that the father, who was employed, should not be solely responsible for the child's expenses. This decision was based on the court's view that the mother had the opportunity to seek employment earlier and could have arranged

---

[72] Ljubljana Higher Court, ruling of 3 September 2021, No. IV Cp 1044/2021, Ljubljana Higher Court, ruling of 15 December 2015, No. IV Cp 3184/2015, Ljubljana Higher Court, ruling of 19 October 2021, No. IV Cp 1475/2021.

[73] Ljubljana Higher Court, ruling of 11 December 2019, No. IV Cp 1996/2019.

[74] Ljubljana Higher Court, ruling of 11 January 2018, No. IV Cp 2379/2017. However, when calculating the parent's assets, the courts decided not take into account the fact that the parent could rent out rooms in his/her own (admittedly large) house. Ljubljana Higher Court, ruling of 15 December 2015, No. IV Cp 3184/2015.

[75] Ljubljana Higher Court, ruling of 22 March 2023, No. I Cp 1676/2022.

[76] Ibid.

[77] Ljubljana Higher Court, ruling of 11 November 2020, No. IV Cp 1805/2020.

[78] E.g. from 2100 EUR to around 1000 EUR. See Ljubljana Higher Court, ruling of 15 June 2022, No. IV Cp 931/2022.

[79] According to Slovenian case law, in order for a parent to obtain a change in the amount of maintenance he or she has to pay, the change in needs or capacity must be substantial, significant and not merely minor. See Ljubljana Higher Court, ruling of 11 November 2020, No. IV Cp 1805/2020.

[80] Ljubljana Higher Court, ruling of 8 March 2018, No. IV Cp 182/2018.

[81] Ljubljana Higher Court, ruling of 8 March 2018, No. IV Cp 354/2018.

for childcare, which would have allowed her to contribute financially.[82] The court emphasised that a parent cannot escape their child support obligations by citing external factors within their control (such as unemployment or lack of childcare) that they could have, and should have, proactively addressed. Parents are expected to use their full capacity to work and should mitigate such circumstances to meet their maintenance responsibilities.[83] Only for parents who genuinely lack[84] the financial capacity to maintain their children, courts in Slovenia set a symbolic maintenance fee, which can be increased later in new court proceedings if circumstances change.[85]

It is also important to note that maintenance obligations have priority over other financial obligations. In Slovenia, Article 195 of the SLFC explicitly provides that, maintenance of children whom the person liable is obliged to maintain shall have priority over maintenance of the maintenance debtor's parents. Therefore, supporting a child not only has priority over supporting the parents, but also over other financial obligations. Thus, the repayment of the loan is not taken into account when calculating the parent's ability to maintain the child. The parent's allegations that the credit loan relates to obligations arising from cohabitation with the ex-partner (the child's other parent) (i.e. the renovation of the property) or it was taken to pay off the purchase of a car[86] are not relevant.[87] Similarly, the court dismissed the father's claim that he did not have sufficient funds to pay the maintenance, when the court found out that he had bought the co-ownership of the boat 2 years ago and that the maintenance of the boat cost 5000 EUR per year, an amount that represented 70% of the annual maintenance for both children.[88] Such a case law confirms that the maintenance of the children takes priority over other expenses.

In Lithuania, relatively similar principles apply regarding the evaluation of parents' financial situation in the context of determining maintenance payments for children. The courts evaluate the factual earnings and also check whether the decrease in factual earnings is not a personal choice or a way to hide income. For instance, in one case, the court underlined that the maintenance debtor had artificially worsened his financial situation by reducing his own salary when he was the head of

[82] Ljubljana Higher Court, ruling of 8 March 2018, No. IV Cp 182/2018.

[83] Ibid.

[84] In situations where parents have above-average means of support that exceed the child's needs, this does not mean that children get unreasonably high maintenance. In such a case, while the parents must also meet the child's above-average needs, the courts are bound to respect the best interests of the child, which includes encouraging the child to learn to be independent. Thus, the child of extremely wealthy parents will not receive child support that significantly exceeds that of the children of non-wealthy parents. Novak et al. (2019), p. 635.

[85] Novak et al. (2019), p. 638.

[86] Ljubljana Higher Court, ruling of 15 December 2015, No. IV Cp 3184/2015.

[87] Ljubljana Higher Court, ruling of 19 January 2017, No. IV Cp 3078/2016.

[88] Ljubljana Higher Court, ruling of 31 August 2021, No. IV Cp 1285/2021.

the company, selling part of his property and gifting the rest of his property to his father.[89]

Similar to Slovenia, in addition to the factual earnings, the parents' behaviour seeking to earn income to support the children is also seen as important when determining maintenance payments. In this regard, a person's ability to improve his or her financial situation is assessed on the basis of both objective and subjective factors: subjective factors are the person's own efforts, willingness, attitudes, and his or her perceived ability to earn an income; objective factors are the person's age, health, the country's economic situation, etc., which are beyond the person's control or responsibility.[90] The ability of a parent to contribute to the maintenance of the child is evaluated by taking into consideration a variety of factors: parent's income, owned movable and immovable property, investments, health, the number of dependents, as well as parent's behaviour seeking to earn and to receive income to support the children.[91] By taking into account both sets of factors, the Lithuanian legal system aims to provide a comprehensive evaluation of a parent's ability to contribute to maintenance payments, ensuring that the parent from whom the maintenance is sought is not manipulating his or her income or is not avoiding his or her duties towards the child.

In line with the case law, in Lithuania, a court may not order child support in excess of what the parents' financial situation objectively allows.[92] In such situations, a minimal maintenance payment is established. It should be noted, however, that if there are reasonable doubts about the true financial situation of the parents and their income, the Lithuanian courts assess it in favour of the child's interests. In such a case, it is assumed that the situation allows for the awarding of maintenance that meets the child's needs. The Supreme Court considers that the behaviour standards of an honest and caring person, who has the duty to maintain their minor child, require taking all available measures to earn an income sufficient for supporting one's children.[93]

3.2.2 Proportionate Distribution of the Maintenance Burden Between Both Parents

After calculating the financial capacity of each parent, the next step (both in Slovenia and Lithuania) is to determine the share of child maintenance that each parent will pay. As noted above, though the obligation of parents to maintain their children is the same for both parents, this does not mean that each of them has to contribute the

[89]LT Supreme Court, ruling of 10 June 2010, No. 3K-3-278/2010.

[90]LT Supreme Court, ruling of 13 February 2015, No. 3K-3-27-686/2015.

[91]LT Supreme Court, ruling of 21 October 2013, No. 3K-3-491/2013.

[92]In case of substantial change of situation (material change in financial situation of the parties), maintenance order might later be reviewed by the court.

[93]LT Supreme Court, ruling of 12 September 2023, No. e3K-3-179-378/2023.

same amount. Under Article 3.192 LT CC, maintenance for children must be provided by both parents proportionally to their financial situation.[94] For example, in one case, the Supreme Court held that the father of the child should pay the greater part of the child's maintenance because the mother of the child was unemployed due to the child's age, had no assets, and her income consisted of social assistance for her children and the support of her siblings living abroad.[95] The situation is similar in Slovenia. Thus, in a case where the father earned between 1600 EUR and 1700 EUR and the mother 660 EUR per month, the court determined that the maintenance burden should be shared 75%:25%.[96]

In both countries, in determining the share of child support responsibilities, courts not only consider the financial capability of each parent but also who has custody of the child. This is seen as an important element because the custodial parent typically carries a heavier load in terms of daily caregiving and financial support for the child. Consequently, courts often assign a smaller portion of maintenance obligations to them. For instance, in Slovenia, in a case where the mother and father had about the same ability to support the child and the child was in the mother's custody, the court decided that the father should financially support 60% and the mother 40% of the child's needs.[97] It can also be inferred that in these situations, the parent with custody of the child contributes more through caregiving efforts, while the other parent compensates by providing greater financial support for the child.

4 Specific Questions Related to Child's Maintenance

4.1 Maintenance in Case of Shared Care of the Child

The practice of shared care has increased in many European countries.[98] Various models of such care are applied across Europe, and the distinction between extended contact with the child and alternative residence is often not entirely clear.[99] A decision may be made for joint custody or a child to live primarily with one parent (residential, custodial parent) while spending up to 50% of their time with the non-resident parent. Though different terminology is used, this latter arrangement can also be interpreted as shared or joint residence. As observed in the doctrine, whether one calls a 50/50 arrangement "residence" or "contact" obviously is, at least

---

[94] However, it has to be noted that the parents' difficult financial situation is relevant only to the amount of maintenance and not to the existence of a maintenance obligation.

[95] LT Supreme Court, ruling of 12 October 2016, No. 3K-3-427-378/2016.

[96] Ljubljana Higher Court, ruling of 19 January 2017, No. IV Cp 3286/2016.

[97] Ljubljana Higher Court, ruling of 31 August 2021, No. IV Cp 1285/2021. Similar also Ljubljana Higher Court, ruling of 11 November 2020, No. IV Cp 1805/2020.

[98] Hakovirta et al. (2023), p. 480.

[99] Rešetar (2011), p. 279.

to a large extent, a semantic game.[100] This is notable in the case of Lithuania and Slovenia, where Slovenia opted for a joint custody concept, while in Lithuania, the option of '50:50 child contact arrangement' exists.[101] Both such models raise questions regarding how child maintenance systems have responded to such child care arrangements and where different approaches lead to different results with regard to child maintenance.

In Lithuania and Slovenia, the established contact arrangements with the separated parent (e.g. if the child has contact with the separated parent every other weekend) do not usually affect the amount of maintenance. However, the situation might be different where shared child care is established. It should be noted that though theoretically shared care refers to an equal division of the time that children stay with either parent, this rule is not strict, and it is widely accepted that the time can range from 25% to 50% with each parent.[102]

When the child spends equal time with both parents, both parents effectively meet the child's needs during this (equally divided) time. In such cases, if the level of contact or the costs of maintaining contact with the child do not affect child maintenance, this suggests that the role of fathers (as noted above, in most cases, it is the father who is paying maintenance) is viewed principally as that of financial provider, with less attention paid to nurturing a social, caring relationship between the father and child.[103]

In this situation, as noted by the Supreme Court of Lithuania, awarding the residential parent with full child maintenance would result in an imbalance between parents' obligations.[104] On the other hand, some child's needs are not limited to everyday expenses (food, clothing); there are also additional expenses (e.g. payment for the child's schooling, or health care costs). In the absence of an agreement between the parents as to the allocation of such costs, the Lithuanian jurisprudence considers that the parent with whom the child's main residence is established is presumed to bear them, and thus, the other parent has a duty to contribute.[105]

The SLFC, in Article 139, determines that when a court issues a settlement or decision on joint custody, it must establish the child's permanent residence, designate which parent will receive mail addressed to the child, and also child's maintenance. Officially, maintenance should, therefore, be established despite joint custody. However, legal theory has a different perspective on this. Some argue that if parents agree on joint custody, they do not have to agree on who will pay

---

[100] Ibid.

[101] Joint custody is not foreseen in the Lithuanian law. However, in recent years, the option of '50: 50 child contact arrangement', very similar to that of joint physical custody, has become a viable possibility for both parents due to changing court practice. For the first cases, see LT Supreme Court, ruling of 19 February 2016, No. 3K-3-99-969/2016; LT Supreme Court, ruling of 19 September 2019, No. 3K-3-279-969/2019.

[102] Hakovirta and Eydal (2020), pp. 43–44.

[103] Rešetar (2011), p. 279.

[104] LT Supreme Court, ruling of 19 September 2019, No. e3K-3-279-969/2019.

[105] LT Supreme Court, ruling of 19 September 2019, No. e3K-3-279-969/2019.

maintenance to whom.[106] In such a case, the child's needs are deemed to be met or paid for equally by both parents. However, if one parent is better off financially, the parents can agree on a monetary payment. In this case, one parent may provide part of the maintenance of a child in work/nature, while the parent with the better maintenance capacity provides the difference in monetary contribution.[107] Finally, it is also possible, in the case of shared custody, for the parents to agree that one parent pays most or all of the costs related to the child and the other parent pays maintenance for a child to that parent.[108]

As a result, we could conclude that both Slovenia and Lithuania have succeeded in establishing a connection between contact or joint custody and maintenance when calculating maintenance contributions.[109] Though the regulation is not yet entirely structured in this regard, and much is left for the judicial margin of appreciation, overall, the current approach could be seen as balanced and properly taking into account the close link between shared care and maintenance duty.

4.2 *Late Request for Maintenance Payments*

Many jurisdictions allow for retroactive claims for child maintenance, meaning that a parent may seek payments for periods prior to the initiation of a formal maintenance order (European E-Justice Portal - Family Maintenance 2024). This possibility, thought with variations, can be seen both in Lithuania and Slovenia.

Pursuant to Article 3.200 of the LTCC, in Lithuania maintenance allowances for a minor child can be ordered for no more than 3 years retroactively from the date of the commencement of the proceedings. When a parent requests retroactive maintenance payments, they can anticipate that the awarded amount will align with what would have been granted if the maintenance had been sought at the time the need arose. Thus, residential parent's delay in asking for child maintenance is not taken into account when determining the amount of maintenance.

In this regard, in 2017, the Supreme Court of Lithuania was asked to establish whether the fact that the resident parent did not initiate maintenance proceedings for a long time means, that the child needed less financial support and that maintenance for the period before the claim was submitted should be lower.[110] In this case, the mother has not requested child maintenance from the father for many years. However, when she did finally apply, she also asked to award maintenance for the last

[106] Novak et al. (2019), p. 424.

[107] Ibid, p. 425.

[108] Ibid, p. 425.

[109] For other jurisdictions see Rešetar (2011), pp. 279–296.

[110] In general, maintenance is awarded from the date from which the right to maintenance exists. If maintenance is claimed for a retrospective period, the law allows it to be recovered only for max 3 years before submission of the claim.

3 years before the submission of the claim. Taking into account the financial situation of both parents and the child's needs, the court of first instance and the court of second instance awarded the maintenance, however, for the last 3 years, the court awarded a smaller amount of maintenance. The lower amount for earlier periods was explained by the fact that the mother of the child, who did not apply for child maintenance for several years, had sufficient funds to meet the child's needs, and therefore the amount of debt requested to be awarded was unreasonably high. The Supreme Court did not agree with the position of the lower courts. It stated that the fact that the mother did not request maintenance for a long time does not mean that the needs of the child were lower. It ruled that the mere fact that one of the parents with whom a minor child lives does not require maintenance of a child from the second parent for a longer time and covers the child's needs alone does not in itself constitute grounds for reducing maintenance since the proceeds of maintenance are the property of the child and not of the resident parent.[111]

In Slovenia, Article 196 SLFC determines that "maintenance shall be assessed in a monthly sum and in advance, and may be claimed from the date of lodging the application or the motion for assessment of maintenance." However, for maintenance covered in the past, Article 199(1) applies. It determines as follows: "Anyone who incurred expenses by maintaining a person they were not liable to maintain shall have the right to claim reimbursement of such expenses from the person who would be liable to maintain such person, provided that such expenses were necessary." The latter article covers a resolution for all situations where the child's maintenance costs had been borne by someone other than the child's parent(s), e.g. grandparents, a man who later turns out not to be the child's father, and, most often, the mother's claims for reimbursement of maintenance costs against the child's father. Hence, past maintenance cannot be claimed; only reimbursement for necessary expenses is allowable. The amount of the necessary expenses is assessed at the time of the decision of the court of first instance and not at the time when the expenses were incurred,[112] however, in addition, the party may also claim statutory default interest.[113]

4.3 *Maintaining a Child with a Physical or Mental Disability*

While adult children are expected to enter employment, earn their own income and become (financially) independent from their parents when they leave school, the prospects are worse for children whose mental or physical disabilities prevent them from doing so. The question thus arises who is responsible for supporting (adult) children with such conditions.

[111] LT Supreme Court, ruling of 30 June 2017, No. e3K-3-288-378/2017.

[112] Novak et al. (2019), p. 662.

[113] Ibid, p. 663.

In Lithuania, the parents' duty to support the child also continues for older than 18 years old if a child has a disability which was established before the age of majority (e.g. if the child was born physically or mentally disabled, or became disabled as a child) and, due to this reason, is not fit to work (unable to engage in employment[114]). In Slovenia, the rules are different. Just like a child without a disability, parents must financially support a child with a disability even after they reach the age of majority, if they continue their education. When such a child leaves an educational institution, the obligation to support the child with a disability is transferred to the state.[115] The state, therefore, has to provide for adults with a physical or mental disability, which applies regardless of the fact that the (adult) child may be placed under the guardianship of his/her parents.

Therefore, it can be noted that legal frameworks in Lithuania and Slovenia regarding the support of children with disabilities after reaching the age of majority highlight significant differences. In Lithuania, the regulation places a continued financial responsibility on the parents, recognising the additional care and support needs of people with disabilities. It implies a recognition of the lifelong challenges faced by individuals with disabilities and the role of family support in mitigating these challenges. However, this continuous duty may also place a significant financial and emotional burden on the parents, potentially affecting their equality compared to parents of healthy children who are expected to become financially independent after reaching adulthood. In contrast, under Slovenian law, once the educational phase is completed, the responsibility for supporting the individual with a disability is transferred to the state. This approach alleviates the long-term financial burden on parents, promoting a more equal footing with parents of non-disabled children. Additionally, by transferring the support obligation to the state, Slovenia emphasises the societal responsibility to care for individuals with disabilities.

4.4 Considering Social Benefits When Determining Maintenance

In the realm of family law, the determination of maintenance obligations often intersects with various forms of state financial support designed to aid to families raising children. This intersection is evident in the contrasting approaches taken by Slovenia and Lithuania regarding child benefits.

[114] If an adult child has been recognised as partially able to work, the award of maintenance is not awarded from parents. See LT Supreme Court, ruling of 17 February 2016, No. 3K-3-91-686/2016. Specific laws on disability regulate what level of incapacity to work is needed to establish that a person is unable to engage in employment—in general, a person whose capacity for work is between 0% and 25% is considered to be unable to engage in employment. It should also be noted that persons with disability receive disability assistance (disability pension), which is counted as covering at least part of their needs.

[115] Novak (2017), pp. 142–143.

In Slovenia, (single- and two-parent) families are, under certain financial conditions, entitled to child benefits ("an income supplement to help parents provide for the maintenance, upbringing and education of the child"—definition of Article 70 of the Parental Protection and Family Benefits Act[116]). This raises the question of whether this child allowance (paid by the state to the residential parent) should be taken into account when determining maintenance to be paid by non-residential parent. The Slovenian jurisprudence is clear in this regard: the child benefit is not intended for the maintenance of the child and is therefore not taken into account when calculating and dividing the amount of maintenance.[117] The right to these benefits depends on the established material situation of the beneficiaries. In determining this, however, maintenance is taken into account as part of the income of a beneficiary, when determining his or her eligibility for the benefit. Therefore, child benefit cannot be taken into account in the assessment of maintenance, as the latter will be taken into account in the subsequent calculation of the amount of child benefit. The maintenance of the non-resident parent is therefore not reduced if the resident parent receives child benefit.[118]

In Lithuania, the approach is different. Each family with children under 18 receives a monthly child benefit, known as 'child money' (lith. *vaiko pinigai*). The child benefit (currently around 96.25 euros per child) is paid without taking into account a family income level. Such child benefit paid by the state is intended to meet the needs of the child and provide financial support to the parents raising the child. Therefore, when the court decides on the amount of child maintenance to be ordered from the parent, the total amount of child support is reduced by the amount of child benefit paid by the state to the child.[119]

5 Concluding Remarks

A comparative analysis of the child support systems in Slovenia and Lithuania reveals a shared foundational philosophy centred on the holistic needs of the child and the financial capacities of parents. Both frameworks strive to balance parental responsibilities and ensure adequate support, yet they diverge in their methodologies. Comparing the national systems of Slovenia and Lithuania, it can be seen that

[116] *Official Gazette* RS, No. 26-1068/2014.

[117] Ljubljana Higher Court, ruling of 11 January 2018, No. IV Cp 2379/2017. Similar Ljubljana Higher Court, ruling of 15 December 2015, No. IV Cp 3184/2015, Ljubljana Higher Court, ruling of 11 November 2020, No. IV Cp 1805/2020, and Ljubljana Higher Court, ruling of 3 September 2021, No. IV Cp 1044/2021.

[118] The same rule (of not-including) applies to all other types of social assistance and state grants. See Ljubljana Higher Court, ruling of 8 March 2018, No. IV Cp 182/2018, Ljubljana Higher Court, ruling of 11 January 2018, No. IV Cp 2379/2017. Regarding (not) including state grants see particular Ljubljana Higher Court, ruling of 31 August 2021, No. IV Cp 1285/2021.

[119] LT Supreme Court, ruling of 2 April 2020, No. e3K-3-164-687/2020.

the core principles guiding the determination of child support are quite similar. The determination of maintenance takes into account the overall needs of the individual child, as well as the financial capacity of his/her parents. In both countries, the final amount of the established financial support for a particular child is divided between the parents taking into account their financial capacity. In this respect, the fact with which parent the child is placed also plays an important role in both countries. However, the starting point of assessing child needs is considerably different in compared countries. While in Lithuania, the indicative amount of child needs is the minimum monthly salary, and each parent can demonstrate higher or lower needs of the concrete child, in Slovenia the calculation starts from zero, to which is added the costs for each individual need of the specific child.

There are also variances in parental obligations beyond childhood. In Lithuania, the support extends to children up to 24 years old if they are still in school, whereas in Slovenia, this age limit is higher, at 26 years. Moreover, a notable distinction arises in how each country handles the responsibility for supporting adult children with disabilities who are no longer attending school. Parents of such children are in a fundamentally different situation in the two countries. In Lithuania, they are obliged to continue to financially support such children, whereas the burden of supporting such adults in Slovenia is transferred to the State and thus does not fall on the parents, even if the parents still have guardianship of their (adult) child. Furthermore, the difference arises as to child benefits, which are included when counting the total amount of expenses for a specific child in Lithuania, but not in Slovenia.

Maintenance is an exceptionally important component of parental care. It ensures that the child's basic and more complex needs are met, and the national rules on the establishment and recovery of maintenance, and their application in case law, are therefore of paramount importance. While the child maintenance systems of Slovenia and Lithuania share foundational principles, they also exhibit distinct differences, and these variances reflect each country's unique approach to family welfare and support. However, there is room for mutual learning and exchanges. For instance, the authors suggest that the Slovenian authorities could consider adopting a certain amount as an indicative benchmark for child needs. This would make it simpler for the court to determine the full extent of the child's needs and the costs involved, while at the same time limiting the parents' obligation to prove that the child's needs are within this amount. On the other hand, justice would undoubtedly be better obtained in Lithuania if it adopted the Slovenian model of support for adult children with disabilities. This approach ensures greater equality between parents of healthy children and those with health issues, avoiding placing an additional burden on the latter.

On the basis of all the above, it can be concluded that the two national legislations compared, although different in parts, pursue well the objective of the best interests of the child, which is one of the greatest values of any developed society.

Legal Acts

Council Regulation (EC) No 4/2009 of 18 December 2008 on jurisdiction, applicable law, recognition and enforcement of decisions and cooperation in matters relating to maintenance obligations. OJ L 7, 10.1.2009, pp. 1–79.
Civil Code of the Republic of Lithuania. *Official Gazette*, 2000, No. 74 with subsequent amendments.
Criminal Code of the Republic of Lithuania. *Official Gazette*, 2000, No. 89-2741, with later amendments.
Slovenian Marriage and Family Relations Act. *Official Gazette* SRS, no. 15-644/1976.
Slovenian Family Code, *Official Gazette* RS, no. 15/17 with subsequent amendments.
Criminal Code of Slovenia, *Official Gazette* RS, no. 55/08 with subsequent amendments.
Slovenian Non-contentious Civil Procedure Act, *Official Gazette* RS, no. 16/19.
Slovenian Parental Protection and Family Benefits Act, *Official Gazette* RS, No. 26-1068/2014.

Slovenian Case Law

SL Supreme Court, ruling of 17 March 1994, No. II Ips 171/94.
Ljubljana Higher Court, ruling of 15 December 2015, No. IV Cp 3184/2015.
Ljubljana Higher Court, ruling of 19 January 2017, No. IV Cp 3078/2016.
Ljubljana Higher Court, ruling of 11 January 2018, No. IV Cp 2379/2017.
Ljubljana Higher Court, ruling of 21 February 2018, No. Cp 314/2018.
Ljubljana Higher Court, ruling of 8 March 2018, No. IV Cp 354/2018.
Ljubljana Higher Court, ruling of 8 March 2018, No. IV Cp 182/2018.
Ljubljana Higher Court, ruling of 23 May 2018, No. IV Cp 1012/2022.
Ljubljana Higher Court, ruling of 6 March 2019, No. IV Cp 50/2019.
Ljubljana Higher Court, ruling of 11 December 2019, No. IV Cp 1996/2019.
Ljubljana Higher Court, ruling of 11 November 2020, No. IV Cp 1805/2020.
Ljubljana Higher Court, ruling of 31 August 2021, No. IV Cp 1285/2021.
Ljubljana Higher Court, ruling of 3 September 2021, No. IV Cp 1044/2021.
Ljubljana Higher Court, ruling of 19 October 2021, No. IV Cp 1475/2021.
Ljubljana Higher Court, ruling of 15 June 2022, No. IV Cp 931/2022.
Ljubljana Higher Court, ruling of 22 March 2023, No. I Cp 1676/2022.

Lithuanian Case Law

LT Supreme Court, ruling of 10 June 2010, No. 3K-3-278/2010.
LT Supreme Court, ruling of 10 November 2009, No. 3K-3-495/2009.
LT Supreme Court, ruling of 12 October 2016, No. 3K-3-427-378/2016.
LT Supreme Court, ruling of 12 September 2023, No. e3K-3-179-378/2023.
LT Supreme Court, ruling of 13 February 2015, No. 3K-3-27-686/2015.
LT Supreme Court, ruling of 17 February 2016, No. 3K-3-91-686/2016.
LT Supreme Court, ruling of 19 September 2019, No. e3K-3-279-969/2019.
LT Supreme Court, ruling of 2 April 2020, No. e3K-3-164-687/2020.
LT Supreme Court, ruling of 2 December 2020, No. e3K-3-495-1075/2020.
LT Supreme Court, ruling of 21 October 2013, No. 3K-3-491/2013.
LT Supreme Court, ruling of 22 June 2016, No. 3K-3-330-378/2016.
LT Supreme Court, ruling of 28 December 2017, No. e3K-3-480-378/2017.
LT Supreme Court, ruling of 29 June 2016, No. 3K-7-231-969/2016.
LT Supreme Court, ruling of 30 June 2017, No. e3K-3-288-378/2017.
LT Supreme Court, ruling of 5 April 2011, No. 3K-3-154/2011.
LT Supreme Court, ruling of 9 February 2010, No. 3K-3-71/2010.
LT Supreme Court, ruling of 19 February 2016, No. 3K-3-99-969/2016
LT Supreme Court, ruling of 19 September 2019, No. 3K-3-279-969/2019.

References

Ahlin Doljak S, Betetto N, Caharijaz Ferme N, Drnovšek K, Felc B, Jambrek P, Jambrek Lampret E et al (2024) Družinski zakonik (DZ): s komentarjem. 1. natis. Ljubljana: Lexpera, GV založba

Antonelli MA, Castaldo A, De Bonis V, Salustri A (2024) Do different household models affect poverty? A dynamic panel analysis in 28 European countries. Appl Econ, 1–15. https://doi.org/10.1080/00036846.2024.2364086

Burkelc F (2023) Postopki Za Varstvo Koristi Otroka in Preživljanje Polnoletnega Otroka. Pravna Praksa, no. 40–41

Calegari E, Fabrizi E, Mussida C (2024) State dependence in material and social deprivation in European single-parent households. Soc Indic Res 172(2):481–498. https://doi.org/10.1007/s11205-024-03317-8

Curry-Sumner I, Montanus P (2012) Child maintenance in the Netherlands. Eur J Soc Secur 14(4): 304–329. https://doi.org/10.1177/138826271201400406

European E-Justice Portal - Family Maintenance (2024). https://e-justice.europa.eu/47/EN/family_maintenance

European Parliament. Directorate General for Internal Policies of the Union (2014) Child maintenance systems in EU Member States from a gender perspective: in depth analysis. LU: Publications Office. https://data.europa.eu/doi/10.2861/10516

Eurostat (2021) How many single-parent households are there in the EU? https://ec.europa.eu/eurostat/web/products-eurostat-news/-/edn-20210601-2

Fernqvist S, Flinkfeldt M, Tegler H (2023) "He Won't Pay": the entanglement of financial abuse and negligence in Swedish child maintenance processes. Violence Against Women, 10778012231185538. https://doi.org/10.1177/10778012231185538

Gabrilo R (1996) Preživljanje otrok. Pravosodni Bilten 17(1–2):125–147

Hakovirta M, Eydal GB (2020) Shared care and child maintenance policies in Nordic countries. Int J Law Policy Family 34(1):43–59. https://doi.org/10.1093/lawfam/ebz016
Hakovirta M, Jokela M (2019) Contribution of child maintenance to lone mothers' income in five countries. J Eur Soc Policy 29(2):257–272. https://doi.org/10.1177/0958928717754295
Hakovirta M, Meyer DR, Salin M, Lindroos E, Haapanen M (2023) Joint physical custody of children in Europe: a growing phenomenon. Demogr Res 49(September):479–492. https://doi.org/10.4054/DemRes.2023.49.18
Končina Peternel M (2019) Postopki za varstvo koristi otroka in vloga otroka v teh postopkih. Pravosodni Bilten:93–105
Kudinavičiūtė-Michailovienė I, Šimkienė V (2018) Vaikų, sulaukusių pilnametystės, išlaikymas: teisinis reguliavimas ir praktika. Jurisprudencija 25(2). https://doi.org/10.13165/JUR-18-25-2-07
Kudinavičiūtė-Michailovienė I, Uusen-Nacke T (2022) Protection of child rights in family cases in Lithuania and Estonia. In: Limantė A, Pūraitė-Andrikienė D (eds) Legal protection of vulnerable groups in Lithuania, Latvia, Estonia and Poland, pp 81–105. https://doi.org/10.1007/978-3-031-06998-7_4
Kudinavičiūtė-Michailovienė I, Vėgelienė J (2012) Child maintenance: several topical theoretical and practical aspects. Jurisprudence / Jurisprudencija 19(1):209–229
Lanza-León P, Cantarero-Prieto D (2024) The loud silent side of single parenthood in Europe: health and socio-economic circumstances from a gender perspective. J Family Econ Issues. https://doi.org/10.1007/s10834-024-09954-y
Moseley Clark C (1999) Imputing parental income in child support determinations: what price for a child's best interest? Cathol Univ Law Rev 49(1):167–200
Natalier K, Hewitt B (2010) "It's Not Just About the Money": non-resident fathers' perspectives on paying child support. Sociology 44(3):489–505. https://doi.org/10.1177/0038038510362470
Nieuwenhuis R (2021) Directions of thought for single parents in the EU. Commun Work Family 24(5):559–566. https://doi.org/10.1080/13668803.2020.1745756
Novak B (2017) Družinski Zakonik. Uradni list RS
Novak B, Čujovič M, Del Fabro A, Dolčič T, Dugar G, Erjavec N (2019) Komentar družinskega zakonika. Uradni list Republike Slovenije, Ljubljana
Pavec B (2006) Določanje višine preživnine za otroka. Pravna Praksa 12:VI–VIII
Rešetar B (2011) The link between child maintenance and contact. In: Boele-Woelki K, Miles JK, Scherpe JM (eds) The future of family property in Europe, 1st edn. Intersentia, pp 279–296. https://doi.org/10.1017/9781839700156.014
Rijavec V (2019) Odločanje o varstvu in vzgoji otrok. Pravni Letopis:57–77
Sagatys G (2005) Tėvų pareiga išlaikyti nepilnamečių vaikus: aktualūs subjektų klausimai. Jurisprudence / Jurisprudencija 67(59)
Sagatys G, Intė O (2017) Vaiko išvežimas iš Lietuvos: teisinis reguliavimas ir praktika. Jurisprudencija 24(1):89–110
Skinner C, Hakovirta M, Davidson J (2012) A comparative analysis of child maintenance schemes in five countries. Eur J Soc Secur 14(4):330–347. https://doi.org/10.1177/138826271201400407
Strobelj T (2020) Odvetnik 94(1):66–68
Trefalt J, Jager Agius I (2014) Pregled Ustavnosodne Presoje Otrokovih Pravic. In: Otrokove Pravice v Sloveniji - Od Normativnih Standardov Do Učinkovitega Varstva, 274. Mednarodno Pravo. Fakulteta za družbene vede, Založba FDV and Ministrstvo za zunanje zadeve Republike Slovenije, Ljubljana, pp 29–60
Weber N (2018) Dogovor o preživljanju v obliki notarskega zapisa. Pravna Praksa 34:23–24
Weber N (2019) Novosti Družinskega zakonika v razmerjih med starši in otroki. Odvetnik 89(1): 7–12
Žalnieriūnas L, Girdenis T (2013) Problematic qualification aspects of the avoidance to maintain a child and alternative ways of child maintenance. Jurisprudence 20(2):707–723. https://doi.org/10.13165/JUR-13-20-2-18

Unpacking the Accountability Dilemma: Individual Criminality for Autonomous Weapon Systems

Swaleh H. Wengo

1 Introduction

One of the debatable issues or questions related to autonomous weapons systems will be to delegate responsibility to either international humanitarian law, international criminal law, or public international law. Two distinct but simultaneously activating regimes form the basis for the assignment of responsibility; individual and state responsibility.[1] If a rule of international humanitarian law is violated, international criminal law deals with the punishment of guilty individuals, while public international law deals with the accountability of states for violation of their obligations. Thus, international responsibility should address "fully and comprehensively, at both international and national levels, the issue of the right to recourse and reparation for victims of flagrant violations of international human rights law and serious violations of international humanitarian law."[2]

The very core of accountability is critical because, without it, deterrence and prevention will suffer, ultimately harming the very essence of the protection of civilians and potential war crime victims while compromising victims' legal redress.[3] Assigning individual responsibility would prove fiendishly difficult if the commission of an international crime was by far attributed to any autonomous weapon system.[4] The term autonomous weapon system according to the ICRC refers to any weapon systems with autonomy in their critical functions-that is-a

[1] Nollkaemper (2003), p. 615.
[2] UN General Assembly (2005), UN Doc A/RES/60/147.
[3] Heyns (2013), UN Doc A/HRC/23/47.
[4] Bo et al. (2022), p. 26.

S. H. Wengo (✉)
Prince Sultan University, Riyadh, Saudi Arabia
e-mail: swengo@psu.edu.sa

Z. Meskić et al. (eds.), *Balkan Yearbook of European and International Law 2024*,
Balkan Yearbook of European and International Law 2024,
https://doi.org/10.1007/978-3-031-89952-2_4

weapon system that can select (that is, search for or detect, identify) and engage (that is, use force against, neutralise, damage, or destroy) targets without human intervention.[5] In other words, it refers to a weapon that selects and engages targets fitting certain predefined criteria without human intervention, following a human decision to deploy the weapon in the understanding that any attack, once launched, cannot be stopped by human intervention.[6] Examples include unmanned AI-driven fighter jets, air defence systems that strike incoming missiles, and loitering munitions developed to destroy military radars, tanks, or armoured vehicles.[7]

Many authors propose that the autonomous capabilities of these weapon systems create an "accountability gap," spawning a whole array of ethical and legally relevant questions.[8] This stems from the understanding that autonomous systems can take their own decisions towards some standard or principle reaction instead of being simply run by fixed rules, misbehaving perhaps unpredictably.[9] The belief, therefore, is that no individual would be held liable for its actions. Are autonomous weapon systems therefore illegal to be used? The answer is no, as international humanitarian law does not make the legality of a weapon and capability of attributing accountability a *sine qua non*.[10] In the group of government experts on lethal autonomous weapons systems, accountability has been carved into its guiding principles directing that accountability for the development, deployment, and use of any new weapons system contained in the Convention is to be guaranteed in accordance with any applicable international law for that matter, including ensuring that these systems are part of a human chain responsible for command and control.[11]

The aim of this chapter is to explore these seemingly conflicting views on the practicality of, and legal issues concerning the attribution of criminal responsibility on the use of autonomous weapon systems. I will address the issues surrounding the attribution of individual responsibility by examining the various modes of participation under the Rome Statute. The chapter demonstrates that while it is challenging to attribute responsibility to the machines due to the ineffectuality and futility of the same, the existing framework of international law provides a path for holding commanders and programmers accountable for violations committed with autonomous weapons.

---

[5]ICRC (2016), p. 1.

[6]The Netherlands (2017) defined AWS as "A weapon that, without human intervention, selects and engages targets matching certain predefined criteria, following a human decision to deploy the weapon on the understanding that an attack, once launched, cannot be stopped by human intervention."

[7]ICRC (2022).

[8]Oimann (2023), p. 7.

[9]Santoni de Sio and Mecacci (2021), pp. 1057–1084.

[10]Dunlap Jr. (2016), p. 63.

[11]UN General Assembly (2019) UN Doc CCW/MSP/2019/9.

2 Individual Responsibility

Individual criminal responsibility is one of the frequently recognized norms in international law, indicating that natural persons can be held criminally liable by reason of committing war crimes.[12] This principle finds its roots in the Lieber Code of 1863,[13] and the Oxford Manual of 1880.[14] According to Professors Gerhard Werle and Boris Burghardt, crimes under international law usually require the collaboration of several individuals to have been committed.[15] This notion includes individuals attempting to commit a crime, instigation, aid and abet, or contribute or facilitate in ways other than those recognized.[16] Also, superior officers could be found criminally liable for omissions or infringements committed by individuals under their control.[17] Thus, international criminal law enables the prosecution of perpetrators and persons who were involved in planning or inciting such crimes.

At this point, it is imperative to narrow down the focus of this analysis to war crimes under the Rome Statute. A commonly cited concern about the utilisation of the automated weapon systems is the harm to civilians. While no one for a moment is suggesting that such autonomous weapon systems cannot be put to use in genocide or crimes against humanity, the likelihood of such occurrences in the foreseeable future, given the current technological capabilities, is too minimal for me to factor into this discussion.

Therefore, my examination will be anchored in Article 8(2)(b)(i) of the Rome Statute, which identifies attacks against civilians as a war crime within the jurisdiction of the ICC.[18] The constituent elements of this crime are as follows: (1) The perpetrator directed an attack; (2) The objective of the attack was a civilian population or civilians not directly participating in hostilities; (3) The perpetrator intended to target the said civilian population or these civilian persons not directly participating in hostilities; (4) The behaviour took place in the context of and was associated with an international armed conflict; (5) The perpetrator was aware of the factual circumstances establishing the existence of an armed conflict.[19]

The first element pertains to the material aspect, the *actus reus*, which denotes the perpetration of the attack.[20] By definition, this offence targets the civilian population, thus necessitating proof in the second element that the attack was aimed at civilians.[21] The moral element represents the third element, otherwise known as

[12] ICRC (2005) R. 151.

[13] Lieber (1863).

[14] Oxford Manual on the Laws of War on Land (1880).

[15] Werle and Burghardt (2014), p. 47.

[16] ICRC (2005), r 151.

[17] Rome Statute (1998), art 28.

[18] Rome Statute (1998), art 8(2)(b)(i).

[19] ICC (2011), art 8(2)(b)(i).

[20] Schabas (2012), p. 125.

[21] Schabas (2012), pp. 125–152.

mens rea, or the "guilty intention" or *dolus directus*.[22] Finally, the other two elements provided by Article 8(2) (b) go for all crimes which are no other than the connection between the perpetrated act and the state of armed conflict, as well as knowledge of the existence of the armed conflict by the perpetrator.

It must be ruled that robots, however autonomous they may be, cannot be held criminally responsible for their actions.[23] Beyond the absurd nature of this proposal, criminal liability simply could not be incurred by robots. As we have just seen, two main elements must be proven to initiate criminal liability in the case of an attack against civilians: *actus reus*, the material commission of the act, and *mens rea*, the intention to commit this act. If an international prosecutor attempts to engage the international responsibility of a robot, the first element of *actus reus* seems possible to demonstrate, but it is quite different for the second element of *mens rea*. As Heyns explains, proving that a robotic system intended to commit a crime is not possible: Robots do not have moral free will and therefore cannot in any way be held responsible if they cause deprivation of life which, if it resulted from a human decision, would call for an invocation of the responsibility of the person concerned.[24]

The ICRC and HRW also ruled out the possibility that a robot could be recognized as criminally responsible.[25] Moreover, the ICC only has jurisdiction over natural persons over the age of 18 at the time of the commission of the crime.[26] An extract from a 1945 Nuremberg International Military Tribunal trial is particularly convincing, although it refers to a completely different subject; it is men and not abstract entities who commit the crimes for which repression is required, as a sanction of the law internationally.[27]

Heyns notes that "software programmers, those who build or sell the hardware, military commanders, subordinates who deploy these systems, and political leaders" could all potentially be found legally responsible.[28] In this regard, the United States accepts the principle that individuals involved in autonomous weapon system operations can be held criminally responsible.[29] Indeed, the U.S. Department of Defense Directive 3000.09 establishes that "Persons who authorise the use of, direct the use of, or operate autonomous and semi-autonomous weapon systems must do so with appropriate care and in accordance with the law of war, applicable treaties, weapon system safety rules, and applicable rules of engagement (ROE)."[30]

---

[22] Schabas (2012), pp. 125–152.

[23] Gless et al. (2016), pp. 412–436.

[24] Heyns (2013), p. 16.

[25] ICRC (2014); Human Rights Watch, Harvard Law School International Human Rights Clinic (2012), p. 45.

[26] Rome Statute (1998), art 25(1).

[27] International Military Tribunal (1994), p. 234.

[28] Heyns (2013), p. 16.

[29] DoD (2012), Directive 3000.09.

[30] DoD (2012), Directive 3000.09.

Moreover, the directive requires that autonomous and semi-autonomous weapon systems are designed to enable commanders and operators to exercise appropriate human judgement over the use of force.

2.1 Responsibility as a Perpetrator

According to Article 25(3)(a) of the Rome Statute, a person is criminally responsible for a crime under the Court's jurisdiction if "that person commits such a crime, whether as an individual, jointly with another or through another person, regardless of whether that other person is criminally responsible."[31] Three forms of commission stem from this article: direct commission, co-perpetration, and indirect commission. Article 25(3)(a) is therefore not limited solely to the concrete and material execution of the criminal act. According to the Pre-Trial Chamber of the International Criminal Court, "the exercise of control over the commission of the crime is a common hallmark of all forms of principal perpetration under paragraph (a) and must be proven for an accused to be considered a principal perpetrator."[32] Let me now examine the extent to which this legal framework may be suitable for attacks against civilians committed using an autonomous weapon system.

2.1.1 Direct Commission

A typical case of direct commission would be a soldier intentionally killing a civilian with a weapon like a rifle. In such a case, the soldier cannot exclude their own liability due to consequences linked to the normal use of the rifle. For some authors, this situation would also apply to autonomous weapon systems. Sassòli believes, for example, that the commander who made the decision to deploy an autonomous weapon system must understand how it works, just as with any other means and method of war.[33] According to him, the causal chain allowing the attribution of responsibility would not be broken by the weapon's autonomy. In this sense, he refutes criticism regarding a lack of responsibility.

Schmitt also admits that any commander who launches an attack with an autonomous weapons system would, as with any other weapons system, be responsible under international criminal law.[34] According to this logic, it is just as fair to hold a robot's commander accountable as to demand accountability from the operator of an assault rifle. It is true that such a scenario may be possible. We can hypothetically conceive that a person who blatantly deploys an autonomous weapons system in a

[31] Rome Statute (1998), art 25(3)(a).

[32] Decision on Confirmation of Charges, *Prosecution v Katanga*, (2008), No.: ICC-01/04-01/07.

[33] Sassòli (2014), p. 308.

[34] Schmitt (2015).

densely civilian-populated location, far from any military objective, could be held criminally responsible for it, in the same way as someone who would deploy a bomb there. In this scenario, this person could have legitimately predicted that deploying an autonomous weapon was not appropriate. A clear causal link could be established between the commander's deployment of the autonomous weapons system and the war crime.[35]

There are, however, areas of in-distinction arising out of the realities of fighting on ground, as well as the intrinsic nature of autonomous weapon systems that might cloud attribution of responsibility. Such was the case where the Kargu-2 drones pursued adversary convoys and units for a certain distance. The longer the delay between activating the system and a possible incident, the more likely the initial circumstances are to be modified, making the link between the operator and the crime tenuous.[36] Considering that the system can commit truly unpredictable acts, the difficulty largely comes from proving that the operator intended to commit the crime.

To overcome this difficulty, Neha Jain suggests modifying the mental element to lower the threshold of *mens rea* to a category of "opaque recklessness", in which the accused knows their conduct is risky but either does not realise or consciously ignores the specific reasons for this risk.[37] If we embrace this more comprehensive concept of recklessness, in which the accused has responsibility even when they are unaware of the specific danger their actions pose, this could be encouraging for assigning responsibility for the harm caused by an Autonomous Weapon System.[38] Hence, notwithstanding the unpredictable character of the AWS's acts, the operator can be held responsible for crimes, even if they were unaware of all the exact risks linked to deploying an autonomous weapon system. Within the context of detrimental autonomous weapon system behaviour, the judge will have to ascertain whether the commander/deploying officer should have been cognisant of a significant and unwarranted risk of harm. Also, it is for the prosecution to show that his failure to address this risk, in light of the circumstances and his knowledge, was such a distinct departure from the duty of care that a reasonable person, in the same situation, would have employed. It is important to indicate that, reducing the *mens rea* levels to recklessness and/or negligence will not encompass all examples of anomalous functioning of AWS, but it will clearly expand the possible range of responsibility to include specific instances. Moreover, this *mens rea* criterion could function as a preemptive measure to discourage the use of an AWS in specific operations. This would involve alerting and motivating commanders and military officers to exercise prudence and actively gather information and understanding about the potential risks and damages that may arise from the autonomous operation of the weapons they deploy.

[35] Gaeta (2023), pp. 1033–1055.

[36] Nasu (2021).

[37] Jain (2016), p. 317.

[38] Bo (2021), pp. 275–299.

In practice, however, states are unlikely to introduce such a new form of responsibility. Ferzan proposed an amendment to the definition of recklessness in the Model Penal Code to include the concept of opaque recklessness.[39] Kenneth Simons observed that this standard of *mens rea* will still require demonstrating a certain degree of subjective consciousness of the extent of behavioural uncertainty associated with Autonomous Weapon Systems conduct which might be difficult to prove in individual cases.[40] Willful blindness could also be invoked, as this norm already exists in international criminal law and applies to civilian superiors in times of war.[41] While the minimum standard for a military leader is that they "should have known", for a civilian superior it is rather that they "deliberately neglected to take into account information".[42] Faced with new realities of war, states could propose lowering the minimum responsibility standard of a military leader to that already existing for a civilian superior.

Another difficulty would also stem from the fact that exercising control over the commission of the crime must be proven. However, Schmitt and Thurnher demonstrate that the simple fact that a human does not control a particular operation does not mean that no human is responsible for the system's actions.[43] For these authors, a person must decide how to program it and when to launch it and is therefore responsible for resulting actions. I agree with these authors that although the Autonomous Weapon System demonstrates machine learning in its choice to target a certain individual or object or in the methods it employs to perform certain operations, these choices are intrinsically linked to the previous human decision to programme it and deploy to perform a task. A direct correlation indicates by a higher level of certainty that control over the commission of a crime transcends a mere pull of the trigger. It ensures only those who played a major role in the commission of the crime are treated as perpetrators.[44] Therefore, the autonomous functions of a weapon cannot be said to bar a person from control over a crime.

In summary, direct commission is a relevant mode of liability for crimes that will be committed using an autonomous weapon system. However, we can surmise that only the most blatant violations of international law, where the intention to commit the crime can be easily proven, will allow recourse to direct commission as the basis for liability. For less clear-cut cases, direct commission may not be a viable pathway to accountability.

---

[39] Ferzan (2001), pp. 597–652.

[40] Simons (2003), p. 179.

[41] Kwik (2023), p. 24.

[42] Fellmeth and Crawford (2022), pp. 1223–1266.

[43] Schmitt and Thurnher (2013), p. 231.

[44] Werle and Burghardt (2014), p. 51.

2.1.2 Co-perpetration

Any person who contributes to the commission of a crime under international law can be held individually liable as a co-perpetrator. According to ICC jurisprudence, this form of liability requires: (1) a group of persons, (2) a common plan involving the commission of an international crime, and (3) an essential personal contribution by the accused.[45] Morally, the co-perpetrator must (1) be aware of the criminal plan and consciously take the risk of further crimes occurring, and (2) personally endorse the subjective aspects of the crime committed by direct perpetrators.[46]

In that regard, manufacturers and programmers engaged in developing autonomous weapons could find themselves liable for co-perpetration.[47] Ultimately, this would imply that the weapon systems were indeed developed with war crimes as their goal, closely coordinated with a commander making certain those systems were used for the purpose. Economically mixed, such a combination seems very unrealistic because experts involved will likely have acted in good faith, not intending to commit international crimes. In addition, their role would shape the behaviour of the weapons, but by no means would conclude with their activation on a battlefield completely separated from any criminal plan.[48]

On the other hand, the accused must also personally bear the mental element (*mens rea*) of the crime, so the issues related to intent mentioned earlier remain. It would be necessary to prove that those who programmed or manufactured the autonomous weapons intended for them to violate the rules of international humanitarian law.[49] This scenario appears very unlikely, especially since numerous people will work on the design, manufacturing, and programming of these systems. Heyns recalls that their development "will certainly involve a large number of people" and that it is "unlikely that any one of them, taken in isolation, understands the complex interactions between the various constituent elements of this robot."[50] Generally speaking, it seems difficult to trace a link between a weapon's development and the commission of a specific crime.

Even if this were possible, a war crime must have been committed in the context of and associated with an armed conflict. According to the fourth point of Article 8 (c) of the Elements of Crimes relating to war crimes, the perpetrator must have had knowledge of the factual circumstances establishing an armed conflict's existence and that the conduct took place in that context.[51] However, it is highly likely that the lengthy process of designing autonomous weapon systems will occur before any

[45] ICC (2007). *Prosecutor v. Lubanga*, Pre-Trial Chamber I, Decision on the Confirmation of Charges, 29 January 2007.

[46] ICC (2007), Para. 1008.

[47] Gless and Whalen-Bridge (2022), p. 2022-08.

[48] McFarland (2020), p. 155.

[49] Gless et al. (2016), pp. 412–425.

[50] Heyns (2013), p. 17.

[51] ICC (2011) Elements of Crime, art 8(c).

armed conflict, i.e., in peacetime.[52] As a result, the programmers and manufacturers who worked on these systems years before an armed conflict could not be found criminally responsible for a war crime, even if they intentionally planned for the robot to contravene international humanitarian law rules. In this regard, McCormack and McFarland could not identify existing jurisprudence from international trials that recognized an individual's criminal responsibility for acts committed before an armed conflict's start.[53] We must therefore remain cautious about the real possibilities that a programmer or weapon manufacturer could be found guilty of a war crime, because their liability "cannot be extended to cover an unlimited number of potential violations that their creation could cause."[54]

2.1.3 Indirect Commission

The same article ultimately establishes a person's guilt if they commit a crime through another person, which is considered indirect commission. Indirect commission of a crime occurs when the accused is "a principal who exercises control over the commission of criminal acts through control over the will of the direct perpetrators."[55] The direct perpetrator, that is, the person who physically or directly performs the act, is defined as a "tool" or "instrument" of the indirect perpetrator.[56] The article states that an indirect perpetrator may be liable regardless of whether the "intermediary" person commits a criminal act.[57] So can we then say that a soldier operating an autonomous weapons system uses a non-human instrument to commit a crime?

The language of Article 25(3)(a) is one constraint which asserts that the intermediary is, in fact, a human character.[58] However, in Halajová's view, since the crime of indirectly perpetrating is independent of the guilt of the direct perpetrator so, however absurdly, it is acceptable to suggest that the autonomous weapon system in executing the crime may be treated like the direct perpetrator as defined by this article.[59] Further, David Jens Ohlin underscores that the views of the ICC on the possibility of attribution under the theory of *Organisationsherrschaft* if a person acted through an organisational apparatus opens up the possibility of attribution when a person acts through control exercised via another mechanism or device.[60]

Indeed, by analogy with the *Organisationsherrschaft* theory, Ohlin puts forward the idea that military commanders can be held responsible under the mode of indirect

[52] Halajová (2020), p. 136.
[53] McFarland and McCormack (2014), p. 377.
[54] Halajová (2020), p. 136.
[55] Werle and Burghardt (2014), p. 58.
[56] Halajová (2020), p. 138.
[57] Fletcher (2000), p. 639.
[58] Fletcher (2000), p. 639.
[59] Halajová (2020), p. 138.
[60] Ohlin (2016), p. 10.

perpetration. The *Organisationsherrschaft*, which can be described as indirect perpetration through a power apparatus, allows recognizing the responsibility of persons "exercising control over the crimes of their subordinates by virtue of their role in a power structure.[61] This power apparatus must be an 'effective structure of quasi-automatic obedience to the injunctions of a superior.'"[62] The accused has a macro-level of control over the commission of the crime: they have the capacity to decide whether the crime will occur, without controlling every aspect of its commission. Each part of the organisation then carries out the assigned task with the required level of discretion.[63] This theory was first designed to accurately reflect criminal liability in bureaucratic dictatorships like the Nazi dictatorship.[64]

We know that autonomous weapon systems can operate independently, particularly by engaging force alone against a target. This is, according to several authors,[65] the main pitfall to recognizing legal responsibility under international criminal law. However, rather than being a difficulty, Ohlin notes that this issue is precisely a characteristic of the *Organisationsherrschaft*.[66] Commanders define the general tasks of autonomous weapon systems, and the latter have discretionary power over how they carry them out, in the same way as individuals within the power apparatus. Geoffrey S. Corn agrees, putting forth that soldiers are also "autonomous weapons" acting within the parameters established by their commanders: "The soldier, like the predicted autonomous weapon system, is capable of exercising cognitive reasoning. This is obviously inherent in any human being. But the soldier is not an 'autonomous actor' in the sense that she may exercise judgement with no parameters. Instead, the soldier operates as an agent of responsible command, and in that capacity must frame her decision-making process within the parameters established by superior command. How the soldier is developed and prepared to exercise this inherently autonomous cognitive capacity without becoming an autonomous actor therefore provides a logical template for the 'preparation' of a weapon system with autonomous cognitive capacity."[67]

To hold a commander liable either for their role in creating the operating conditions that led to the illegal behaviour or for the failure to impose appropriate limits on the autonomous system's ability to act seems sensible. However, this cannot cover a scenario where the commander deploys an autonomous weapon system without a specific criminal intent in mind.[68] Indeed, it must still be proven that the person personally endorses all the subjective elements of the crime and had knowledge of the circumstances attesting to their control over the perpetrators.

[61] Werle and Burghardt (2014), p. 58.
[62] Werle and Burghardt (2014), p. 58.
[63] Ohlin (2016), p. 10.
[64] Lanza (2017), p. 12.
[65] Tudosia (2024).
[66] Ohlin (2016), p. 10.
[67] Corn (2016), p. 221.
[68] Halajová (2020), p. 140.

Simply deploying the autonomous system, without more, may not meet the required thresholds for establishing indirect perpetration liability under international criminal law.[69]

All in all, this theory demonstrates the flexibility of international law and could be used as a starting point for developing a form of accountability adapted to systems autonomous weapons. Among the three forms of article 25 (3) al. a) of the ICC Statute, it appears that indirect commission is the most promising avenue for recognizing the responsibility of people who commit crimes using weapons systems autonomously.

2.2 *Accessory Forms of Participation*

Paragraphs (b), (c), and (d) of Article 25(3) provides different levels of culpability of individuals who have not directly committed the crime but have aided it or contributed something to its commission;[70] These individuals are treated as accomplices, rather than the perpetrators. Specifically, paragraph (b) concerns the act of instigation of the crime through orders, solicitation, or encouragement. Paragraph (c) concerns assistance, abetting, or aiding the crime. Any other form of contribution to the group crime is described in paragraph (d). Each of these accessory forms of participation will be discussed briefly in this section. However, it is pertinent to record here that there are certain accountability issues they raise in common with those regarding the liability of the perpetrator: for example, the required mental element under Article 30, or the existence of armed conflict.

2.2.1 Order, Solicitation or Encouragement

The utilisation of autonomous weapons systems seems not to present any peculiar challenges towards appropriate accusatives for instances of ordering, soliciting or encouraging criminal acts exploiting the first accessory mode in paragraph (b).[71] Should the evidence show an accused had ordered, solicited, or encouraged another individual to initiate the attack on the civilian, determining the proper level of mental element on the prosecutor's part should become easier.[72] However, direct orders given to an armed autonomous robotic system will probably incur different responsibilities, indisputably as the principal rather than the accessory.

[69] Werle and Burghardt (2014), p. 58.

[70] Werle and Burghardt (2014), p. 63.

[71] Rome Statute (1998), art 25(3)(b).

[72] Haider (2018), p. 27.

2.2.2 Competition, Help or Any Other Form of Assistance

The process of developing autonomous weapon systems is rather connected with how they will act after being launched. One of the key differences to note is that designers of autonomous system weapons have a certain amount of control over what their systems do once they have been released.[73] This leads to considering how the manufacturer and programmers might be prosecuted for failure to give assistance in attack against civilians under the form of responsibility prescribed in the Article 25(3)(c) related to aiding and abetting crimes.[74] As prescribed by the Rome Statute, such assistance must have been rendered with a view to the perpetration of the crime, although the accused is under no obligation to have apprehended the same unlawful intent as that of the principal offender. This mode of liability does not require the victim to have actual knowledge of any other participant's intent to kill, but it is enough that the main perpetrator did so.[75]

According to McFarland, invoking the aiding and abetting mode of liability would require a degree of shared control between the operator and manufacturer of an autonomous weapon system.[76] Unlike other weapon types, the possibilities for shared responsibility are greater because the programming that governs the robot's autonomy directly impacts its future actions. As the author explains, the degree of control and responsibility attributable to the manufacturer depends on the level of autonomy exhibited by the system regarding a particular action.[77] Technological autonomy implies that the operators and developers gradually exchange various degrees of control and accountability for the system's actions and outcome. As long as an operator has a substantial ability to impact the weapon system's operation, control remains divided between the developer and operator.[78]

In order for the manufacturer to be held liable under aiding and abetting, they would have to have played a part but not the "dominant" part in the running of the autonomous system.[79] Of course, according to McFarland there are significant hindrances that would make such responsibility difficult to recognize. First of all, the temporal conditions may not be fulfilled because activities which took place prior to the existence of an armed conflict cannot consequently lead to individual criminal responsibility pursuant to the IHL. Some components to establish criminal responsibility are that the criminal conduct was committed in the context of and related to an armed conflict which would not be included in weapon system manufacturers. Additionally, existing case law does not cover situations where an accused "assisted" the physical perpetrator before the latter intended to commit the crime.

[73] McFarland (2020), p. 152.

[74] Rome Statute (1998), art 25(3)(c).

[75] Werle and Burghardt (2014), p. 63.

[76] McFarland (2020), p. 157.

[77] McFarland (2020), p. 156.

[78] McFarland (2020), p. 156.

[79] McFarland (2020), p. 157.

In other words, at the time the assistance was provided, it must be proven the physical perpetrator already intended the crime.[80] Surely, manufacturers do not design weapon systems with such a mental picture of the future operators' criminal intentions. Furthermore, article 25(3)(c) defines a special mental element, namely that the assistance was rendered with a view to facilitate the commission of such a crime. Thus for instance to convict the accused, the prosecutor would have to prove not only that the accused aided in the crime while having knowledge of the perpetrator's intent for instance by manufacturing or selling an autonomous weapon system but also that he or she intended to facilitate the said crime.[81]

Jack Beard notes that it can be challenging to apply aiding and abetting liability to manufacturers, at least when the products they manufacture are not illegal per se.[82] We can extend this reasoning further. As discussed above, it is the responsibility of each state to ensure the legality of any new war technologies they intend to use. If we determine that a war crime occurred and the fault lies entirely or partially with the manufacturers, would that not imply the state was using an inherently illegal weapon?

All considerations taken into account, there is little likelihood that manufacturers will be held responsible under the aiding and abetting mode of liability. Even if they were, we can at the very least note that the potential liability of a programmer in no way excludes the responsibilities of those involved in the final deployment of the weapon system.[83]

2.2.3 Residual Forms of Contribution to Group Crime

Article 25(3)(c) of the Rome Statute extends a new form of participation to assist in prosecuting a person who in any other way took part in the commission or attempted commission of a crime. As Werle and Burghardt points out this can include other kinds of indirect support like funding of criminal activities by the group.[84] However, the authors maintain that this rule "is still imprecise and its application against an accused before the ICC is currently uncertain."[85] This view is shared by many other scholars.[86] Moreover, this form of liability would likely be of little relevance for the use of autonomous weapon systems, particularly because it would require proving some kind of conspiracy between programmers, manufacturers, and operators.

80 McFarland (2020), p. 157.
81 McFarland (2020), p. 157.
82 Beard (2014), p. 649.
83 Chengeta (2015), p. 23.
84 Werle and Burghardt (2014), p. 182.
85 Werle and Burghardt (2014), p. 182.
86 Beard (2014), p. 647.

2.3 *The Responsibility of Military Leaders and Other Hierarchical Superiors*

In addition to being responsible for crimes they order, commanders bear responsibility for crimes committed by their subordinates if: (1) they knew or had reason to know the subordinates were committing or about to commit such crimes, and (2) they failed to take all necessary and reasonable measures within their power to prevent the crimes' execution.[87] The significance of this rule of customary international humanitarian law is even further underlined in the Commentary on the Additional Protocols, where it is noted that at the troop level, such measures must be taken as are necessary to ensure proper respect for the Conventions and Protocols and to prevent a fatal distance from the commitment of the parties on the one hand and of the individual on the other.[88] Since commanders cannot, to some extent, directly control troops during combat, they need to demand enough discipline for the rules to be followed even when the troops are not under the commander's supervision. Finally, one can conclude that without commanders monitoring and engagement, the rules are hardly useful.[89]

Article 28 of the Rome Statute establishes the responsibility of military commanders and other superiors in the hierarchy. It distinguishes between two types of superior responsibility: that of military commanders and that of civilian superiors. For the purposes of this chapter, we will only focus on the responsibility of military commanders, as it is foreseeable that military forces will primarily deploy autonomous weapon systems.

In order to hold a military commander accountable for crimes committed by subordinates, the following conditions must be met: (a) the existence of a superior-subordinate relationship, (b) the commander's knowledge of subordinates' involvement in a crime, (c) the commander's failure to prevent the commission of the crime or to punish the subordinates, and (d) the subordinates' commission of the crime resulting from the commander's failure to exercise control over these forces.[90] The commander is not accused of directly contributing to the actual commission of the crime nor did the commander order the crime, but rather of failing in their duty as a superior to exercise control. The mental element requires actual or potential knowledge—the commander knew or should have known.

The lower *mens rea* requirement is precisely what makes the doctrine of superior responsibility relevant to the use of autonomous weapon systems. Given the difficulties in proving criminal intent for acts autonomously committed by a system, it seems relevant to assess the possibility of holding a commander responsible if they knew or should have known that crimes were going to be or were being committed

[87] Rome Statute (1998), art 28.

[88] Pilloud et al. (1986), p. 1042.

[89] Pilloud et al. (1986), p. 1042.

[90] Halajová (2020), p. 142.

and failed to take appropriate preventive or suppressive measures.[91] Could a military commander's responsibility be triggered under this provision for a crime committed by an autonomous weapon system? Two hypothetical scenarios mentioned in the literature explore this; one considering the commander's responsibility for a subordinate's deployment of such a system, and the other viewing the person deploying an autonomous system as the superior to that system.

In the first scenario, even though a system is autonomous, it will not affect the relevant law already in existence. A military commander is accountable if he or she knew, or had reason to know, that one of his or her subordinates intends to or is in the process of performing a war crime, it will be the legal duty of the commander to take all necessary and reasonable to prevent the execution of such act where the subordinate will be using any weapon.[92] On this basis, therefore, Jain regards the application of Article 28 as prima facie legitimate.[93] In addition, the commander would also be guilty under international criminal law, if they were aware that an AWS was unable to respect the principles and rules of international humanitarian law but did nothing to stop its use.[94]

In the second scenario, one could argue that the relationship between the person deploying an autonomous robot and the robot itself is akin to a military commander-subordinate relationship.[95] At the outset, if this person intended for a crime to be committed, invoking Article 28 should be rejected. Sassoli for this reason was right in claiming that this would justify holding the person responsible as a principal perpetrator under Article 25(3)(a). Moreover, to the extent a soldier uses the weapon with ill purpose, his action is equally as unlawful as if that soldier were to directly commit a crime with any other tool rather than making what can be thought of as an omission error.

Alessandra Spadaro also disagrees in respect of command responsibility for autonomous weapons.[96] She argues that the doctrine of superior responsibility is not applicable to AWS under international law due to the absence of a superior-subordinate relationship between humans and machines. Still traditionally attributed to military commanders, this doctrine rests its success on the capacity of the superior to effectively control human subordinates. Yet, as Spadaro notes, such control is of a different kind than control over weapons and AWS cannot be viewed as legal subjects, who could be subordinate to people.[97]

This argument fails to appreciate that changes in technological agency have occurred and are expected in warfare affairs. Peter Margulies argues that as elements of the military command system, while not being human themselves, AWS act as

[91] Bo (2021), pp. 275–299.

[92] Rome Statute (1998), art 28.

[93] Jain (2016), p. 313.

[94] Schmitt and Thurnher (2013), p. 277.

[95] Toscano (2015), p. 67.

[96] Spadaro (2023), pp. 1119–1136.

[97] Spadaro (2023), pp. 1119–1122.

instruments of a superior, in the same way; it means their use is an extension of the commander's decisions.[98] In this view, AWS could be considered subordinates in a broader sense. What Margulies fails to consider is that a commander's accountability is to all elements of command, human or mechanical and that the interpersonal dynamic is only one element of a much larger issue, which is that AWS, just like human soldiers are reflections of the commander's choices.[99]

The second major argument Spadaro makes is that superior responsibility presupposes the commission of a crime by a punishable subordinate. Since AWS lack the *mens rea* required for criminal responsibility, no direct or indirect crime can be ascribed to them under current international law.[100] The author points out that even if AWS can independently execute an act fulfilling the requirements of a war crime, AWS itself cannot possess the necessary intent to commit a war crime, thus, it is impossible to incriminate their human operators for acts that AWS commits autonomously.[101] This also poses a basic question in the effectiveness of using superior responsibility as a legal instrument in the context of AWS.

Spadaro's assertion that AWS lacks the *mens rea* necessary for committing a crime is correct in a strict legal sense, but the doctrine of superior responsibility could evolve to encompass negligence or failure to prevent AWS from causing harm. Nehal Bhuta[102] and Rebecca Crootof[103] argue that accountability in the use of AWS should not hinge on whether the machine itself forms intent but on the human decision-makers who authorised or failed to control their actions. Bhuta acknowledges that AWS functions in a system created by their human masters and if AWS' use leads to a breach of international law then the designers, the deployers or those who failed to oversight the AWS should be held responsible.[104] In other words, the mental element of war crimes could have been connected to the human decisions which were behind the AWS's actions, thus avoiding the problem of the machine's cognitive capabilities.

Alternatively if the person who deployed the autonomous weapon system has no criminal intent then Article 28 can be more readily invoked but the issue remains whether the provision would apply. According to Jain, retaining superior responsibility in this case would breed redundancy and end up with every soldier considered a superior whenever complex arms are deployed to fulfil orders.[105] In general, it might be assumed that the persons who use autonomous weapon systems will be higher-ranked officers rather than junior soldiers since the costs of these technical means and potential consequences of their application are high. Furthermore, if we

[98] Margulies (2016), p. 19.
[99] Margulies (2016), p. 19.
[100] Spadaro (2023), pp. 1128–1131.
[101] Spadaro (2023), pp. 1128–1131.
[102] Bhuta and Pantazopoulos (2016), pp. 284–300.
[103] Crootof (2016), p. 1347.
[104] Bhuta and Pantazopoulos (2016), pp. 284–300.
[105] Jain (2016), p. 312.

determine that the autonomous system is under similar control as the subordinate to a military superior, applying the superior responsibility doctrine to such soldiers would not be unreasonably done. These arguments temper the worries enumerated by Jain.

Regarding the burden of proof, an international prosecutor would have to prove that the commander knew or should have known that the system was about to commit or was committing a crime, and that they "failed to take all necessary and reasonable measures within their power to prevent or repress its execution or to refer the matter to the competent authorities for investigation and prosecution."[106] Diederik-Jan Posthuma believes the "should have known" requirement is incompatible with autonomous systems' use, because the military commander lacks the necessary technological knowledge to foresee how an algorithm controlling a weapon would behave in the field.[107] However, we can qualify his arguments: autonomous weapons will not act in a completely unpredictable manner, and it is in the armed forces' interest that commanders are sufficiently familiar with the operation of weapons they will deploy—they will at minimum be responsible for the decision to deploy them.

The arrangement of the military hierarchy structure makes sure that the decisions made by a group of soldiers are contained with the result of a decision that has been made by a higher-duty officer in the chain of command. In other words these human soldiers are even "more 'autonomous'" than weapon systems themselves—no software can control their autonomy and the manner in which they can act. However, their bosses always remain liable for the actions of such soldiers and for the crimes themselves. It can be regarded as historical practice for the leaders of the troops which used weapons against civilians to be punished for such actions; for instance, Germain Katanga is one of the persons who was convicted by the ICC for planning an attack on the civilians as the commander of the troops.[108] For McFarland, this extends to commanders of military forces that allegedly use autonomous weapons against civilians during armed conflict.[109] It is my argument that the unpredictability of autonomous weapon systems is not a sufficient reason to preclude military commanders' responsibility.

In conclusion, while it remains unlikely the ICC would accept this analogy, it demonstrates international law's full potential flexibility. Military commander responsibility seems a promising avenue to consider a new form of liability adapted to the autonomous weapons reality. In particular, the "knew or should have known" mental element allows recognizing a lower level of culpability than the modes in Article 25. It will be important to establish, among other factors, whether military commanders can sufficiently understand the complex programming of autonomous weapons to justify criminal liability.

[106] Rome Statute (1998), art 28(b)(iii).

[107] Posthuma (2019), p. 36.

[108] *Prosecutor v Germain Katanga* (n.d.) (ICC-01/04-01/07, Trial Judgment, 7 March 2014).

[109] McFarland (2020), p. 143.

3 Gaps in the Rome Statute

While the literature as a whole blames accountability vices on systems of autonomous weapon on their own, one fact that stands out is that there are certain holes within the Rome Statute that lead to such accountability deficits. For example, one of the key notions for using Article 25 to attribute individual criminal liability i.e. intentionality, is with no provision for lesser degrees of guilt, including negligence. This is to say that the omission was deliberate by the drafters of the Statute, because the jurisdiction of the Court only extends to, 'the most serious crimes which affect the entire International community'.[110] The goal being to call for justice for the worst crimes. Finally, the ICC is complementary to national courts in addressing the issue.[111] If a person committed manslaughter during warfare, he or she could be taken through a national court of law and thus not regulated by the ICC.

Although weapons experimentation and testing may demonstrate that an autonomous weapons system can theoretically comply with international humanitarian law, it would be inappropriate to hold anyone accountable if a failure occurs. No justice system operating under the rule of law would want to criminally charge individuals when a machine performs an action that was truly unpredictable.[112] Similar questions emerge in other domains of automation, such as when a Tesla vehicle operating on autopilot causes a fatality.[113]

States are required to use weapons that are lawful under the international humanitarian law; these should be weapons that can be used in compliance with standards like the proportionality and indeed the necessity. States also have no reason to use unpredictable or faulty weapons. However, where an unforeseeable failure or an act which could not reasonably have been foreseen within a reasonable degree of risk occurs, there should be no one culpable. All attempts to apportion blame must be dismissed. As Daniele Amoroso states, "In dealing with questions of responsibility, we must always be careful not to confuse the fight against impunity with the scapegoating of human beings."[114] It would appear entirely unfair to hold an individual guilty to the highest degree of responsibility for an act that they did not intend and had no possibility of foreseeing. Schmitt and Thurnher believe that the more likely scenario would be the criminal misuse of these weapons, such as an operator who cannot distinguish between civilians and combatants but still deploys an autonomous weapon system in an area where the two are intermingled.[115]

In other words, people will always remain responsible for the use of AWS. Although such activities will be delegated to these systems, control of their proper utilisation shall remain in the jurisdiction of humans as the orders to use such

[110] Rome Statute (1998), art 25.

[111] Rome Statute (1998), art 25.

[112] Posthuma (2019), p. 33.

[113] Rosenthal (2022).

[114] Amoroso (2020), p. 143.

[115] Schmitt and Thurnher (2013), p. 278.

systems and decisions on how to program them shall come from humans.[116] For this reason, "any recklessness or criminal misuse will result in liability through the same war crimes mechanisms that already exist under the law of armed conflict."[117] In other cases, it could potentially involve a failure or a state's use of a weapon that contravenes international humanitarian law.

4 Conclusion

In conclusion, many questions remain unanswered and subsequently, about the AWS in general including but not limited to ethical, juridical and accountability issues. Because the technology in military application is trending towards more and more automated, such issues are beginning to demand the attention of the international community. Concerns arising from AWs should not be treated lightly and efforts to address these as soon as possible should be a priority because should they spread faster than the legal and policy frameworks that seek to govern their usage, legal remedies would be hard to come by. Combining the ethical question of who should be allowed to decide on certain issues in armed conflict with the problem of properly holding the responsible perpetrators to international law account in the best not easy, and so requires anticipation.

The issue of individual accountability for crimes committed by autonomous systems poses another challenge; this brings into the question of who ought to take 'individual responsibility'. Placing responsibility on the machine in itself will never be acceptable. Machines lack moral agency; holding a machine accountable will never alleviate the anguish it brings that could be done against the victim, nor will it serve to deter future offences. Assigning accountability to the human actors will probably be the next most sensible step, but such a proposition also brings with it hurdles. Whereas an operator is normally called on in the use of autonomous weapons, it is the commander or superior officer who bears general responsibility from practical and legal standpoints for operations carried out under their authorisation and oversight. Because the commander has a broader perspective and greater authority than the operator, he is considered more accountable, especially in situations where the acts of an autonomous system become difficult for an operator to predict or control.

The programmers were actually scrutinised in this paper, especially if some evidence were established that they were intentionally creating a system in order to commit unlawful acts. However, only a few years later, as the systems become more autonomous, the line between negligence on the part of the programmers and autonomous decision-making choices of the system has become increasingly subtle. This dynamic makes assigning blame difficult and the proof of intention to propose

[116] Schmitt and Thurnher (2013), p. 280.

[117] Schmitt and Thurnher (2013), p. 280.

some liable for a criminal action, difficult. In short, commanders may prove to be the most plausible candidates to attribute responsibility; however, future progressed military technological interests may warrant a more valid legal framework that allows for clarification of the inherent difficulty of autonomous systems in the context of armed conflict.

References

Amoroso D (2020) Autonomous weapons systems and international law: a study on human-machine interactions in ethically and legally sensitive domains. Nomos Verlagsgesellschaft mbH & Co. KG, Baden-Baden

Beard J (2014) Autonomous weapons and human responsibilities. Georgetown J Int Law 45:617–681

Bhuta N, Pantazopoulos S-E (2016) Autonomy and uncertainty: increasingly autonomous weapons systems and the international legal regulation of risk. In: Bhuta N, Beck S, Geiß R, Liu H-Y, Kreß C (eds) Autonomous weapons systems: law, ethics, policy. Cambridge University Press, Cambridge, pp 284–300

Bo M (2021) Autonomous weapons and the responsibility gap in light of the mens rea of the war crime of attacking civilians in the ICC statute. J Int Crim Just 19(2):275–299

Bo M, Bruun L, Boulanin V (2022) Retaining human responsibility in the development and use of autonomous weapon systems: on accountability for violations of international humanitarian law involving AWS. Stockholm International Peace Research Institute, Stockholm

Chengeta T (2015) Accountability gap, autonomous weapon systems and modes of responsibility in international law. Denver J Int Law Policy 45:1–50

Corn GS (2016) Autonomous weapons systems: managing the inevitability of "taking the man out of the loop". In: Bhuta N et al (eds) Autonomous weapons systems: law, ethics, policy. Cambridge University Press, Cambridge, pp 209–242

Crootof R (2016) War torts: accountability for autonomous weapons. Univ Pa Law Rev 164:1347–1402

Department of Defense (DoD) (2012) Autonomy in weapon systems. Directive 3000.09. Department of Defense, Washington, D.C.

Dunlap CJ Jr (2016) Accountability and autonomous weapons: much ado about nothing? Temple Int Comp Law J 30:63–76

Fellmeth A, Crawford E (2022) "Reason to know" in the international law of command responsibility. Int Rev Red Cross 104(919):1223–1266

Ferzan KK (2001) Opaque recklessness. J Crim Law Criminol 91(3):597–652

Fletcher GP (2000) Rethinking criminal law. Oxford University Press, Oxford

Gaeta P (2023) Who acts when autonomous weapons strike? The act requirement for individual criminal responsibility and state responsibility. J Int Crim Just 21(5):1033–1055

Gless S, Whalen-Bridge H (eds) (2022) Human-robot interaction in law and its narratives: legal blame, criminal law, and procedure. Cambridge University Press, Cambridge

Gless S, Silverman E, Weigend T (2016) If robots cause harm, who is to blame? Self-driving cars and criminal liability. N Crim Law Rev 19(3):412–436

Haider A (2018) Autonomous weapon systems in international humanitarian law. JAPCC J 27

Halajová L (2020) Individual criminal responsibility for war crimes resulting from the use of autonomous weapons systems. Lawyer Q 10:134–146

Heyns C (2013) Report of the Special Rapporteur on extrajudicial, summary or arbitrary executions. UN Document A/HRC/23/47

Human Rights Watch & Harvard Law School International Human Rights Clinic (2012) Losing humanity: the case against killer robots

International Committee of the Red Cross (ICRC) (2005) Customary international humanitarian law
International Committee of the Red Cross (ICRC) (2014) Autonomous weapon systems—Q & A
International Committee of the Red Cross (ICRC) (2016) Views of the International Committee of the Red Cross (ICRC) on autonomous weapon systems
International Committee of the Red Cross (ICRC) (2022) What you need to know about autonomous weapons
International Criminal Court (ICC) (2007) *Prosecutor v. Lubanga*, Pre-Trial Chamber I, Decision on the Confirmation of Charges, 29 January 2007, ICC-01/04-01/06-803
International Criminal Court (ICC) (2011) Elements of crimes. UN Document PCNICC/2000/1/Add.2
International Military Tribunal (1994) Trial of the major war criminals before the International Military Tribunal, Nuremberg, 14 November 1945–1 October 1946. Official text, T. Mage
Jain N (2016) Autonomous weapons systems: new frameworks for individual responsibility. In: Bhuta N, Beck S, Geiß R, Liu H-Y, Kreß C (eds) Autonomous weapons systems: law, ethics, policy. Cambridge University Press, Cambridge, pp 301–324
Kwik J (2023) The conceptual roots of the criminal responsibility gap in autonomous weapon systems. Melbourne J Int Law 24
Lanza G (2017) Indirect perpetration and organisationsherrschaft. PhD thesis, Università degli Studi di Verona
Lieber F (1863) Instructions for the government of armies of the United States in the field (general orders no. 100). United States War Department, Washington, D.C.
Margulies P (2016) Making autonomous weapons accountable: command responsibility for computer-guided lethal force in armed conflicts. In: Ohlin JD (ed) Research handbook on remote warfare. Edward Elgar Press, Cheltenham, pp 263–285
McFarland T (2020) Autonomous weapon systems and the law of armed conflict: compatibility with international humanitarian law. Cambridge University Press, Cambridge
McFarland T, McCormack TLH (2014) Mind the gap: can developers of autonomous weapons systems be liable for war crimes? Int Law Stud 90:361–385
Nasu H (2021) The Kargu-2 autonomous attack drone: legal & ethical dimensions. Lieber Institute
Nollkaemper A (2003) Concurrence between individual responsibility and state responsibility in international law. Int Comp Law Q 52:615–640
Ohlin JD (2016) The combatant's stance: autonomous weapons on the battlefield. Int Law Stud 92: 1–30
Oimann AK (2023) The responsibility gap and LAWS: a critical mapping of the debate. Philos Technol 36(3):1–25
Oxford Manual on the Laws of War on Land (1880) Manual published by the Institute of International Law at Oxford, Brussels
Pilloud C et al (1986) Commentary of additional protocols of June 8, 1977, to the Geneva Conventions of August 12, 1949. Martinus Nijhoff, Leiden
Posthuma DJ (2019) Autonomous weapons systems and command responsibility: addressing the Specter of impunity. PhD thesis, Tilburg University
Prosecutor v. Germain Katanga, (n.d.) ICC-01/04-01/07, Trial Judgment, 7 March 2014
Rome Statute of the International Criminal Court (1998) 2187 UNTS 3
Rosenthal E (2022) When a Tesla on autopilot kills someone, who is responsible? The Driven, 11 March
Santoni de Sio F, Mecacci G (2021) Four responsibility gaps with artificial intelligence: why they matter and how to address them. Philos Technol 34:1057–1084
Sassòli M (2014) Autonomous weapons and international humanitarian law: advantages, open technical questions and legal issues to be clarified. Int Law Stud 90:308–340
Schabas W (2012) Mens rea, actus reus, and the role of the state. In: Unimaginable atrocities: justice, politics, and rights at the war crimes tribunals. Oxford University Press, Oxford, pp 197–220

Schmitt M (2015) Regulating autonomous weapons might be smarter than banning them. Just Security

Schmitt M, Thurnher J (2013) Out of the loop: autonomous weapon systems and the law of armed conflict. Harv Natl Secur J 4:231–281

Simons KW (2003) Should the model penal code's mens rea provisions be amended? Ohio State J Crim Law 1:179–205

Spadaro A (2023) A weapon is no subordinate: autonomous weapon systems and the scope of superior responsibility. J Int Crim Just 21(5):1119–1136

The Netherlands (2017) Examination of various dimensions of emerging technologies in the area of lethal autonomous weapons systems, in the context of the objectives and purposes of the convention. CCW/GGE.1/2017/WP.2

Toscano CP (2015) Friend of humans: an argument for developing autonomous weapons systems. J Natl Secur Law Policy 8:1–44

Tudosia M (2024) Autonomous weapon systems: is a practical approach possible? European Security & Defense

UN General Assembly (2005) Fundamental principles and guidelines concerning the right to a remedy and reparation for victims of flagrant violations of international human rights law and serious violations of international humanitarian law. UN Document A/RES/60/147

UN General Assembly (2019) Final report: meeting of the high contracting parties to the convention on prohibitions or restrictions on the use of certain conventional weapons which may be deemed to be excessively injurious or to have indiscriminate effects. UN Document CCW/MSP/2019/9

Werle G, Burghardt B (2014) Establishing degrees of responsibility: modes of participation in Article 25 of the ICC Statute. In: Van Sliedregt E, Vasiliev S (eds) Pluralism in international criminal law. Oxford University Press, Oxford, pp 301–324

Part III
European Law

EU Succession Regulation vs. Member State Treaties with Third States: Insights from CJEU Judgment C-21/22

Slavko Đorđević and Jovan Živanović

1 Introduction

The primary objective for the adoption of Regulation (EU) No 650/2012 of the European Parliament and of the Council of 4 July 2012 on jurisdiction, applicable law, recognition and enforcement of decisions, and acceptance and enforcement of authentic instruments in matters of succession and on the creation of a European Certificate of Succession[1] (so-called EU Succession Regulation, hereinafter: abbr. 'ESR') was to facilitate proper functioning of the internal market by removing the obstacles to the free movement of persons who face difficulties in asserting their rights in cross-border succession cases and enabling citizens to organize their succession in advance.[2] In order to ensure the achievement of this objective, the uniform jurisdiction and conflict-of-law rules of ESR have been created to follow the principle of unity of succession (the court seized should apply one applicable national law to the succession as a whole) which is tailored around the last habitual residence of the deceased as a main connecting factor (Art. 4 and 21 of ESR) and complemented by the *Gleichlauf* principle (court seised should apply its law to the

[1]Council Regulation (EU) 650/2012 of 4 July 2012 on jurisdiction, applicable law, recognition and enforcement of decisions and acceptance and enforcement of authentic instruments in matters of succession and on the creation of a European Certificate of Succession, OJ L 201, 27.7.2012, p. 107.
[2]See Recital 7 of ESR.

S. Đorđević (✉)
University of Kragujevac, Faculty of Law, Kragujevac, Serbia
e-mail: slavko@jura.kg.ac.rs

J. Živanović
University of Miskolc Déak Ferenc, Doctoral School of Law, Central European Academy, Budapest, Hungary
e-mail: jovan.zivanovic@centraleuropeanacademy.hu

Z. Meskić et al. (eds.), *Balkan Yearbook of European and International Law 2024*, Balkan Yearbook of European and International Law 2024,
https://doi.org/10.1007/978-3-031-89952-2_5

succession as a whole),[3] although there are certain deviations from these principles mainly accustomed for the cases closely connected to third States. However, the achievement of this objective may be undermined by bilateral treaties concluded between Member States and third States before the adoption of ESR, since they, according to Art. 75(1) of ESR, take precedence over ESR insofar their scopes of application overlap.[4] Most of these bilateral treaties contain jurisdiction and conflict-of-law rules that employ the nationality of the deceased and the location of estate assets as main connecting factors, usually following the principle of scission of succession,[5] meaning that they apparently contravene the principles and rules of ESR which could have as a consequence that the courts of a Member State bound by such treaty establish jurisdiction and determine applicable law in certain cases in accordance with the set of rules that completely differ from those of ESR applied in other Member States, thus creating the possibility that the decisional harmony and proper functioning of internal market within EU be jeopardized.[6]

Bearing the above in mind, the goal of this chapter is to contribute to the assessment of the potential adverse impact of Member States' bilateral treaties with third States on the proper functioning of the internal market and decisional harmony that ESR aims to establish. After the brief discussion on default principles and rules of ESR and their comparison with those of bilateral treaties with third States to identify the incompatibilities between them, the chapter will focus on the interpretation of Art. 75 of ESR in conjunction with Art. 351 of Treaty on the Functioning of the European Union (hereinafter: abbr. 'TFEU')[7] which, on the one hand, allows derogation from the principle of primacy of EU law in relation to international treaties concluded between Member States and third States prior to their EU membership,[8] while, on the other hand, limits the freedom of Member States to continue to be committed to these treaties if they are not compatible with EU law.[9] Such approach provides for the possibility to ascertain in which way the EU and/or Member States have to deal with the incompatibilities between ESR and bilateral treaties with third States if the latter impair proper functioning of internal market and decisional harmony within the EU, whereas the special attention, in addition to the settled case law of the Court of Justice of European Union (hereinafter

[3] See Recital 27 of ESR.

[4] Art. 75(1) of ESR: "This Regulation shall not affect the application of international conventions to which one or more Member States are party at the time of adoption of this Regulation and which concern matters covered by this Regulation."

[5] The texts of most of the treaties concluded between Member States and third States regulating succession matters having cross-border implications can be found in Dutta and Wurmnest (2019b), pp. 357–459.

[6] See Dutta (2019), pp. 319–321; Wurmnest (2019), pp. 341–344; Looschelders (2019), pp. 164, 168.

[7] In that regard see Dutta (2019), pp. 324–326; Süß (2014), pp. 197–198.

[8] Art. 351 (1) of Treaty on the Functioning of the European Union of 13 December 2007 – consolidated version, OJ C 202, 7.6.2016, pp. 47–360.

[9] Art. 351 (2) of the TFEU.

'CJEU'), will be given to the analysis of the recent OP case (C-21/22) that primarily addresses the divergent regimes of the ESR and bilateral treaty between Poland and Ukraine through the interpretation of Art. 75(1) of ESR.

2 EU Succession Regulation (ESR) and Bilateral Treaties with Third States: Identifying Incompatibilities

2.1 EU Succession Regulation (ESR)

ESR harmonizes rules on jurisdiction of Member State courts,[10] determining applicable law,[11] recognition and enforcement of decisions and authentic instruments rendered by Member State courts or other authorities in succession matters[12] as well as on creation of a European Certificate of Succession,[13] whereby term 'succession' covers all forms of transfer of assets, rights and obligations by reason of death, either under a disposition of property upon death or through intestate succession.[14] It should be noted that jurisdiction and conflict-of-law rules of ESR have replaced those of national private international laws of Member States, while the rules on recognition and enforcement of ESR have been tailored for circulation of the decisions and authentic instruments within the EU only, meaning that national laws of Member States apply to recognition and enforcement of decisions and authentic instruments rendered in third States.

2.1.1 Grounding (Key) Principles

ESR introduces the last habitual residence of the deceased as a main connecting factor for determining both jurisdiction of Member State courts and law applicable to the succession which has to be interpreted autonomously, i.e. *lege fori europea*, considering all circumstances of the case (particularly, the duration and regularity of the deceased's presence in the State concerned and the conditions and reasons for that presence).[15] The main grounding principle on which the jurisdiction and conflict-of-law rules of ESR are based is the principle of unity of succession which should provide for the succession as a whole to be ruled by the court of one

[10]See Art. 4 – 19 of ESR.

[11]See Art. 20 – 38 of ESR.

[12]See Art. 39 – 61 of ESR.

[13]See Art. 62 – 73 of ESR.

[14]See Art. 3(1) (a) of ESR.

[15]See Recital 23 and 24 of ESR; see also Köhler (2024), pp. 61 et seq.; Solomon (2014), pp. 21 et seq.; Dutta (2013), p. 11.

Member State ('unity of succession on jurisdiction level')[16] and to be governed by one national law ('unity of succession on conflict-of-law level').[17] This principle is complemented by the so-called *Gleichlauf* principle which is reflected in an attempt of EU legislator to create such jurisdiction and conflict-of-law rules in ESR whose application in most cases should lead to the result that the Member State court seized applies its law/*lex fori* ('parallelism between forum and ius).[18] However, although jurisdiction and conflict-of-law rules of ESR strive to maintain these principles (particularly, the principle of unity of succession), some deviations from them are intentionally regulated by the provisions of ESR or seem to be necessary to occur in certain succession cases (especially, in those closely connected to third States) which prompted European legislator to enact specific provisions in ESR for such cases in order to enable the principle of scission of succession be exceptionally established. While briefly discussing jurisdiction and conflict-of-law rules of ESR in this chapter, proper attention will be given to their alignment with the grounding principles.

2.1.2 Jurisdiction and Conflict-of-Law Rules

The rule on general jurisdiction contained in Art. 4 of ESR provides that 'the courts of the Member State in which the deceased had his habitual residence at the time of death shall have jurisdiction to rule on a succession as a whole', which means that it establishes the principle of unity of succession 'on jurisdiction level' since the courts of that Member State shall rule on deceased's whole estate, irrespective of whether the assets belonging to the estate are located in that Member State, the other Member States or third States.[19] Considering that the general conflict-of-law rule (Art. 21(1) of ESR) provides for the same connecting factor (i.e. the last habitual residence of the deceased) which refers to 'the succession as a whole' too, it can be concluded that ESR strongly intends to follow the principle of unity of succession on both jurisdiction and conflict-of-law levels, aiming to ensure the achievement of *Gleichlauf* principle. As concerns other jurisdiction rules of ESR, which are outlined below and may be marked as exemptions from the rule on general jurisdiction, they provide the possibility for the courts of a Member State in which the deceased did not have a last habitual residence to establish the jurisdiction and are primarily designed to uphold the grounding principles, even though some intentional deviations are provided in certain situations.

[16] For the principle of unity of succession on the jurisdiction level, see Dutta (2024a) Artikel 4, para. 13; Đorđević (2020), p. 29; Đorđević (2010), pp. 377–399; Lagarde (2015), paras. 7–14, pp. 24–26.

[17] About the principle of unity of succession on the conflict-of-law level, see more Dutta (2024d) Artikel 21, para. 9; Köhler (2024), p. 60; Fuchs (2015), p. 120.

[18] See Recital 27 of ESR; Dutta (2024f) Vorbemerkung zu Artikel 4, para 2–5; Fuchs (2015), pp. 119–120; Köhler (2024), pp. 41–42.

[19] Đorđević (2020), p. 26; Radoja Knol (2019), pp. 52 et seq.; Popescu (2014), p. 39.

The rule on choice-of-court agreement contained in Art. 5 of ESR enables the parties concerned (e.g. heirs and beneficiaries) to agree that the courts of a Member State whose law was chosen by the deceased as his/her *lex nationalis* in accordance with Art. 22 of ESR[20] 'are to have exclusive jurisdiction to rule on any succession matter'. By referring that such agreement may relate to the ruling 'on any succession matter' and not exclusively to 'the succession as a whole', this rule provides the possibility for abandoning the principle of unity of succession by the will of the parties concerned,[21] although striving to maintain the *Gleichlauf* principle.[22] On the other hand, the rules on subsidiary jurisdiction of Art. 10 of ESR contend to follow the principle of unity of succession as far as possible and apply to cases in which the last habitual residence of the deceased was in a third State, but the assets of his/her estate are located in a Member State.[23] In such cases the courts of that Member State can establish jurisdiction to rule on 'the succession as a whole' if the deceased had the nationality of that Member State at the time of death or his/her previous habitual residence was in that Member State (provided that the change of his/her habitual residence occurred in the last 5 years).[24] However, if no court in a Member State can establish jurisdiction to rule on the succession as a whole in accordance with the cited conditions, the courts of a Member State in which assets are located shall have jurisdiction to rule only on those assets[25] while the other assets of estate fall within the jurisdiction of third States, which causes the scission of succession on 'jurisdiction level' between Member State courts and third State courts.[26] Finally, the rule on necessity jurisdiction of Art. 11 of ESR applies to cases where no court in a Member State has jurisdiction pursuant to other jurisdiction rules of ESR and it provides that in such (very rare)[27] cases the jurisdiction of courts of a Member State may be exceptionally established if the given case has sufficient connection with that Member State and the proceedings cannot be reasonably brought or conducted or would be impossible in a third State to which the case is closely connected.[28] It may

[20] The rule of Art. 5 of ESR covers the cases in which the deceased, a national of one Member State, chose the law of that Member State as the law applicable to his/her succession but had last habitual residence in another Member State or in a third State.

[21] The ruling on 'any succession matter' can be related either to the entire estate or to one or more estate assets located either in Member States or third States. See Đorđević (2020), p. 30.

[22] See Hess (2014), p. 137.

[23] About Art. 10 of ESR see more Dutta (2024b) Artikel 10, para 1, etc.; Köhler (2024), pp. 48–49; Panopoulos (2017a) Article 10, pp. 145 et. seq.; Buonaiuti (2016a) Article 10, pp. 186 et seq.; Dutta (2024b) Artikel 10, para. 1 et. seq.; Đorđević (2020), p. 29.

[24] Art. 10(1) of ESR.

[25] Art. 10(2) of ESR.

[26] See Đorđević (2020), p. 29.

[27] There is a relatively small number of cases where Member Sates' courts could not establish the jurisdiction either on Article 4 or Article 10 (see more Buonaiuti (2016b), pp. 201 et seq.; Panopoulos (2017b), pp. 145 et. seq.)

[28] For Art. 11 of ESR, see more Buonaiuti (2016b) Article 11, pp. 199 et seq.; Dutta (2024c) Artikel 11, para. 1 et.; Panopoulos (2017b) Article 11, pp. 154 et seq.

be spotted that this rule addresses solely the assets of the estate located in a third State[29] and that its *ratio legis* is not to follow either the principle of unity of succession or *Gleichlauf* principle, but rather to prevent the denial of justice in very rare and exceptional cases.

It should be noticed that the above-presented jurisdiction rules of ESR allow derogation from the principle of unity of succession in very few groups of cases, mainly in those that are closely connected to third States. However, there are still a certain number of similar cases in which the unity principle is preserved, although it seems that its derogation would be preferable. Namely, Member State courts may, under most of the above-presented rules, have jurisdiction to rule on the succession as a whole in cases having a close connection with third States, such as those in which the assets of the deceased who had last habitual residence in a Member State are located in a third State. In such cases the positive jurisdiction conflicts between Member State and third State courts may occur if the jurisdiction of the latter is based on different criteria, which may further lead to the refusing of recognition and enforcement of Member State court's decision in a third State if the courts of that third State have exclusive jurisdiction over immovable assets located on its territory.[30] For that reason, the EU legislator introduced the rule of Art. 12 of ESR which provides the possibility for limitation of the succession proceedings in a way that the Member State court seized to rule on the succession may, at the request of one of the parties, decide not to rule on one or more of assets located in a third State if it may be expected that its decision in respect of those assets will not be recognized and, where applicable, declared enforceable in that third State.[31] This rule may be marked as a general exemption from the principle of unity of succession on jurisdiction level created only for certain specific succession cases, whereas it must be highlighted that it does not limit the jurisdiction of the Member State court established under a certain jurisdiction rule of ESR, but rather the subject matter of the proceedings by excluding certain assets from its ruling.[32]

As concerns conflict-of-law rules of ESR, they are of a universal nature which means that any law specified by them shall be applied whether or not it is the law of a Member State (Art. 20 of ESR). The general conflict-of-law rule is contained in Art. 21 of ESR which sets the last habitual residence of the deceased as a main connecting factor and combines it with the escape clause.[33] Pursuant to Art. 21(1) of ESR, the law applicable to the succession as a whole shall be the law of the State in which the deceased had his habitual residence at the time of death, meaning that this provision follows the principle of unity of succession on 'conflict-

[29] See Đorđević (2020), pp. 29–30.

[30] See Đorđević (2020), pp. 30–31; Lein (2014) pp. 215–218; Panopoulos (2015), pp. 102–103.

[31] For interpretation and application of Art. 12 of ESR, see in detail Đorđević (2020), pp. 30 et seq.; Panopoulos (2015), pp. 99 et seq.

[32] See Đorđević (2020), p. 31; Panopoulos (2015), pp. 105–106.

[33] About Art. 21 of ESR see more Solomon (2014), pp. 20–36; Köhler (2024), pp. 60–67; Dutta (2024d) Artikel 21, para. 1 et. seq.

of-law level' and enables the achievement of *Gleichlauf* principle since it is based on the same connecting factor as the rule on general jurisdiction of Art. 4 of ESR. However, Art. 21(2) of ESR provides that where, by way of exception, it is clear from all the circumstances of the case that, at the time of death, the deceased was manifestly more closely connected with a State other than the State of his/her last habitual residence, the law applicable to the succession shall be the law of that other State. This escape clause also preserves the principle of unity of succession but enables the deviation from the *Gleichlauf* principle.[34] Nevertheless, the application of law referred by Art. 21 of ESR may be avoided if the deceased, during his/her lifetime, did use the right provided by Art. 22 of ESR to choose as the law to govern his/her succession as a whole the law of the State whose nationality he/she possessed at the time of making the choice or at the time of death[35] (in case of possessing nationalities of several States he/she may choose the law of any of them).[36] Apparently, this 'limited' choice of law rule of Art. 22 of ESR, as an exemption from the general rule of Art. 21 of ESR, refers to 'the succession as a whole' likewise, strictly following the principle of unity of succession, while providing the possibility for deviation from *Gleichlauf* principle which, however, may be re-established in cases where the deceased chose the law of a Member State whose nationality he/she possessed, providing that heirs and beneficiaries agreed, in accordance with Art. 5 of ESR, to confer the jurisdiction to the courts of that Member State.[37] In addition, ESR contains the special conflict-of-law rules on dispositions of property upon death and agreements as to succession (Art. 24-25 of ESR which refer to and are in line with the provisions of Art. 21 and 22 of ESR) and on their formal validity (Art. 27), as well as other rules that regulate a number of conflict-of-law issues in cross-border succession matters,[38] including those belonging to the general part of private international law.[39] It should be noted that some of them may cause the deviation from the principle of unity of succession on 'conflict of law level', such as the rule of Art. 30 of ESR on application of rules imposing restrictions affecting the succession in respect of certain assets and the rule on *renvoi* of Art. 34 of ESR.[40]

---

[34] See also Kunda et al. (2020), p. 115 et seq.

[35] Pursuant to Art. 22(2) of ESR, such a choice has to be made in a declaration in the form of a disposition of property upon death.

[36] About Art. 22 of ESR see more Solomon (2014), pp. 37–45; Köhler (2024), pp. 67–74; Dutta (2024e), Artikel 22, para. 1 etc.; Szilágyi (2021); Viarengo (2020).

[37] See and compare Viarengo (2020), p.: Kunda et al. (2020), pp. 113 et seq.

[38] Rules on the law applicable to the formal validity of acceptance or waiver of the succession (Art. 28), the appointment of an administrator of the estate (Art. 29), restrictions of succession in respect of certain assets (Art. 30), the adaptation of rights in rem (Art. 31), commorientes (Art. 32), an estate without claimant (Art. 33).

[39] Rules on the application of special restricting rules that concern or affect the succession (Art. 30), *renvoi* (Art. 34), public policy (Art. 35), and issues arising from complex legal systems (Art. 36 and 37).

[40] *Renvoi* rule of Art. 34 of ESR can lead to the scission of succession in cases in which the conflict-of-law rules of the law of a third State referred to by Art. 21(1) of ESR provide different connecting

2.1.3 Recognition/Enforcement and European Certificate of Succession

Finally, in order to secure the decisional harmony and proper functioning of the internal market within the EU, ESR introduces rules on recognition/acceptance and enforcement of decisions and authentic instruments rendered in Member States (Art. 39-61 of ESR). As concerns the recognition of decisions, they shall be recognized without any special procedure being required (the principle of ex lege recognition[41]), whereby any interested party could raise the issue of recognition[42] in the simplified procedure[43] in which a few explicitly listed grounds for non-recognition[44] may be invoked. On the other hand, an authentic instrument issued in one Member State shall have the same evidentiary effects in another Member State or the most comparable effects (ex lege acceptance), unless this is manifestly contrary to the public policy of the latter Member State.[45] The authenticity of an authentic instrument may be challenged before the courts of the Member State of origin,[46] while legal acts or relationships recorded in such instrument before the courts having jurisdiction under the rules of ESR.[47] The same simplified procedure has been provided for the declaration of enforceability of both decisions and authentic instruments, if these are enforceable in the Member State of origin.[48]

Following the same aim of achievement of decisional harmony within the EU, ESR has introduced the European Certificate of Succession (hereinafter: 'Certificate') as a 'sui generis legal instrument' which strives to ensure uniform legal effects with regard to succession in all Member States.[49] Though the use of Certificate is optional and does not replace internal documents rendered in Member State for same or similar purposes, it is an overly valuable instrument. Once issued upon application of heirs and/or beneficiaries, the Certificate produces its effects ex lege in all Member States, with no need for additional acceptance procedures. It carries a

factors for immovable and movable assets of the estate (e.g. *lex rei sitae* for immovables and *lex domicili or lex nationalis* for movables). See Lein (2014), pp. 211–212.

41 See Art. 39(1) of ESR.

42 See Art. 39(2) of ESR.

43 See Art. 45–58 of ESR.

44 See Art. 40 of ESR.

45 See Art. 59(1) of ESR.

46 See Art. 59(2) of ESR.

47 See Art. 59(3) of ESR.

48 See Art. 43 and 60 of ESR.

49 Council Document (EU) 10126/11 of 20 May 2011 on proposal for a Regulation of the European Parliament and of the Council on jurisdiction, applicable law, recognition and enforcement of decisions, and acceptance and enforcement of authentic instruments in matters of succession and on the creation of a European Certificate of Succession – Political guidelines for the future work, p 12. Available at: https://data.consilium.europa.eu/doc/document/ST-10126-2011-INIT/en/pdf. Issuance of the Certificate, as highlighted in Art. 63 of ESR, enables heirs, legatees, executors of wills, and administrators of estate to establish their legal position in other Member States.

presumption of accuracy under the law applicable to succession, protects the legal position of third parties and creditors, and serves as a property ownership record.[50]

2.2 *Bilateral Treaties with Third States and Their Incompatibilities with ESR*

The above brief discussion on provisions of ESR has shown that this regulation has adopted uniform private international law rules in succession matters with the explicit aim of facilitating the free movement of persons concerning their succession rights and estate planning in order to achieve the decisional harmony and proper functioning of the internal market within EU. However, numerous bilateral treaties concluded between Member States and third States exhibit apparent deviations from the ESR regime, especially with regard to the rules on jurisdiction and on determining applicable law. Therefore, this section seeks to expound the differences arising from these treaties and to assess how they might compromise the harmonization effects envisaged by ESR.

2.2.1 Jurisdiction and Conflict-of-Law Rules of Bilateral Treaties: An Overview

Inference of the Member States' bilateral treaties with third States in succession matters had not been extensively analyzed until the commencement of the study in 2019 that was undertaken under the auspices of a working group established jointly by the Universities of Augsburg and Munich.[51] The study compiled country reports from various EU Member States and third States,[52] which analyze the scope of application and rules of these bilateral treaties and evaluate their influence on the operation of the ESR. With a carefully designed research methodology, thorough data analysis, and high-quality findings, the results provide substantial evidence, implying their certitude.[53]

Even though bilateral treaties with third States vary in the subject matter, their general objectives were to establish equal treatment for citizens of the Contracting States, provide access to their courts, and facilitate the smooth flow of emigrants

[50] Art. 69 of ESR; About this instrument see in detail Dutta (2015), p. 42.

[51] See Dutta and Wurmnest (2019b), pp. 357–459.

[52] See Ibid; Besides the reports from Austria, Belgium, Croatia, the Czech Republic, Finland, France, Germany, Italy, Sweeden, Estonia, and Greece, the study also contains contributions from Iran, Turkey, Switzerland as well as the States of the former Yugoslavia that are not EU Member States – Bosnia & Herzegovina, Serbia, Montenegro, and North Macedonia).

[53] See Dutta and Wurmnest (2019a), Introduction, pp. 1–4; Dutta and Wurmnest (2019b), Questionnaire, pp. 5–7; Dutta (2019), pp. 319–328; Wurmnest (2019), pp. 329–356.

from one country to another.[54] However, as observed in the study, the jurisdiction and conflict-of-law rules in succession matters delineated in these treaties diverge from those of ESR, as they are founded upon completely different private international law concepts and, as such, may impair the harmonization effects of ESR. As concerns the rules on recognition and enforcement of decisions contained in these bilateral treaties, they are usually designed to enable the circulation of judicial decisions between a given Member State and respective third State only, meaning that they do not affect the rules on recognition and enforcement of decisions contained in ESR.[55]

Regarding international jurisdiction, examined bilateral treaties generally follow the principle of scission of succession 'on jurisdiction level', granting exclusive jurisdiction over a succession of immovable property to judicial authorities of the Contracting State in which property is located, and either elective or also exclusive jurisdiction over a succession of movable property to judicial authorities of Contracting State whose nationality the deceased possessed at the time of death or in which the deceased had a domicile at the time of death. For instance, the Treaty on mutual legal assistance in civil, family and criminal matters between Yugoslavia and Hungary from 1968,[56] which is still in force between successor states[57] of Yugoslavia and Hungary, now a Member State, confers exclusive jurisdiction over immovable estate to the courts of the Contracting State where the property is situated and elective jurisdiction over movable property to the courts of the Contracting State whose nationality deceased possessed at the time of death.[58] On the other hand, the Treaty between Czechoslovakia and Soviet Union on legal assistance and legal relations in civil, family and criminal matters of 1982,[59] which is still in force between Czech Republic (a Member State) and Russian Federation, provides that judicial authorities of the Contracting State in whose territory the deceased had domicile at the time of death shall have jurisdiction to rule on succession to movable property, while the exclusive jurisdiction over immovable property is, as in

[54]They can be classified as (a) agreements that foster friendship, reciprocity, and commerce between contracting parties; (b) agreements on consular relations; (c) agreements on regional cooperation; (d) agreements on legal assistance; and (e) agreements regulating the situation of State dissolution and de-colonialization (see Wurmnest (2019), pp. 333–340).

[55]See also Dutta (2019), p. 319.

[56]Treaty between the People's Republic of Hungary and the Socialist Federal Republic of Yugoslavia on mutual legal assistance of 7 March 1968, Službeni list SFRJ – Dodatak: Međunarodni ugovori i drugi sporazumi, br. 3/68.

[57]Successor States are Serbia, Montenegro, Bosnia and Herzegovina, and North Macedonia. About this treaty see more Djordjevic and Meškić (2019), pp. 227–228, 235–236, 245–246.

[58]See Art. 44 and 45 of the Treaty.

[59]Treaty between the Czechoslovak Socialist Republic and the Union of Soviet Socialist Republics on Legal Assistance and Legal Relations in Civil, Family and Criminal Matters of 12 August 1982, Vyhláška ministra zahraničních věcí č. 95/1983 Sb (about this treaty see more Pfeiffer (2019), pp. 99–101).

previously mentioned treaty, conferred to judicial authorities of the Contracting State in which that property is located.[60]

As concerns determining the applicable law, some of these treaties adopt the principle of unity of succession ('on conflict-of-law level'), providing for a single connecting factor to determine the law applicable to succession of both immovable and movable property. For instance, aforementioned Treaty on mutual legal assistance between Yugoslavia and Hungary employs nationality as a single connecting factor for both immovable and movable estate assets,[61] establishing the principle of unity of succession that can be truly achieved only if the court of one Contracting State has jurisdiction to rule on the whole estate, which might happen, for example, if the deceased was a national of Serbia and all immovable and movable assets belonging to him/her are located in Hungary. However, most other bilateral treaties follow the principle of scission of succession, providing for different conflict-of-law rules on succession of movable and immovable property, whereas *lex rei sitae* is typically applied to immovable property, while *lex nationalis* to movable property.[62] This holds, for example, in the case of the Treaty between Yugoslavia and Soviet Union on legal assistance in civil, family and criminal matters from 1962,[63] which is now in force between Croatia (as a successor State of Yugoslavia and a Member State)[64] and Russia. This treaty follows the principle of scission of succession by employing the conflict-of-law rules that refer in regard to the succession of the movable estate to the law of the Contracting State of which the deceased was a national at the time of death, while in regard to the succession of immovable property to the law of the Contracting State in which immovable property is situated.[65] Also, certain bilateral treaties provide for the last domicile of the deceased as a connecting factor for determining the law applicable to succession to movable property, such as the aforementioned Treaty between Czechoslovakia and the Soviet Union.[66] Finally, it should be emphasized that none of the bilateral treaties examined in the study regulates the testator's right to choose the applicable law for their succession, which implies that a party autonomy in succession matters is generally prohibited.

---

[60] See Art. 43 of the Treaty.

[61] See Art. 41 of the Treaty (for a brief commentary on this provision see Đorđević and Meškić (2019), p. 235).

[62] See Wurmnest (2019), pp. 337–338.

[63] Treaty between the Federal People's Republic of Yugoslavia and the Union of Soviet Socialist Republics on Legal Assistance in Civil, Family and Criminal Matters of 24 February 1962, Službeni list SFRJ – Dodatak: Međunarodni ugovori i drugi sporazumi, br. 5/63.

[64] It also binds other successor States of Yugoslavia.

[65] See Art. 37 of the Treaty; About this treaty see more Babić and Hoško (2019), pp. 69 et. seq.

[66] See Art. 40(1) of the Treaty.

2.2.2 Incompatibilities

Having in mind that bilateral treaties with third States, pursuant to Art. 75 of ESR, take precedence over ESR if their scopes of application overlap, Member States courts bound by such treaties encounter conceptually different jurisdiction and conflict-of-law rules from those of ESR,[67] which can significantly impair the achievement of decisional harmony within the EU. As discerned above, the fundamental difference between bilateral treaties and ESR lies in the fact that bilateral treaties are based on traditional private international law concepts that follow the principle of scission of succession, either on jurisdiction level or on both jurisdiction and conflict-of-law levels, by employing *locus rei sitae* for immovable estate and nationality (or domicile) of the deceased for the movable estate as connecting factors, and, in case the unity principle is followed at conflict-of-law level, provide for *lex nationalis* as a general conflict-of-law rule, whereas the possibility of choosing the applicable law is not regulated at all.[68] Such concepts are evidently incompatible with the modern concept of ESR grounded in the principles of unity of succession and *Gleichlauf*, the last habitual residence of the deceased as a main connecting factor for determining both jurisdiction and applicable law and in the limited possibility of choosing the applicable law. From a general perspective, these incompatibilities imply that the same cross-border succession case would have been decided differently by the court of a Member State bound by a bilateral treaty with a third State and the court of another Member State which is not bound by such treaty, since the one would apply the rules of bilateral treaty and the other the rules of ESR, which leads to the conclusion that the decisional harmony within EU and proper functioning of the internal market might be compromised.[69]

The harsh disharmonies arising *in concreto* from the incompatibilities between ESR and bilateral treaties become particularly obvious in cross-border succession cases which are connected not only to the Member State and third State which are Contracting States bound by bilateral treaty, but also to at least one more Member State.[70] For example, in the case where the deceased, a national of Serbia (third State), owned immovable property in Hungary (Member State) but had the last habitual residence in Slovenia (Member State), the Hungarian courts would, in accordance with rules of bilateral treaty between Hungary and Serbia, have exclusive jurisdiction over immovable property located on its territory as *forum rei sitae*[71] and would apply Serbian law as deceased's *lex nationalis*.[72] On the other hand, the courts of Slovenia not being bound by this bilateral treaty would decide on the case by applying the rules of ESR pursuant to which they would have jurisdiction (Art.

[67] See also in that regard Szilágyi (2021), pp. 164–165.

[68] See and compare Wurmnest (2019), p. 341.

[69] See and compare Ibid.

[70] See and compare Ibid, pp. 342–343; Looschelders (2019), p. 173.

[71] Art. 44 of the Treaty.

[72] Art. 41 of the Treaty.

4 of ESR) to rule on the succession as a whole and would apply Slovenian law (Art. 21(1) of ESR), since the last habitual residence of the deceased was in Slovenia. If a Slovenian court establishes jurisdiction and determines applicable law in this case in accordance with the rules of ESR, the enforcement of the decision rendered by the Slovenian court might be refused in Hungary where immovable estate is located, because Hungarian courts could claim that such decision violates its obligation under international law to apply the bilateral treaty concluded between Hungary and Serbia (third State),[73] which could be interpreted as a violation of Hungarian public policy representing a ground for non-recognition (non-enforcement). This example shows that the free movement of decisions and functioning of the internal market within the EU can be seriously hampered when the application of bilateral treaties is involved. Another (to a certain extent similar) problem may arise, for example, in a case where a person, a national of a third State, having habitual residence in Member State A bound by the bilateral treaty with that third State and owning the immovable assets located in Member State A and Member State B, wants to draw up a notarial will which contains a provision on choosing his/her *lex nationalis*, i.e. the law of third State whose nationality he/she possessed, as the law applicable to the succession as a whole.[74] If that person requests the notary in Member State A to draw up such will, the notary would, with regard to immovable assets located in Member State A, apply the conflict-of-law rules of bilateral treaty which do not provide the possibility of choosing the applicable law, meaning that the notary should refuse to introduce a requested provision in a will. However, if this person decides to visit the notary in Member State B which is not bound by a bilateral treaty, this notary would apply the rule of Art. 22 of ESR that allows a person to choose his/her *lex nationalis* as the law applicable to succession, which means that the provision on choice of law might be contained in a notarial will. Therefore, this example shows that the existence of different conflict-of-law regimes in succession matters within the EU (embedded in bilateral treaties and ESR) may encourage persons to choose to draw up a notarial will either before a notary in a Member State bound by a bilateral treaty or before a notary in a Member State which applies ESR, depending on which regime they more prefer (this could be marked as a forum shopping situation). Also, it should be noticed that in the scenario in which a person decides to draw up a notarial will in Member State B (not being bound by a bilateral treaty), the problem could arise when the enforcement of such a notarial will is sought in Member State A (with regard to immovable assets located there) after the death of that person since Member State A is bound by bilateral treaty which do not allow choice of applicable law and its judicial authorities could find that the provision on choice of applicable law contained in a notarial will is null and void.

---

[73] See and compare from the German perspective (with regard to the German-Iranian bilateral treaty): Süß (2014), p. 190; Wurmnest (2019), p. 342.

[74] The idea for this hypothetical case came from the Judgment of 12 October 2023, *OP v. Notariusz Justyna Gawlica*, C-21/22, EU:C:2023:766.

In addition, there are a lot of other situations where the application of bilateral treaties may cause problems that potentially could impair decisional harmony and raise legal issues being difficult to resolve, such as, for example, those in which the different parts of the deceased's estate have to be decided by the courts of two or more Member States.[75] However, many authors particularly emphasize that the most apparent discordant effect of the application of these bilateral treaties lies with the interference with the European Certificate of Succession (the Certificate), since this instrument can operate effectively only if the certified inheritance position of the successors (or other succession position such as administrator of the estate) is assessed in all Member States on the basis of the same applicable law determined by the rules of ESR.[76] If the courts of a Member State bound by bilateral treaty having precedence over ESR is requested to issue the Certificate that would also relate to estate assets located in other Member States, the legal position of successors and beneficiaries would not be established in accordance with the law applicable under the rules of ESR, but rather by the law determined by conflict-of-law rules of that bilateral treaty, which represents the obstacle for operation of such Certificate in other Member States.[77] The literature has proposed that this problem could be resolved by restricting the Certificate to the assets of estate which are located in other Member States not being bound by bilateral treaty, in which case the applicable law shall be determined by conflict-of-law rules of ESR.[78] On the other hand, the problem may also arise in case where the Certificate issued in a Member State which is not bound by bilateral treaty has to be used in a Member State bound by bilateral treaty with third State where some assets of the deceased who was a national of respective third State are located. In this case, such a Certificate might be ineffective or challenged in a latter Member State on the ground that its obligation under international law toward a third State has been violated.[79] Therefore, it is obvious that the aim of having information provided by the Certificate to be the same in all Member States[80] is compromised which raises the concern to the existence of bilateral treaties.

[75]Looschelders (2019), pp. 170–172; Dutta (2019), p. 320; Wurmnest (2019), pp. 342–343.

[76]Dutta (2019), p. 320.

[77]Ibid.

[78]Looschelders (2019), pp. 170–171; Süß (2014), pp. 186 et. seq.

[79]See and compare Dutta (2019), p. 320; Looschelders (2019), pp. 171–172.

[80]This is indicated in the Judgment of 25 March 2021, *Generics (UK) Ltd v Commission*, C-588/16 P, EU:C:2021:242, pp. 36 et. seq.

3 Possible Solutions for Removing or Avoiding the Incompatibilities: Focusing on the Interpretation of Art. 75(1) of ESR in Conjunction with Art. 351 of TFEU

3.1 Introductory Remarks

Even though the severe incompatibilities between the bilateral treaties and ESR described in the previous section have shown that the bilateral treaties diminish the harmonization effects of ESR and jeopardize the proper functioning of the internal market, it seems that their application remains unaffected since Art. 75 (1) of ESR clearly states that they take precedence over ESR:

> This Regulation shall not affect the application of international conventions to which one or more Member States are party at the time of adoption of this Regulation and which concern matters covered by this Regulation.[81]

This provision, visibly, adheres to the public international law rule of '*pacta sunt servanda*',[82] which is also explicitly expressed in the first paragraph of Art. 351 of TFEU that generally provides for precedence of international treaties with third States over EU law if those have been concluded before the respective Member States acquired their EU membership:

> The rights and obligations arising from agreements concluded before 1 January 1958 or, for acceding States, before the date of their accession, between one or more Member States on the one hand, and one or more third countries on the other, shall not be affected by the provisions of the Treaties.[83]

On the other hand, it must be borne in mind that the second paragraph of Art. 351 of TFEU refers to situations in which the incompatibilities between such international treaties and EU law arise and provides certain guidance for resolving these conflicts in order to preserve the proper functioning of the internal market and fundamental principles of EU law:

> To the extent that such agreements are not compatible with the Treaties, the Member State or States concerned shall take all appropriate steps to eliminate the incompatibilities established. Member States shall, where necessary, assist each other to this end and shall, where appropriate, adopt a common attitude.[84]

[81] Art. 75(1) of ESR.

[82] Vienna Convention on the Law of Treaties of 27 January 1969, United Nations, Treaty Series, vol. 1155, p 331, Art. 26: "Every treaty in force is binding upon the parties to it and must be performed by them in good faith."

[83] Article 351(1) of the TFEU.

[84] Article 351(2) of the TFEU.

Therefore, although Art 75(1) of ESR does not explicitly mention Art. 351 of TFEU (as is the case with some other regulations[85]), it undoubtedly appears that these provisions are interrelated and have to be interpreted together, whereas the existing case law of CJEU pertaining to the interpretation of provisions of Art. 351 of TFEU and Art. 71 of Regulation No 44/2001/Brussels I Regulation[86] (which follows a similar logic to that of Art. 75 of ESR) as well as to the requirement of Member States to comply with principles of EU law,[87] must be taken into account. Following this path, it should be ascertained in which way the EU itself and/or Member States have to deal with the incompatibilities produced by bilateral treaties with third States enclosing different jurisdiction and conflict-of-law provisions from those of ESR in order to ensure the ongoing compatibility of the Member States' private international laws with the EU law.[88]

3.2 *Providing for Solutions 'Shaped' in Accordance with Settled Case Law*

It is quite clear that Art. 351(1) of TFEU allows a derogation from the principle of primacy of EU law only in relation to international treaties concluded prior to EU membership and, in principle, only to treaties between Member States and third countries,[89] which is in line with Art. 75(1) of ESR.[90] According to the settled case law, the purpose of such rule is to establish that the application of EU law does 'not affect the duty of the Member State concerned to respect the rights of non-member countries under a prior treaty and to perform its obligations thereunder'.[91] However, it is advocated that Member State could not be given 'carte blanche' to continue operating on the basis of conflicting rules forever since that would constitute disproportionate interference with *une certaine idée de l'Europe*.[92] In the famous *Kadi* case, which pertained to the status of sanction rulings issued by the UN

[85] Such as, for example, Art. 69 of Council Regulation (EC) 4/2009 of 18 December 2008 on jurisdiction, applicable law, recognition and enforcement of decisions and cooperation in matters relating to maintenance obligations, OJ L 7, 10.1.2009, p 1 (which mentions ex-Art. 307 now Art. 351); Art. 62 of Council Regulation (EU) 2016/1103 of 24 June 2016 implementing enhanced cooperation in the area of jurisdiction, applicable law and the recognition and enforcement of decisions in matters of matrimonial property regimes, OJ L 183, 8.7.2016, p. 1.

[86] Council Regulation (EC) No 44/2001 of 22 December 2000 on jurisdiction and the recognition and enforcement of judgments in civil and commercial matters, OJ L 12, 16.01.2001, p. 1.

[87] See and compare Varga (2021), p. 260 et seq; Traser et al. (2020), pp. 152–174; Claes (2015), pp. 178–199.

[88] In that regard see also Dutta (2019), pp. 323–328.

[89] Rosas (2011), p. 1321.

[90] Rylski (2020), p. 96.

[91] See Judgment of 14 July 1980, *Attorney General v. Burgoa*, C-812/79, EU:C:1980:231, para. 8; citing Judgment of 27 February 1962, *Commission v. Italy*, Case C-10/61, EU:C:1962:2.

[92] Ehrlich et al. (2013), p. 121; See also Varga (2021), p. 260 et seq; Traser et al. (2020), pp. 152–174.

Security Council within EU law, the CJEU asserted that the EU's legal framework encompasses certain 'core constitutional principles' intrinsic to the foundational base of the Union's legal structure, with particular emphasis on safeguarding fundamental rights, and that Art. 351 of TFEU may 'in no circumstances permit any challenge' to those principles,[93] emphasizing that neither the EU institutions nor Member States can avoid conformity interpretation of their acts that proceed from international obligations since these 'cannot affect the autonomy of the Community legal system'.[94] Also, in the *Fediol* and *Nakajima* cases the CJEU followed the same approach for the purpose of a legality review concerning the EU measure or principle that intend to incorporate a non-directly effective international rule into the EU legal order,[95] while in the case *Commission v Germany* clearly confirmed that any agreement (treaty) concluded by Member States needs to comply with the EU law, especially if the application of its provisions may result in discriminatory effects or violate the principle of equal treatment.[96] Finally, in a number of other cases the CJEU took the stance that international treaties concluded by Member States with third States cannot be, in relations between Member States, detrimental to the objectives of EU law.[97] Hence, it follows from the above presented case-law that Article 351 (2) safeguards not only the primary law of the Treaties but also the secondary law established to fulfill the objectives envisaged by the Treaties, which is particularly the case where such legislation adopts the rules designed to facilitate the achievement of rights based on the fundamental principles of EU law.

As concerns international treaties in the area of judicial cooperation in civil and commercial matters, the judgment of CJEU in the case *TNT Express Nederland*[98] seems to be the most important one. In this case, the CJEU had to rule on whether Art. 71 of Regulation No 44/2001 must be interpreted as meaning that the rules of CMR[99] governing jurisdiction, recognition, and enforcement shall be applied instead

[93] Judgment of 3 September 2008, *Kadi and Al Barakaat International Foundation v Council and Commission*, Joined Cases C-402/05 and 415/05, EU:C:2008:461, paras. 303-304; Additionally, in the Judgment of 5 November 2002, *Commission v United Kingdom of Great Britain and Northern Ireland*, C-466/98, EU:C:2002:624, para. 23, CJEU stated that Article 351 is applicable to any international agreement, irrespective of the subject matter.

[94] Joined Cases C-402/05 and 415/05, paras. 281–282.

[95] See Judgment of 22 June 1989, *Fediol v Commission*, Case 70/87, EU:C:1989:254, paras. 19–22; Judgment of 7 May 1991, *Nakajima v Council*, Case 69/89, EU:C:1991:186, par. 31.

[96] Judgment of 21 January 2010, *Commission v Germany*, C-546/07, EU:C:2010:25, paras. 42, 47–52.

[97] See e.g. Judgment of 12 October 2023, *OP v. Notariusz Justyna Gawlica*, C-21/22, EU:C:2023:766; Judgment of 22 September 1988, *Ministère public v Gérard Deserbais*, C-286/86 ECR 4907, EU:C:1988:434, par. 18; Judgment of 22 October 2009, *Irène Bogiatzi v Deutscher Luftpool and Others*, C-301/08, EU:C:2009:649, par. 19.

[98] Judgment of 4 May 2010, *TNT Express Nederland BV v AXA Versicherung AG*, C-533/08, EU:C:2010:243.

[99] Convention on the Contracts for the International Carriage of Goods by Road, signed at Geneva on 19 May 1956, amended by the Protocol signed at Geneva on 5 July 1978 (the CMR), United Nations, Treaty Series, vol. 399, p. 189.

of those contained in this regulation. In order to provide the answer, the CJEU at first reminded that according to settled case law, in interpreting a provision of EU law it is necessary to consider not only its wording but also the context in which it occurs, and the objectives pursued by the rules of which it is part'.[100] Then it stated that the wording of Art. 71 of Regulation No 44/2001 gives, in principle, the precedence to international treaty over regulation if the dispute falls within the scope of both instruments, but explicitly emphasized that the application of international treaty 'cannot compromise the principles which underlie judicial cooperation in civil and commercial matters in the European Union',[101] adding that 'Art. 71 of Regulation No 44/2001 cannot have a purport that conflicts with the principles underlying the legislation of which it is part'.[102] It also referred that 'this finding is consistent with settled case law that conventions concluded by Member States with non-member countries cannot, in relations between the Member States, be applied to the detriment of the objectives of European Union law'.[103] Finally, the CJEU concluded that the rules governing jurisdiction, recognition, and enforcement set out in specialized convention referred to in Art. 71 of Regulation No 44/2001, such as the CMR, can be applied in the European Union only to the extent that the principles of this regulation are observed and not compromised[104] and ruled that it has no jurisdiction, in preliminary rulings proceedings, to interpret neither the rules of CMR[105] nor the rules of other treaties concluded between Member States and third States,[106] although it apparently may examine whether they undermine the fundamental principles of EU law. Since the same stance and opinions have been confirmed by the CJEU in the preliminary rulings proceedings in cases *Nipponkoa Insurance Co. (Europe) Ltd*[107] and *Nickel & Goeldner Spedition GmbH*,[108] one could claim that Member State courts should, in case the international treaty detriments principles underlying EU legislation, apply the rules of that EU legislation instead of those of international treaty even though the provision contained in that piece of EU legislation and Art. 351(1) of TFEU initially provide for precedence of that international treaty. However, it must be taken into account that in all mentioned cases the

[100] C-533/08, par. 44.

[101] C-533/08, par. 49.

[102] C-533/08, par. 51.

[103] C-533/08, par. 52 (CJEU referred to the following cases: Judgment of 22 September 1988, *Ministère public v Gérard Deserbais*, C-286/86 ECR 4907, EU:C:1988:434, par. 18; Judgment of 6 April 1995, *RTE and ITP* v *Commission*, Joined Cases C-241/91 P and C-242/91 P, EU:C:1995:98, par. 84; and Judgment of 22 October 2009, *Irène Bogiatzi v Deutscher Luftpool and Others*, C-301/08, EU:C:2009:649, par. 19.)

[104] C-533/08, par. 53 and 55.

[105] C-533/08, par. 63.

[106] C-533/08, par. 61.

[107] Judgment of 19 December 2013, *Nipponkoa Insurance Co. (Europe) v Inter-Zuid Transport BV*, C-452/12, EU:C:2013:858.

[108] Judgment of 4 September 2014, *Nickel & Goeldner Spedition GmbH v 'Kintra' UAB*, C-157/13, EU:C:2014:2145.

CJEU discussed conflicts between Regulation No 44/2001 and CMR only in relations between Member States and has not explicitly ruled that the Member States must ignore their obligations arising from international treaties and automatically apply the rules of EU law only because the former undermine the principles of the latter. The same conclusion can be drawn from the latest OP case (C-21/22 which will be discussed in the next section) where the CJEU dealt with the interpretation of Art. 75 of ESR and observed alleged incompatibilities between ESR and the bilateral treaty concluded between Poland and Ukraine.[109]

Bearing the above in mind, it seems that, in case of concurrence between rules of ESR and those of bilateral treaties concluded between Member States and third States, Art. 75(1) of ESR in conjunction with Art. 351(1) of TFEU can be interpreted in a way that the application of bilateral treaties takes precedence over ESR unless they are incompatible with ESR to the extent that the rules of the former undermine the fundamental principles of the latter. Also, it is clear that the CJEU does not have jurisdiction to interpret the rules of bilateral treaties (which are to be interpreted by Member State courts as a part of their domestic laws), but it can consider them in order to determine whether they are incompatible with ESR (i.e. whether they undermine principles underlying ESR) since such approach can be regarded as an interpretation of the principles and rules of ESR (i.e. EU law). If the detrimental incompatibilities were determined in a given case, it cannot be claimed at this moment that the rules of ESR should be automatically applied instead of those of a bilateral treaty since the CJEU has not yet provided such a ruling. This implies that the courts of a Member State bound by the bilateral treaty whose detrimental incompatibility with ESR has been determined by the CJEU will, pursuant to Art. 75(1) of ESR, continue to apply such bilateral treaty until that Member State takes an action under the provision of Art. 351(2) of TFEU to which it is obliged to. As cited above, Art. 351(2) of TFEU provides that *'the Member States... concerned shall take all appropriate steps to eliminate the incompatibilities established'*,[110] which means that a Member State bound by the incompatible bilateral treaty must terminate it or amend it in order to bring its principles and rules in line with those of ESR.[111] Finally, it should be mentioned that EU itself can, pursuant to Art. 3(2) of the TFEU,[112] engage in negotiations with a third State to conclude the treaty that would override the existing bilateral treaty between Member State and that third State, as well as that the European Commission can, pursuant to Art. 258(1) of the

[109] See Opinion of Advocate General Campos Sanchez-Bordona delivered on 23 March 2023, Case C-21/22, *OP v. Notariusz Justyna Gawlica*, EU:C:2023:247, paras. 41–43.

[110] Pursuant to the second sentence of Art. 351(2) of TFEU, 'Member States shall, where necessary, assist each other to this end and shall, where appropriate, adopt a common attitude'.

[111] See and compare Dutta (2019), pp. 325–326; Süß (2014), pp. 197–198; Rylski (2020), pp. 97–98.

[112] Art. 3(2) of TFEU: "The Union shall also have exclusive competence for the conclusion of an international agreement when its conclusion is provided for in a legislative act of the Union or is necessary to enable the Union to exercise its internal competence, or in so far as its conclusion may affect common rules or alter their scope."

TFEU, request the Member States to terminate or attempt to renegotiate their bilateral agreements if they are incompatible with the EU law (so-called ‘infringement procedure’)[113] which would comply with the obligation enshrined in the Art. 351 (2) of TFEU.[114]

4 Analysis of Judgment C-21/22 of CJEU (the OP case)

4.1 Circumstances of the Case and Referred Questions

On 12 October 2023, the CJEU responded to a request for a preliminary ruling from the Regional Court of Opole, Poland (Sąd Okręgowy w Opolu), regarding the interpretation of Art. 22 and 75 of ESR. This inquiry, encapsulated in Judgment of 12 October 2023, *OP v. Notariusz Justyna Gawlica*, C-21/22, EU:C:2023:766C-21/22, (the OP case), concerns a situation where a Ukrainian national residing in Poland, who co-owns immovable property situated in Poland, requested Polish deputy notary to draw up a notarial will containing a clause that the law applicable to her succession shall be the Ukrainian law. The deputy notary refused to draw up such a will on two grounds. First, Art. 22 of ESR, read in the light of Recital 38 of ESR, confers the right to choose the applicable law only on nationals of EU Member States. Second, Art. 37 of the 1993 Bilateral Agreement between Poland and Ukraine on legal assistance and legal relations in civil and criminal matters (hereinafter: ‘Bilateral Agreement’), which supersedes ESR pursuant to Art. 75(1) of ESR, provides that the law applicable to succession of movable property is the law of the State whose nationality the deceased possessed and the law applicable to succession of immovable property is the law of the State in which that property is situated, whereas this Bilateral Agreement contains no provision on testator’s right to choose the law applicable to succession, meaning that such choice is not allowed.[115] Thus, the Polish deputy notary concluded that in respect of immovable property which OP co-owns in Poland the law applicable to her succession would be the Polish law.[116]

[113] Art. 258 (1) of the TFEU: “If the Commission considers that a Member State has failed to fulfill an obligation under the Treaties, it shall deliver a reasoned opinion on the matter after giving the State concerned the opportunity to submit its observations.”

[114] See also Dutta (2019), pp. 324–325.

[115] Article 37 of the Agreement between Poland and Ukraine on legal assistance and legal relations in civil and criminal matters of 24 May 1993: “(1) Legal relations in respect of the succession of movable property shall be governed by the law of the Contracting Party of which the decedent was a national at the time of his or her death. (2) Legal relations in respect of the succession of immovable property shall be governed by the law of the Contracting Party in whose territory the property is situated. (3) The determination of whether an item included in the estate is movable property or immovable property shall be governed by the law of the Contracting Party in whose territory the item is situated.” Available at: https://treaties.un.org/Pages/showDetails.aspx?objid=08000002805c4784.

[116] C-21/22, paras. 12 and 13.

As a reaction to this refusal, OP brought an action before the Regional Court in Opole (hereinafter: 'the referring court'), arguing that Art. 22 of ESR allows a 'person' to choose his/her national law as the law applicable to his/her succession.[117] In addition, OP expressed that the purpose of Art. 75(1) of ESR is to preserve the conformity of ESR with the obligations arising from agreements concluded by Member States with third States, but claimed that the application of Art. 22 of ESR is not incompatible with the Bilateral Agreement since this agreement does not govern the testator's right to choose the applicable law.[118] Considering the circumstances of the case, the referring court decided to stay the proceedings and referred the following questions to the CJEU for a preliminary ruling:

(1) Must Article 22 of Regulation No 650/2012 be interpreted as meaning that a person who is not a citizen of the European Union is entitled to choose the law of his or her native country as the law governing all matters relating to succession?
(2) Must Article 75, in conjunction with Article 22, of Regulation No 650/2012 be interpreted as meaning that, in the case where bilateral agreement between a Member State and a third State does not govern the choice of law applicable to a case involving succession but indicates the law applicable to that case involving succession, a national of that third State residing in a Member State bound by that bilateral agreement may make a choice of law?'[119]

In the ensuing analysis, we will closely examine the court's judgement and assess its legal reasoning, with due consideration given to the viewpoint presented by Advocate General Campos Sánchez-Bordona (hereinafter referred to as 'AG') in his Opinion on this case.[120]

4.2 Interpretations and Standpoints of CJEU

The response to the first question posed minimal challenges for the CJEU. It started with the literal interpretation of Art. 22 of ESR which grants the right to choose the applicable law to 'any person', without making any distinction between nationals of the EU and those of third States, observed it in conjunction with Art. 20 of ESR (which provides for 'universal' nature of conflict-of-law rules)[121] and some other provisions of the ESR,[122] and concluded that Art. 22 of ESR must be interpreted as meaning that a third State national residing in an EU Member State may choose the

[117] C-21/22, par. 14.

[118] C-21/22, par. 14.

[119] C-21/22, par. 15.

[120] Opinion of Advocate General Campos Sanchez-Bordona delivered on 23 March 2023, Case C-21/22, *OP v. Notariusz Justyna Gawlica*, EU:C:2023:247.

[121] See C-21/22, par. 21.

[122] Such as Art. 5, 6, 12, and 34 and recitals 57 and 38 of ESR (see C-21/22 paras. 21–23).

law of that third State as the law governing his/her succession as a whole.[123] However, the response to second question required more extensive consideration since there are concurrent provisions pertaining to the effect: under Art. 22 of ESR OP is entitled to choose the law of her nationality (Ukrainian law) to govern the succession as a whole, while under Art. 37 of the Bilateral Agreement that choice seems to be prohibited because the agreement is silent on that issue and, instead, provides for default rules—*lex rei sitae* for immovable estate and *lex nationalis* of deceased for the movable estate. So, for the first time, the CJEU had to interpret Art. 75(1) of ESR and to take into consideration the principles and rules of the Bilateral Agreement in order to determine whether they are incompatible with those of ESR to the extent that the former undermines the latter. It addressed several lines of argumentation in that context.

Initially, the CJEU confirmed that if the Member State is a party to a bilateral treaty concluded with a third State before the entry into force of ESR, and that bilateral treaty contains provisions laying down rules applicable to succession, it is those provisions which, in principle, are intended to apply according to Art. 75 of ESR and not those of ESR in that regard.[124] However, it immediately stated, by referring to the Opinion of AG,[125] that Art. 75 of ESR 'is not an isolated provision in the EU instruments on judicial cooperation in civil and commercial matters' since many other EU regulations and conventions include provisions which follow a similar logic to that of Art. 75 of ESR,[126] and that such provisions 'cannot have a scope which conflicts with the principles underlying the EU legislation of which it forms part'.[127] This seemingly implies that the rules of a bilateral treaty, although having precedence in the application, cannot compromise the principles underlying the ESR and judicial cooperation in civil and commercial matters within EU. In other words, the bilateral treaty can be applied only to the extent that these principles are observed (the standpoint taken in the case *TNT Express Nederland*, C-533/08, to which CJEU referred in this case[128]), which has to be discussed and determined by the CJEU in this case too.

Discussing on the aforementioned issue with regard to the question posed in this case, the CJEU stated that the purpose of ESR is 'to remove the obstacles to the free movement of persons who may face difficulties in asserting their rights in the context of a succession with cross-border implications, in particular by laying down rules on jurisdiction and applicable law in the matter, and on the recognition and

[123] C-21/22, par. 24; Similarly, AG articulated in his opinion that the response to the first question does not seem to evoke any uncertainties: Excluding third state' nationals from the option to select the applicable law for their succession would contravene not only the literal language of Art. 22 but also the universal scope of applicability inherent in the ESR. Likewise, it is noteworthy that the Court specifically tasked the AG with providing an opinion solely on the second question, presuming the clarity of the response to the first question.; See Opinion of AG in C-21/22, par. 3.

[124] C-21/22, par. 27.

[125] Opinion of AG in C-21/22, paras. 29–30.

[126] C-21/22, par. 28; See regulations cited in footnote 84.

[127] C-21/22, par. 29.

[128] See C-21/22, paras. 26 and 29.

enforcement, in a Member State, of judgments and acts of other Member States' (which is cited in recitals 7 and 59 of ESR).[129] It also pointed out that Art. 21 of ESR has been established as a general rule 'containing a default connecting factor which is determined by reference to the habitual residence of the deceased at the time of death', while the possibility of choosing the national law of deceased, governed by Art. 22 of ESR, 'must be regarded as a derogation from the general rule' laid down in Art. 21 of ESR[130] and, therefore, 'cannot be regarded as a principle underlying ESR and judicial cooperation in civil and commercial matters within the European Union of which it is an instrument'.[131] The context of such argumentation undoubtedly provides for the conclusion that in this case the CJEU took the stance that the rules of Bilateral Agreement between Poland and Ukraine do not conflict (compromise/ undermine) the 'limited' choice-of-law rule of Art. 22 of ESR since this rule does not represent the underlying (fundamental) principle of ESR, but rather the exemption from such principle laid down in Art. 21 of ESR. So the CJEU answered that Art. 75 of ESR, read in conjunction with Art. 22 of ESR, must be interpreted as not precluding a national of a third State, residing in a Member State bound by bilateral agreement with that third State, from not being able to choose the law of that third State to govern his or her succession as a whole.[132] This means that a national of a third State residing in a Member State cannot choose the applicable law under Art. 22 of ESR if the existing bilateral treaty between Member State and third State, which takes precedence pursuant to Art. 75 of ESR, prohibits such choice because the rule of Art. 22 of ESR does not represent a principle underlying the ESR. Whether the bilateral treaty prohibits the right to choose applicable law, can be determined only by the courts of a Member State bound by that treaty since the CJEU does not have jurisdiction in that regard.[133]

The CJEU also observed one of the key principles of ESR and provided a general opinion on its (in)compatibility with different concepts established in bilateral treaties with third States, such as the Bilateral Agreement between Poland and Ukraine. Namely, the CJEU upheld the standpoint taken in its earlier judgments (such as C-80/19 and *Oberle* C-20/17) 'that the general objective of that regulation, which seeks to ensure the mutual recognition of decisions given in the Member States in matters of succession, is linked to the principle of a single estate' (i.e. 'the principle of unity of succession'), but claimed that this principle 'is not absolute'[134] since, in its view, Art. 12(1) of ESR 'expressly introduces a derogation from that principle by allowing the court having jurisdiction not to rule on property located in third States' if the judgment will not be recognized or enforced in those third

[129] C-21/22, par. 30.

[130] C-21/22, par. 31.

[131] C-21/22, par. 33.

[132] C-21/22, par. 38.

[133] In that regard see also Lehmann (2023), p. 840.

[134] C-21/22, par. 34.

States.[135] Following this argumentation, the CJEU concluded that 'the EU legislature expressly intended to comply, in certain specific cases, with the split model of succession that could be implemented in relations with certain third States',[136] which means that 'the principle of scission of succession' (i.e. 'split model') is not generally incompatible with ESR. Such view of CJEU mainly relies on the reasoning of the AG expressed in his Opinion on this case, where he stated that the principle of unity of succession (i.e. single estate principle) is, indeed, the 'backbone' of the ESR, but it is still not the absolute principle because the avoidance of fragmentation of the estate is only intended and not absolutely required.[137] AG argues that the possibility of occurrence of such fragmentation has been already foreseen in certain provisions of ESR, especially in situations in which the adoption of the principle of unity of succession, without any reservations, is doomed to failure, such as those in which an estate includes immovable property situated in third States which follow the principle of scission of succession.[138] In that regard, AG particularly emphasized that the rule of Art. 12(1) of ESR, which provides the possibility for Member State courts not to rule on estate assets located in third States, demonstrates the acceptance of the plurality of models (principles) concerning the treatment of succession having cross-border implications within the EU,[139] and seemingly took the view that this rule reflects the intention and willingness of EU legislator to respect the principle of scission of succession established not only in the laws of third States but also in the bilateral treaties between Member States and third States (having in mind that these treaties, pursuant to Art. 75(1) of ESR, cannot be in principle affected by the rules of ESR).[140] Therefore, it may be concluded that AG finds that ESR is 'friendly' to the principle of scission of succession because some of its rules provide for 'rupture' of the principle of unity of succession,[141] which CJEU accepted in its judgment.[142]

Finally, it should be mentioned that AG, unlike CJEU, has also provided an opinion on how to deal with conflicts between the principles laid down in ESR and the Bilateral Agreement between Poland and Ukraine if the CJEU had found that such conflicts existed. After rejecting the possibility that the rules of ESR should automatically prevail,[143] AG took the view that the solution is to be found in the interpretation of Art. 75(1) of ESR in the light of Art. 351 of TFEU,[144] which would require the Polish courts to avoid any incompatibility by bringing the interpretation of the Bilateral Agreement into line with ESR to the extent possible and in

[135] C-21/22, par. 35.

[136] C-21/22, par. 36.

[137] Opinion of AG in C-21/22, par. 69.

[138] Opinion of AG in C-21/22, par. 70–77.

[139] Opinion of AG in C-21/22, par. 71.

[140] Opinion of AG in C-21/22, par. 78–79.

[141] Ibid.

[142] See C-21/22, par. 35 and 36.

[143] Opinion of AG in C-21/22, par. 43.

[144] Opinion of AG in C-21/22, par. 80–84.

compliance with international law.[145] If this is not possible, Poland would have to take an action in order to terminate or amend the Bilateral Agreement with Ukraine.[146]

4.3 Concluding Comments

With regard to the above-presented rulings and argumentation on the interpretation of Art. 75(1) of ESR provided in the judgment of CJEU in the OP case, we find it necessary to provide a few concluding comments.

In our view, it is crucial that in all future cases concerning the interpretation of Art. 75 of ESR, the CJEU maintains the stance (already established in its previous judgments in similar cases) that bilateral treaties with a third States, which in principle take precedence over ESR, cannot compromise the principles underlying the ESR and judicial cooperation in civil and commercial matters in EU. This undoubtedly means that the CJEU can take the rules and principles of a bilateral treaty with third States into consideration solely to determine whether they compromise the rules and underlying principles of ESR in a given case, which should be exclusively understood as an interpretation of ESR and not of a bilateral treaty. In that regard, we support the CJEU's interpretation that Art. 22 of ESR, which provides for the right to a person to choose his/her *lex nationalis* as the law applicable to succession, cannot be regarded as a principle underlying the ESR since such 'limited' choice of law rule represents an exemption from the primary conflict-of-law rule of Art. 21(1) of ESR, providing for the last habitual residence of the deceased as a default connecting factor.

On the other hand, we find that the CJEU's argumentation concerning the principle of unity of succession had to be more profound. Namely, the CJEU stated that the general objective of ESR, which seeks to ensure the mutual recognition of decisions in succession matters within the EU, is strongly linked to the principle of unity of succession, but also claimed that this principle is 'not absolute' since certain rules of ESR derogate it, and concluded that ESR intended to comply, in certain specific cases, with the model of scission of succession. Although it is undisputable that ESR provides for intentional deviations from the principle of unity of succession in certain cases, the main problem with the CJEU's finding is that it did not expressly state whether and to which extent this principle and its links to the general objective of ESR represent the underlying principle of ESR. In our view, the principle of unity of succession should be regarded as the underlying principle of ESR as far as it is a guarantee for the achievement of the proper functioning of the internal market in cross-border succession cases, which is also reflected in the free circulations of decisions in succession matters within EU. The derogation from this principle

[145] Opinion of AG in C-21/22, par. 85.

[146] Opinion of AG in C-21/22, par. 86.

provided by certain rules of ESR, such as Art. 12(1), has been exclusively created to enable Member States courts to successfully cope, while applying the provisions of ESR, with different concepts in private international laws of third States and not with concepts provided in bilateral treaties concluded between Member States and third States. This means that the derogation from the grounding principle of unity of succession established in ESR caused by bilateral treaties employing the principle of scission of succession has a substantially different meaning and must be observed in a different context since such derogation can undermine the proper functioning of the internal market (decisional harmony) within EU and create the obstacles for mutual recognition and enforcement of decisions in Member States (which has already been discussed above in Sect. 2.2.). Therefore, we find that the CJEU needed to clarify its view in this or a similar manner in order to encourage Member State courts to examine their bilateral treaties with third States in every single case and, where applicable, submit the request for preliminary ruling proceedings in which the CJEU would decide whether the rules of bilateral treaties compromise the underlying principles of ESR.

Nevertheless, to avoid any difficulties regarding the interpretation of whether the underlying principles of ESR have been compromised by bilateral treaties with third States, every Member State bound by such treaty should try to renegotiate its jurisdiction and conflict-of-law provisions in succession matters with respective third State in order to terminate them or to amend them in line with principles and rules of ESR (which has already been suggested by AG in respect to Poland and explained as a solution in Sect. 3.2.).

Legal Documents

Vienna Convention on the Law of Treaties of 27 January 1969, United Nations, Treaty Series, vol. 1155, pp 331–512

Council Regulation (EU) 1215/2012 of 12 December 2012 on jurisdiction and the recognition and enforcement of judgments in civil and commercial matters (recast), OJ L 351, 20.12.2012, pp 1–49

Council Regulation (EU) 2016/1103 of 24 June 2016 implementing enhanced cooperation in the area of jurisdiction, applicable law and the recognition and enforcement of decisions in matters of matrimonial property regimes, OJ L 183, 8.7.2016, pp 1–30

Council Regulation (EC) 4/2009 of 18 December 2008 on jurisdiction, applicable law, recognition and enforcement of decisions and cooperation in matters relating to maintenance obligations, OJ L 7, 10.1.2009, pp 1–88

Agreement between Republic of Poland and Ukraine on legal assistance and legal relations in civil and criminal matters of 24 May 1993. Available at: https://treaties.un.org/Pages/showDetails.aspx?objid=08000002805c4784

Convention on the Contract for the International Carriage of Goods by Road, signed at Geneva on 19 May 1956, amended by the Protocol signed at Geneva on 5 July 1978, United Nations, Treaty Series, vol. 399, pp 189–239

Council Document (EU) 10126/11 of 20 May 2011 on proposal for a Regulation of the European Parliament and of the Council on jurisdiction, applicable law, recognition and enforcement of decisions and acceptance and enforcement of authentic instruments in matters of succession and on the creation of a European Certificate of Succession – Political guidelines for the future work, Available at: https://data.consilium.europa.eu/doc/document/ST-10126-2011-INIT/en/pdf

Council Regulation (EC) No 44/2001 of 22 December 2000 on jurisdiction and the recognition and enforcement of judgments in civil and commercial matters, OJ L 12, 16.01.2001, pp 1–23

Council Regulation (EU) 650/2012 of 4 July 2012 on jurisdiction, applicable law, recognition and enforcement of decisions and acceptance and enforcement of authentic instruments in matters of succession and on the creation of a European Certificate of Succession, OJ L 201, 27.7.2012, pp 107–135

Treaty between the Czechoslovak Socialist Republic and the Union of Soviet Socialist Republics on Legal Assistance and Legal Relations in Civil, Family and Criminal Matters of 12 August 1982, Vyhláška ministra zahraničních věcí č. 95/1983 Sb

Treaty between the People' Republic of Hungary and the Socialist Federal Republic of Yugoslavia on mutual legal assistance of 7 March 1968, Službeni list SFRJ – Dodatak: Međunarodni ugovori i drugi sporazumi, br. 3/68

Treaty between the Federal People's Republic of Yugoslavia and the Union of Soviet Socialist Republics on Legal Assistance in Civil, Family and Criminal Matters of 24 February 1962, Službeni list SFRJ – Dodatak: Međunarodni ugovori i drugi sporazumi, br. 5/63

Treaty on the Functioning of the European Union of 13 December 2007 – consolidated version, OJ C 202, 7.6.2016, pp 47–390

Case-Law

Opinion of Advocate General Campos Sanchez-Bordona delivered on 23 March 2023, Case C-21/22, *OP v. Notariusz Justyna Gawlica*, EU:C:2023:247

Judgment of 27 February 1962, *Commission v. Italy*, Case C-10/61, EU:C:1962:2

Judgment of 14 July 1980, *Attorney General v. Burgoa*, C-812/79, EU:C:1980:231

Judgment of 22 September 1988, *Ministère public v Gérard Deserbais*, C-286/86 ECR 4907, EU:C:1988:434

Judgment of 22 June 1989, *Fediol v Commission*, Case 70/87, EU:C:1989:254

Judgment of 7 May 1991, *Nakajima v Council*, Case 69/89, EU:C:1991:186

Judgment of 6 April 1995, *RTE and ITP* v *Commission*, Joined Cases C-241/91 P and C-242/91 P, EU:C:1995:98

Judgment of 5 November 2002, *Commission v United Kingdom of Great Britain and Northern Ireland*, C-466/98, EU:C:2002:624

Judgment of 3 September 2008, *Kadi and Al Barakaat International Foundation v Council and Commission*, Joined Cases C-402/05 and 415/05, EU:C:2008:461

Judgment of 22 October 2009, *Irène Bogiatzi v Deutscher Luftpool and Others*, C-301/08, EU:C:2009:649

Judgment of 21 January 2010, *Commission v Germany*, C-546/07, EU:C:2010:25

Judgment of 4 May 2010, *TNT Express Nederland BV v AXA Versicherung AG*, C-533/08, EU:C:2010:243

Judgment of 19 December 2013, *Nipponkoa Insurance Co. (Europe) v Inter-Zuid Transport BV*, C-452/12, EU:C:2013:858

Judgment of 4 September 2014, *Nickel & Goeldner Spedition GmbH v 'Kintra' UAB*, C-157/13, EU:C:2014:2145

Judgment of 25 March 2021, *Generics (UK) Ltd v Commission*, C-588/16 P, EU:C:2021:242

Judgment of 12 October 2023, *OP v. Notariusz Justyna Gawlica*, C-21/22, EU:C:2023:766

References

Literature

Babić D, Hoško T (2019) Croatia. In: Dutta A, Wurmnest W (eds) European private international law and member state treaties with third states: the case of the european succession regulation. Intersentia, Cambridge, pp 67–83

Buonaiuti FM (2016a) Article 10. In: Caravaca CAL, Davi A, Mansel HP (eds) The EU succession regulation: a commentary. Cambridge University Press, Cambridge, pp 186–198

Buonaiuti FM (2016b) Article 11. In: Caravaca CAL, Davi A, Mansel HP (eds) The EU succession regulation: a commentary. Cambridge University Press, Cambridge, pp 199–208

Claes M (2015) The primacy of EU law in European and national law. In: Arnull A, Chalmers D (eds) The Oxford handbook of European Union law. Oxford University Press, Oxford, pp 178–211

Djordjevic S, Meškić Z (2019) The relations of Bosnia and Herzegovina, Serbia, North Macedonia and Montenegro with EU Member States. In: Dutta A, Wurmnest W (eds) European private international law and member state treaties with third states: the case of the European succession regulation. Intersentia, Cambridge, pp 209–251

Đorđević S (2010) O problemima nekoordiniranog raspravljanja zaostavštine jednog lica u različitim pravnim porecima. In: Bejatović S (ed) Pravni sistem Srbije i standardi Evropske unije i Saveta Evrope. Faculty of Law, Kragujevac, pp 377–399

Đorđević S (2020) Some remarks on prevention and resolution of positive jurisdiction conflicts between Croatian (member state) and Serbian courts in cross-border succession cases – from Croatian (EU) and Serbian point of view. Pravni vjesnik – J Law Soc Sci Faculty Law Josip Juraj Strossmayer University of Osijek 36(2):25–49

Dutta A (2013) Novo međunarodno nasljedno pravo Evropske unije – prvo čitanje Uredbe o nasljednom pravu. Nova pravna revija, Časopis za domaće, njemačko i evropsko pravo 2013(2):9–22

Dutta A (2015) The European certificate of succession: a new European instrument between procedural and substantive law. Int J Proced Law 5(1):38–50

Dutta A (2019) The perspective of the European Union. In: Dutta A, Wurmenst W (eds) European private international law and member state treaties with third states: the case of European succession regulation. Intersentia, Cambridge, pp 319–328

Dutta A (2024a) Artikel 4. In: MüKoBGB, EuErbVO, Band 6. Aufl. C. H. Beck, München, para. 1–14

Dutta A (2024b) Artikel 10. In: MüKoBGB, EuErbVO, Band 12, 9. Aufl. C. H. Beck, München, para. 1–18

Dutta A (2024c) Artikel 11. In: MüKoBGB, EuErbVO, Band 12, 9. Aufl. C. H. Beck, München, 2024, para. 1–3

Dutta A (2024d) Artikel 21. In: MüKoBGB, EuErbVO, Band 12, 9. Aufl. C. H. Beck, München, para. 1–9

Dutta A (2024e) Artikel 22. In: MüKoBGB, EuErbVO, Band 12, 9. Aufl. C. H. Beck, München, para. 1–39

Dutta A (2024f) Vorbemerkung zu Artikel 4. In: MüKoBGB, EuErbVO, Band 12, 9. Aufl. C. H. Beck, München, para. 1–56

Dutta A, Wurmnest W (2019a) Introduction. In: Dutta A, Wurmnest W (eds) European private international law and member state treaties with third states: the case of the European succession regulation. Intersentia, Cambridge, pp 1–4

Dutta A, Wurmnest W (2019b) Questionnaire. In: Dutta A, Wurmnest W (eds) European private international law and member state treaties with third states: the case of the European succession regulation. Intersentia, Cambridge, pp 5–7

Ehrlich SA, Ginter C, Tigane T (2013) Loyalty to the EU and the duty to revise pre-accession international agreements. Juridicum International, Näituse 2013(20):121–132

Fuchs A (2015) The new EU succession regulation in a nutshell. ERA Forum 16(2):119–124

Hess B (2014) Die internationale Zuständigkeit nach der Erbrechtsverordnung. In: Dutta A, Herrler S (eds) Die Europäische Erbrechtsverordnung. C. H. Beck, München, pp 131–142

Köhler A (2024) In: Gierl W, Köhler A, Kroiß L, Wilsh H (eds) Teil 1 EuErbVO. Internationales Erbrecht, Baden-Baden, pp 21–156

Kunda I, Winkler S, Pertot T (2020) Jurisdiction and applicable law in succession matters. In: Ruggeri L, Giobbi M, Cazorla Gonzales M, Škerl Kramberger J, Ruggeri L (eds) Property relations of cross-borders couples in the European Union. Edizioni Scientifiche Italiane, Napoli, pp 99–131

Lagarde P (2015) Introduction. In: Bergquist U, Damascelli D, Frimston R, Lagarde P, Odersky F, Reinhartz B (eds) EU regulation on succession and wills – commentary. Otto Schmidt, Köln, pp 20–38

Lehmann D (2023) Ausschluss der Rechtswahl durch einen in einem EU-Mitgliedstaat wohnhaften Drittstaatsangehörigen bei nach Art. 75 EuErbVO vorrangigen Abkommen; Anm. zu EuGH (Dritte Kammer), Urt. v. 12.10.2023– C-21/22 23, ZEV, pp. 840–841

Lein E (2014) Die Erbrechtsverordnung aus Sicht der Drittstaaten In: Dutta A, Herrler S (Hrsg) Die Europäische Erbrechtsverordnung. C. H. Beck, München, pp 199–220

Looschelders D (2019) Germany. In: Dutta A, Wurmnest W (eds) European private international law and member state treaties with third states: the case of the European succession regulation. Intersentia, Cambridge, pp 149–173

Panopoulos G (2015) Limitation of proceedings under Article 12 succession regulation (2012): an impossible codification of the improbable. Elte Law J 2015(2):99–106. Available at: https://eltelawjournal.hu/wp-content/uploads/2016/10/2015-2-07-Georgios-Panopoulos.pdf

Panopoulos G (2017a) Article 10. In: Pamboukis H (ed) P (eds) EU succession regulation No 650/2012 – a commentary. Nomiki Bibliothiki – C. H. Beck – Hart – Nomos, Athens, pp 145–153

Panopoulos G (2017b) Article 11. In: Pamboukis HP (ed) EU succession regulation No 650/2012 – a commentary. Nomiki Bibliothiki – C. H. Beck – Hart – Nomos, Athens, pp 154–160

Pfeiffer M (2019) Czech Republic. In: Dutta A, Wurmnest W (eds) European private international law and Member State treaties with third states: the case of the European succession regulation. Intersentia, Cambridge, pp 85–120

Popescu DA (2014) Guide on international private law in successions matters. Ministry of Justice. Magic Print, Oneşti, pp 1–130

Radoja Knol K (2019) Deviations from the principle of the unity of succession in the EU regulation on succession. Pravni Vijesnik 35(2):49–65

Rosas A (2011) The status in EU law of international agreements concluded by EU Member States. Fordham Int Law J 34(5):1303–1345

Rylski R (2020) The influence of bilateral treaties with third states on jurisdiction and recognition of decisions in matters on succession – polish perspective. Problemy Prawa Prywatnego Międzynarodowego 26:91–105

Solomon D (2014) Die allgemeine Kollisionsnorm (Art. 21, 22 EuErbVO) In: Dutta A, Herrler S (Hrsg) Die Europäische Erbrechtsverordnung. C. H. Beck, München, 2014, pp 19–45

Süß R (2014) Der Vorbehalt zugunsten bilateraler Abkommen mit Drittstaaten. In: Dutta A, Herrler S (eds) Die Europäische Erbrechtsverordnung. C. H. Beck, München, pp 181–198

Szilágyi F (2021) The option to choose the law applicable to succession under the EU Succession Regulation. Iustum Aequum Salutare, Budapest 17(1):149–190

Traser SJ, Béres N, Marinkas G, Pék E (2020) The principle of the primacy of EU Law in light of the case law of the constitutional courts of Italy, Germany, France and Austria. Central Eur J Comp Law 1(2):151–175

Varga C (2021) Rule of law, contesting and contested. Central Eur J Comp Law 2(1):245–278

Viarengo I (2020) Planning Cross-Border Successions: The Professio Juris in the Succession Regulation. Rivista Di Dritto Internazionale Privato E Processuale, p. Available at: https://air.unimi.it/retrieve/dfa8b9a5-0053-748b-e053-3a05fe0a3a96/01_RDINT_3_2020_Viarengo%20DEF.pdf

Wurmnest W (2019) Comparative report and policy perspectives. In: Dutta A, Wurmnest W (eds) European private international law and member state treaties with third states: the case of the European succession regulation. Intersentia, Cambridge, pp 329–356

Representations and Warranties in M&A Transactions Under Bosnian Law: How Do We Tackle Unknown Territory?

Almir Gagula

1 Introduction

In recent years, the M&A market in Bosnia and Herzegovina has experienced a significant upswing, presenting a wealth of promising opportunities for foreign investors. The post-war economic development has catalyzed a surge in foreign investments, with many investors choosing to establish new entities, particularly limited liability companies, through green-field investments.

Other investments were related to M&A transactions in limited liability companies and public companies (stock companies). Investments in particular business fields, such as the banking sector, were primarily focused on acquisitions of domestic players and their integration into larger banking systems.

The corporate law in Bosnia and Herzegovina, though intricate, is a well-defined system split between the regulations of the laws in two Bosnian entities: the Federation of Bosnia and Herzegovina (FB&H) and the Republic of Srpska (RS). While some distinct features exist between the general regime of establishing companies in these entities, most of the general issues are comparable. Both entity's laws define two forms of capital incorporated companies: limited liability and public company, with similar corporate body structures and divisions of the powers between them.

While the corporate peculiarities of the Bosnian system may seem unfamiliar, our focus is on the contract law issues related to share-purchase agreements under Bosnian law. Looking at Bosnian law from this perspective, the view becomes much clearer and closer to the comfort zone where foreign investors, especially Europeans, operate when entering into business in Bosnia and Herzegovina. The

A. Gagula (✉)
University of Zenica and Law Office Gagula, Zenica and Sarajevo, Bosnia and Herzegovina
e-mail: almir.gagula@gagula.ba

Z. Meskić et al. (eds.), *Balkan Yearbook of European and International Law 2024*,
Balkan Yearbook of European and International Law 2024,
https://doi.org/10.1007/978-3-031-89952-2_6

dispositive nature of pertinent provisions allows parties to adapt contractual responsibility for the shares sold to suit their needs, giving them a sense of control and empowerment.

This chapter provides an overview of the legal basis for introducing the standard set of representations and warranties in share-purchase transactions under Bosnian law. We will start by discussing the applicable rules to share-purchase transactions in Limited Liability Companies and then explore warranties in share-purchase agreements.

It is worth noting that, albeit the term M&A covers both mergers and acquisitions, it is often used interchangeably or more often to refer to acquisitions. However, given the merger of the companies under Bosnian law also has a contractual basis,[1] the reasons set out in this chapter also apply to mergers of companies.

One additional introductory note is necessary. In Bosnia and Herzegovina, legal writing and case law regarding the general regime of material and legal defects are substantive. Plenty of the doctrinal works from the region (Slovenia, Croatia, Serbia, Montenegro, Republic of North Macedonia) on the issues of Law on Obligations are almost directly effective for use in the Bosnian legal system given the joint legal heritage of these countries. However, nearly none of the doctrines on specific issues of representation and warranties exist in M&A settings. This is why the author considered it necessary to cover this issue.

No matter how limited the case law or scholarly works on the issue are, the problem can be relatively easily tackled by using the concepts of responsibility for material defects as construed for the standard purchase agreement of the goods. Due to the lack of domestic reading on the issue, we shall also support our findings with a comparative approach.

2 Applicable Rules to Share-Purchase Transactions in Limited Liability Companies

The legal framework in Bosnia and Herzegovina provides clear guidelines for share-purchase transactions of limited liability companies (Ltd). The provisions of the Law on Companies in both the Federation of Bosnia and Herzegovina and the Republic of Srpska establish a comprehensive framework.[2] Law on Companies FB&H[3] defines the shares of the shareholders in Ltd companies as transferable, either by contract or

[1] Art. 40 of the Law on registration of business entities in Federation of Bosnia and Herzegovina (Official Gazette, No. 27/2005, 68/2005, 43/2009, 63/2014, 32/2019); Art. 53. of the Law on registration of business entities in Republic of Srpska (Official Gazette, No. 67/2013, 15/2016 i 84/2019).

[2] Bosnia and Herzegovina has two entities: the Federation of B&H and the Republic of Srpska, each with its competencies in civil law in general.

[3] Official Gazette of Federation of Bosnia and Herzegovina No. 81/2015 and 75/2021.

by inheritance.[4] In the former case, other shareholders are granted the right of first refusal with 30 days' notice.[5] The right of first refusal falls into the category of *ius dispositivum*, meaning that the shareholders of the limited liability company have a right to exclude or define in significant detail rights and obligations related to the right of first refusal.[6] The provisions of the Law on Companies of the Republic of Srpska define a similar construct of transferring the shares via contract.[7]

The transfer of the shares requires two transactions between the buyer and the seller. The share purchase agreement (SPA) is a contractual basis for the later transfer of the shares. Although the SPA is the most frequent basis for transferring shares, the shares under Bosnian law can be transferred based on the donation agreement. The shares likewise can be inherited.[8]

On the other hand, the share-transfer agreement (STA) is purely procedural and transfers the shares in the court register from the previous owner to the new owner.[9]

There is a slight formal distinction between the rules applicable in the Federation and the Republic of Srpska. Namely, following the decision of the Constitutional Court of the Federation, mandatory rules providing for notarial acts for SPA and STA are declared unconstitutional.[10] Therefore, unlike before, SPA and STA in the Federation of Bosnia and Herzegovina must be in written form, with confirmation of the parties' signature by a competent authority (municipality or notary).[11] The parties to the agreement can submit the agreements to further formal requirements (*e.g.*, requesting a notarial act instead of confirming the parties' signatures).[12] In the Republic of Srpska, the Law on Companies RS specifically requires that SPA and STA be concluded in written form, with the parties' signatures confirmed by a public notary.[13]

It is important to emphasize that the parties are not obligated to submit SPA to the authorities to transfer the shares to the Ltd companies. The seller and the buyer are only under the obligation to submit STA to the court, leaving the provisions of SPA fully confidential.

---

[4] Art. 320 Law on Companies FB&H.

[5] Bikić and Gagula (2019), p. 155.

[6] Art. 321 Law on Companies of FB&H.

[7] Art. 120–123 Law on Companies or RS (Official Gazette of Republic of Srpska No. 127/2008, 58/2009, 100/2011, 67/2013, 100/2017, and 82/2019).

[8] Art. 235 Law on Companies FB&H.

[9] Bikić and Gagula (2019), p. 154.

[10] Decision of the Constitutional Court of FB&H No. U-22/16. Following this decision, a new draft of the changes of Law on Registration of Business Entities in FBiH has been prepared by the government, pending further legislative procedure.

[11] The Law on Companies of FB&H does not explicitly refer to the form of SPA or STA. However, in practice, the courts request confirmation of the signature through analogous application of Art. 305 of the Law on Companies of FB&H.

[12] Art. 69 LOO.

[13] Art. 123(1) Law on Companies of RS.

Leaving aside this minor distinction between the Law on Companies and related laws on the level of Bosnian entities, the core legislation applicable to the substantial part of SPA and STA are identical. The sale agreement or the donation can establish the basis for transferring the shares in Ltd.[14] The Law on Obligations (Federation and Republic of Srpska) applies to the SPA.[15] The Law on Obligation is almost entirely the same as declared by the Socialistic Federative Republic of Yugoslavia,[16] which Bosnia and Herzegovina was part of until its independence in 1992. Later, in the Federation[17] and the Republic of Srpska[18] the Law on Obligations was changed several times, but its core remained untouched. Apart from minor distinctions such as the general statute of limitation (Federation of Bosnia and Herzegovina 5 years, Republic of Srpska 10 years), the Law on Obligation is almost identical, and further references in this chapter to the Law on Obligation (LOO) apply equally to regulation in both Bosnian entities.

The Law on Obligations also applies to M&A transactions in the region. For example, in Croatia, the rules of the Law on Obligations for the purchase contract apply to the sale of shares, and likewise, the rules regarding defects apply to the sale of shares.[19]

3 Warranties for Material Defects in Purchase Agreement

Under Bosnian law, the warranties are divided into two groups: (i) the warranties for material and (ii) legal defects. The warranties for material and legal defects are natural, implied terms of any bilaterally binding agreement.[20] Due to its unilaterally binding nature, this generally excludes the warranties for material defects in the donation contract.[21] However, the donor shall be held responsible for the legal defects of the donated goods or rights if he or she knows that the third party owns the goods or rights and decides to conceal that information.[22] This is to say that in rare cases where the donation agreement achieves the transfer of the shares, dispositive rules on the warranties for purchase agreements are generally not applicable.

[14] The Bosnian LOO does not provide provisions for the donation contract. Instead, the rules of ABGB are still directly applicable to rights and obligations arising out of the donation (Art. 938–956).

[15] Džidić (2010), p. 504.

[16] Official Gazette of SFRY, No. 29/78, 39/85, 46/85, 45/89, and 57/89.

[17] Official Gazette of RB&H No. 2/1992, 13/1993, and 13/1994. Official Gazette of FB&H No. 29/2003, and 42/2011.

[18] Official Gazette of RS, No. 17/1993, 3/1996, 37/2001, 39/2003, and 74/2004.

[19] Barbić (2013), p. 106.

[20] Art. 121 LOO.

[21] Bikić and Bikić (2011), p. 56.

[22] Art. 945 ABGB. It is noted that the rules of the Austrian Civil Code (ABGB) are still applicable to, among others, donation contracts.

Bosnian law does not provide any regulation specifically concerning the responsibility of the seller in share-purchase transactions and the legal and material defects of the shares. The Law on Companies provides that the shares can be transferred by agreement or inheritance[23] and provides for minimal regulation of the right of first refusal.[24] Even concerning the share purchase agreement form, the Law on Companies does not establish detailed rules. Namely, it only regulates the form of the Foundation Act of the company[25] (*i.e.*, the Articles of Association). Still, it leaves the remaining issues of the form and the substance of the share-purchase agreement unregulated.[26] However, it is a general practice of the courts in FBiH to accept the foundation act and the SPA in written form with the certified signature of the parties to the agreement.

Therefore, the LOO is the primary source of the legal provisions concerning the SPA. According to Art. 454(2) LOO, the seller of the right undertakes an obligation to transfer certain rights to the buyer. This also includes selling any rights other than movables or real estate.[27] This is the primary source of direct applications of the provisions of LOO regarding the sale agreement onto SPA.

4 Material Defects and the Seller's Responsibilities

Concerning material defects of the right sold, LOO defines that the object of the sale agreement has a defect if (i) it does not have necessary properties for the usual usage of the right or legal traffic, (ii) it does not have necessary properties for specific usage for which a buyer acquires a right which was known to the seller, or he must be aware of it, (iii) it does not have properties which were explicitly or implicitly agreed or regulated by the law or (iv) the goods are not compliant with the sample or the model of the goods presented unless the sample or the model are provided only for informative purposes.[28]

If the parties to the agreement fail to specify, the seller must deliver the goods acceptable for usual usage. The typical usage is a practical question to be determined in each case.[29]

---

[23] Art. 320 Law on Companies of FB&H.

[24] Art. 321 Law on Companies of FB&H.

[25] Art. 305 Law on Companies of FB&H.

[26] It is crucial to note that the Law on Registration of the Commercial Entities in FB&H (Official Gazette 27/05, 68/05, 43/09, and 63/14) stipulates a notarial act for both the foundation act and the share-transfer agreement. However, a landmark decision by the Constitutional Court of FBiH No. U-22/16, dated 6 March 2019, has clarified that the notarial act is not a formal condition for acceptance of the foundation act for registration at the court. This decision significantly impacts the legal landscape.

[27] Blagojević-Krulj (1980), p. 947.

[28] Art. 479 LOO.

[29] Bikić and Bikić (2011), p. 21.

Sometimes, the buyer intends to use the goods for purposes different from the usual usage. In such a case, to be responsible for non-compliance with the goods for that particular purpose, the seller must be aware of the intended purpose of the buyer's end.[30]

The case of expressly or tacitly agreed-upon properties of the goods sold is most important for our topic. Namely, the parties are entitled to agree on specific properties of the good. In such a case, the seller will be held responsible if it delivers goods that do not conform to the agreed-upon properties between the parties. In cases where the law defines the specific property, any deviation will be considered a material defect.[31]

Lastly, but least applicable to our topic, the seller is responsible for material defects in the goods if they are non-conforming with the sample or the model shown.[32]

Given the definition of the material defects above, one might wonder what might constitute material defects over the share from the perspective of the LOO. The Bosnian case law and literature are tacit on the issue. The buyer acquires the company's shares to generate profit with the company.[33] In order to do so, the company must have its employees, equipment, office space, etc. This is all necessary for running the business. Therefore, some general properties must exist for the company to be used in the usual manner. In effect, if the target company does not have all the requirements to continue the normal course of the business before the purchase, the buyer might consider that it lacks properties necessary for the usual usage of the rights resulting from the share. However, this responsibility does not extend vastly beyond and behind the share. It could not be taken as an all-encompassing liability of the seller for all the rights or obligations of the company. The seller, *ex lege* warrants for the share itself, not the company's economic value behind the share.

This is, in our view, truly comparable with the textbook's example of the material defects of the car. Given the general purpose, as long as the car runs as any other car, it will be deemed that the car is defect-free. If the buyer wishes to ensure the car has certain properties (e.g., maximum speed), the buyer must agree with the seller on these properties. Likewise, if the buyer of the share wishes that the seller's responsibility for the material defects goes beyond the usual share usage, it will have to ask for specific warranties for specific economic properties of the company.[34]

---

[30] Bikić and Bikić (2011), p. 21.

[31] Bikić and Bikić (2011), p. 22.

[32] Bikić and Bikić (2011), p. 22.

[33] Art. 2(1) Law on Companies FB&H.

[34] Art. 479(3) LOO.

5 Inspection Duty, Visible and Hidden Defects, and the Buyer's Knowledge

Under Bosnian law, the buyer must inspect the goods as soon as possible and inform the seller about any visible defects without delay to preserve its rights.[35] If the seller fails to inspect or notify the seller in a timely manner, it shall be considered that it waives its rights regarding the defects. The buyer will likewise bear the consequences of failing to use the required level of care when inspecting the goods.

The seller's responsibility is different in the case of hidden defects. When the defect is not visible at the inspection but becomes apparent only afterward, the buyer must inform the seller about the defects without delay.[36] Otherwise, the buyer will forfeit its rights.

In both cases, the buyer's notification must contain a detailed description of the defect and an invitation for the seller to inspect the goods.[37]

On this issue, it is evident that the LOO follows the Swiss law approach.[38] Under Swiss law, the inspection and notification obligation of the buyer[39] is equally valid for all different kinds of purchase contracts, *i.e.,* for the purchase of shares in a company, and this applies to all types of "defects", *i.e.,* also to the presence or absence of a warranted attribute of the purchased object. In other words, the buyer may not merely rely on a warranted attribute of the purchase object but must check—as soon as feasible—whether a warranted attribute is present.[40]

If the buyer discovers a "defect" in the purchased object—*e.g.*, the absence of a warranted attribute—for which the seller is liable under warranty - the buyer must notify the seller without delay. The buyer must give the seller a substantiated notice of a concrete "defect". The notice must put the seller in a position to determine the extent of the complaint.[41] A general notice of defects is not sufficient. It must state the extent to which the purchased item does not meet the contractually stipulated or guaranteed characteristics. The notice must also state that the buyer wants to demand a warranty or refuse acceptance of the goods.[42]

The period in which the buyer must notify the seller is relatively short. Obvious "defects" must be reported to the seller immediately after delivery, *i.e.,* in two to

---

[35] Art. 481(1) LOO.

[36] Art. 481(2) LOO.

[37] Art. 484 LOO.

[38] It is noted that Swiss Law on Obligation was one of the key role models for Yugoslavian Law on Obligation; hence, the comparison between Bosnian law and Swiss law approach to the matter at hand is not to show a different approach but to be informative for interpretation of certain issues that were not recorded in Bosnian case law yet.

[39] Art. 201 para. 1 CO.

[40] Honsell (2015), Art. 201, para. 3.

[41] Swiss Federal Supreme Court (BGE), BGE 22 I 498, p. 503, para. 2.

[42] Honsell (2015), Art. 201, para. 10.

three working days.[43] Notices sent seven, fourteen,[44] seventeen or twenty[45] days after the discovery of the defects are belated. Defects that only become apparent during an inspection shall be reported immediately. Hidden (concealed) defects, *i.e.*, those not detectable by proper inspection, must be reported immediately after discovery.

The purchased object is deemed accepted if the buyer does not comply with his statutory inspection and notification obligation.[46] In other words, failure to comply with the timely inspection and complaint obligations leads to a deemed approval: the purchased item is considered approved regarding the "defect", *i.e.,* any potential warranty claims lapse.[47] Art. 201 CO is of a dispositive nature: The parties to a purchase agreement are free to contractually exclude, mitigate, or sharpen the application of Art. 201 CO.[48] However, unless the parties to a purchase agreement have agreed otherwise, the rule of Art. 201 CO applies without restriction.

Under Bosnian law, the buyer's knowledge of the defects cancels the seller's responsibility for the defects (Art. 480 LOO). Similarly, in a case where the seller is aware of the defects and fails to inform the buyer accordingly, the buyer does not waive its rights if it (a) fails to inspect the goods promptly, (b) fails to notify the buyer thereof or (c) the defect becomes apparent only after expiration of six months after the delivery.[49]

Otherwise, the seller's responsibility for the defects ceases six months after the delivery, provided the parties have not agreed on a more extended deadline.[50] Indeed, provisions on the seller's responsibility for visible and hidden defects are of a dispositive nature.

Under Swiss law, the seller cannot be held liable for any defects and/or for the absence of any warranted attributes of the purchased object that were known to the buyer when the share purchase agreement was concluded.[51] In other words, if the buyer of shares knew, at the time the share purchase agreement was concluded, that any warranted attribute of the company was missing, the seller's liability is statutorily excluded under Art. 200 para. 1 CO from the outset.[52] Art. 200 para. 1 CO is of a dispositive nature: The parties to a purchase agreement are free to contractually exclude, mitigate, or sharpen the application of Art. 200 para. 1 CO.[53] However,

[43] BGE 4D_4/2011, para. 4.1; BGE 4A_367/2009, para. 1.2; Walter (2019), p. 76.

[44] BGE 4A_251/2018, para. 3.3.

[45] BGE 4C.205/2003, para. 3.2.

[46] Art. 201 para. 2 CO.

[47] Honsell (2015), Art. 201, para. 13.

[48] Honsell (2015), Art. 201, para. 13.

[49] Art. 485 LOO.

[50] Art. 482(2) LOO.

[51] Art. 200(1) CO.

[52] Honsell (2015), Art. 200, para. 2.

[53] Honsell (2015), Art. 200, para. 5.

unless the parties to a purchase agreement have agreed otherwise, the rule of Art. 200 para. 1 CO applies without restriction.

6 Buyer's Remedies

The buyer who informs the seller in a timely manner shall have certain rights due to the material defects of the goods sold. Firstly, the buyer shall be entitled to request fulfillment of the contract, requiring the seller to remedy the defects or deliver the goods without defects. Secondly, the buyer shall be entitled to demand a price reduction. Thirdly, the buyer can terminate the contract.[54]

It is generally understood that the buyer is entitled to the alternative remedies described above. The buyer can choose between the remedies but is not entitled to cumulate its rights. However, irrespective of the remedy selected by the buyer, it will be entitled to damages suffered due to the seller's breach of the contract.

It should be noted that the buyer is not fully free to select remedies for material defects. Firstly, it is under obligation to request the seller to fulfill the contractual obligation. Only after the seller fails to comply with the contract fully shall the buyer be entitled to require either a price reduction or termination of the contract by notifying the seller, in cumulative, with the right to compensation for the damages suffered.[55]

The seller can fulfill the contract as agreed by removing the defect on the goods or by delivering the goods without defects. Even here, the buyer can ask for the removal of the defect on the goods delivered, provided that the defect can be cured objectively and within a reasonable time. If the seller fails to remedy the defect, the buyer shall be entitled to engage a third party for the same at the seller's expense. It is, therefore, obvious that reparation in this manner is most often taken in the case of *species*. In contrast, the delivery of new goods most often happens in the case of generic goods (*genera*).[56]

Furthermore, the buyer is entitled to ask for a price reduction based on the difference between the value of the goods with and without the defect.[57]

Finally, the buyer's most drastic right is the right to terminate the contract. However, to enforce this right, the buyer must grant the seller reasonable additional time to fulfill the contract. The law does not define the duration of such a period but must be assessed in each case, considering the surrounding circumstances.[58]

As noted above, each alternative chosen by the buyer shall be entitled to restitution of the damages suffered due to the seller's breach of the contract. The damages

[54] Art. 488 LOO.

[55] Bikić and Bikić (2011), p. 25.

[56] Bikić and Bikić (2011), p. 25 and 26.

[57] Bikić and Bikić (2011), p. 26.

[58] Bikić and Bikić (2011), p. 26.

for the buyer can relate to the damages to the goods themselves and the pertaining services (storage, montage, *etc.*). The damages also include the right to the lost profit that the buyer would generate had the seller delivered the goods without the defects in the first place.[59]

From a comparative perspective, the order of the buyer's rights in such a scenario in Croatia has changed slightly due to the implementation of the Directive 2019/771 EU in Croatian Law on Obligations.[60] The buyer's rights follow the hierarchy defined by Art. 410 Croatian Law on Obligations. The buyer is only entitled to the price reduction or the contract's termination if the seller fails to remedy the defects. This seems like a reasonable approach, given the gravity of the termination of the contract. However, it must be noted that the rules on material and legal defects under Croatian law are also dispositive.[61] Therefore, the parties enjoy rather wide discretion in altering the dispositive rules of the Croatian Law on Obligation.[62] This, in turn, entitles the parties to regulate their rights and obligations in terms of representations and warranties as best suit their needs in an M&A transaction.

7 Dispositive Nature of Pertinent Provisions

The provisions of the LOO regulating the material defects on the goods sold are dispositive. This means the parties are entitled to depart from the legal regime and adapt contractual responsibility for the shares sold to suit their needs. For example, the parties are entitled, in the alternative or in cumulative, to (a) exclude responsibility for the defects entirely, (b) extend the responsibility and create a stricter regime (*e.g.*, provide for the seller's responsibility for a more extended period even for visible defects), (c) extend deadlines for the inspection by the buyer or notification to the seller, *etc.* As explained in more detail below, this overriding quality of LOO's pertaining provisions is crucial for a meaningful contractual regime on the representation and the warranties in the setting of the M&A transactions.

It is generally understood that the rules regulating the buyer's duty to notify any defects timely are of a dispositive nature. Therefore, the rules regulating the notification duty, including any time restrictions, are also dispositive.[63] That is logical, given that the rules of dispositive nature are dominant in LOO.[64] The same applies to

[59] Without going into the details, it is noted that the scope of the restitution of the lost profit under Bosnian law squarely fits into an explanation of the same right under the Art. 74. CISG. Advisory Council Opinion No. 6, Calculation of Damages under CISG, 3.3 and 3.4., accessible at cisg-online.org.

[60] Law on Obligations of Croatia (Official Gazzette, No. 35/05, 41/08, 125/11, 78/15, 29/18, 126/21, 114/22, 156/22, 155/23).

[61] High Commercial Court of the Republic of Croatia No. Pž-7279/05-3.

[62] Gorenc (2014), p. 703.

[63] Fišer-Šobot (2009), pp. 128 and 145.

[64] Art. 20 LOO.

the rules regarding the guarantee of the quality of technical equipment.[65] On a more general level, the contractual liability rules are also dispositive.[66] Likewise, agreeing on the notification period for legal defects is possible.[67] This does not diminish the quality of the notification period rules. Regardless of whether the parties agreed on a specific notification period or the dispositive rules from LOO apply, it will be considered a preclusive deadline.[68] The buyer shall waive its rights by failing to meet notification deadlines, agreed or legal.[69]

Even on a regional level, where certain ex-Yugoslav countries introduced new Laws on Obligations, the quality of the pertaining rules remained unchanged. Therefore, the rules regulating material defects under Croatian Law on Obligations are still dispositive.[70] There is a consensus among scholars that these rules are dispositive.[71] Even more specifically, the provision of Art. 486(1) LOO explicitly entitles parties to limit or even completely exclude the seller's liability for material defects. In that case, it is even more understandable that the parties are entitled to what could be considered "less than exclusions of the responsibilities" *i.e.*, amending the legal regime, including the notification periods defined in LOO.[72] Even a unilateral extension of the notification period, solely by the seller, shall be deemed legal.[73] The extension of the notification period to five years will allow the buyer to notify the seller about the material defects even after the expiration of the six-month deadline defined by Art. 482. LOO.[74]

It is evident from the outset that the LOO's provisions on material defects are not directly applicable to M&A transactions. There are several reasons why the legal regime cannot be applied accordingly, without further contractual regulation by the parties, to the representation and warranties: (i) unrecorded obligations of the company will often become apparent more than six months after the transfer of the shares and control onto the buyer, (ii) even the inspection of the financial records of the company will necessarily take longer than a few days which LOO anticipates for inspection of the goods, (iii) depending on the scope of the breach of the

---

[65] Klarić and Vedriš (2009), pp. 417 and 425.

[66] Klarić and Vedriš (2009), p. 606.

[67] Art. 515 LOO; Trifković (2004), p. 88.

[68] Art. 482 LOO.

[69] Supreme Court of B&H Rev. 569/83; Supreme Court of Serbia Pž. 6/07; Supreme Court of FB&H Pž. 204/99; Supreme Court of B&H Rev. 21/94; Slakoper (2007), p. 366; Vujisić (2009), p. 78.

[70] Petrić (2006), p. 123.

[71] Slakoper (2007), p. 366.

[72] But there are differing voices on this: the author argues that the preclusive effect of untimely notification from Art. 482(1) LOO suggests that the rules are mandatory, not of a dispositive nature. Interestingly, the author refers to the Swiss Law on Obligations (Art. 201(1)) to support its line of reasoning. However, precisely under the Swiss law, Art. 201(1) CO is dispositive. For this plainly wrong approach, see Hiber (2022), pp. 471 and 472.

[73] Supreme Court of Montenegro No. Rev-252/87.

[74] Perović (1995), p. 920.

representations and warranties, the buyer will necessarily need more time to assess the situation and gain complete knowledge about the scope of the breach and additional time to prepare adequate notification to the seller, *etc.*

It is noted that the freedom of contract entitles the parties to define the issue of responsibility for the material and legal defects in great detail and thus depart from the legal regime provided under LOO. The seller, therefore, can guarantee specific properties of the company, *e.g.*, that the company's grounds are not polluted, that the machines owned by the company are in good order, that the company's claims are chargeable, etc. In case of breach of such guarantees, the seller shall be responsible to the buyer as defined under the SPA.[75]

For the reasons explained above, and to set a meaningful regime, the parties will often need to modify the legal regime and provide detailed regulation defining in great detail (i) representations, (ii) warranties, (iii) inspection and notification duty, (iv) duration of the seller's warranty, (v) the remedies that the buyer will be entitled to, *etc.*

In essence, the parties' contractual freedom entitles them to define specific guarantees, remedies, and the order of use of such remedies.[76]

Issues of the remedies are also quite specific: the buyer will rarely want to use the termination as a first remedy. Instead, it would agree on a reduction of the price of the shares. Suppose more is needed to remedy the buyer fully. In that case, it will often insist on full reimbursement of either the buyer or the company for any loss suffered or expense made for the unrecorded obligations, or for that matter, any other breach of the contract that could qualify as the breach of the representations and warranties.

This is also the case in Switzerland. The statutory rules of Art. 197 *et seq.* CO are mostly dispositive and can be derogated if the parties to a purchase contract agree.[77] If and to the extent that the parties to a purchase contract have not agreed on deviating rules, the statutory rules of Art. 197 *et seq.* CO shall apply with full force and without restriction. This also applies to the inspection duty. Namely, Art. 201 CO is of a dispositive nature: the parties to a purchase agreement are free to contractually exclude, mitigate, or sharpen the application of Art. 201 CO.[78]

8 Warranties for Legal Defects

Regulating warranties for legal defects under Bosnian law is less of an issue for M&A transactions. Namely, the dispositive rules of LOO already provide for sufficiently comprehensive regulation of legal defects. The seller is responsible to

[75] Barbić (2008), p. 258.

[76] Barbić (2008), p. 258.

[77] Honsell (2015), Art. 197–210, para. 4.

[78] Honsell (2015), Art. 201, para. 13.

the buyer if a third person has rights over the shares that exclude, decrease, or limit the buyer's right over the share.[79] If a third person has some right over the share, the buyer is under obligation to inform the seller and ask to remove the third party's rights or claims.[80]

If the seller does not act accordingly and fails to provide relief to the third party's claims, the buyer shall be entitled to contract termination or a price reduction. In any case, the buyer shall be entitled to damages. However, if the buyer was aware of the potential claims of the third party, it shall not be entitled to damages but shall be entitled to restitution of the price paid.[81]

As with the material defects, the buyer must inform the seller of the third party's claims. If it does not notify the seller but instead decides to enter into legal proceedings with the third party, it still retains all the rights unless the seller can demonstrate that the seller had the means to ensure the dismissal of the third party's claims.[82]

Another significant similarity with the regulation on material defects is that the warranties for legal defects are also dispositive. Any contractual provision excluding or limiting the seller's liability shall be null and void in case of the seller's bad faith. If the seller knew or could have known the third party's rights, it shall not be protected by such a clause.[83]

Any rights of the buyer shall be extinguished after one year after the third party's right comes to the buyer's attention.[84]

Therefore, it is evident that the legal regime provided for in LOO already sufficiently covers the issue of legal defects over the share. The buyer is already adequately protected even in M&A transactions. The dispositive nature of the pertaining provisions here also entitles the parties to modify the legal regime to suit the specifics of their transaction.

9 Standard Representation and Warranties

In M&A transactions, the seller's (and buyer's) representations and warranties are among the most essential parts of the SPAs. These representations and warranties are to be considered statements and connected warranties concerning the target company's legal and factual matters, aiming to establish the seller's responsibility if such representations and warranties prove wrong.[85]

---

[79] Art. 508 LOO.

[80] Art. 509 LOO.

[81] Art. 510 LOO.

[82] Art. 511 LOO.

[83] Art. 513 LOO.

[84] Art. 515 LOO.

[85] Esin (2015), p. 277.

Representations and warranties typically cover areas such as licenses, undisclosed legal proceedings, outstanding tax and other liabilities, validity of intellectual property rights, supply agreements, books and records, and accuracy and completeness of financial statements.[86] The list of representations can also include environmental representations,[87] warranties for the nonexistence of significant contracts except disclosed, pending undisclosed proceedings, *etc.*[88]

These representations and warranties can easily be classified as material defects under the LOO. In all of the instances described above, they would be considered the properties that the parties explicitly agreed to in the SPA. In our opinion, this would allow the buyer to argue that the seller guaranteed the existence of a specific property of the object of the transaction (in this case, the shares). On the other hand, a breach of this guarantee could be seen as a material defect, with all the resulting consequences outlined in the LOO or fine details in the SPA.

This is the same approach used in comparative law. For example, in Turkey, the representations and warranties stated in the SPA are considered warranties against defects.[89] Under Swiss law, the seller is, in principle,[90] liable to the buyer for (1) a breach of warranty of quality and (2) for any defects that would materially or legally negate or substantially reduce the value of the object or its fitness for the designated purpose in accordance with the statutory regulations. These principles of the seller's liability also apply to a "share deal", *i.e.,* when the object of the purchase are shares in a company. However, in a "share deal", the shares—and not the company behind the shares—are the object of the purchase. Accordingly, the Swiss Federal Supreme Court ruled that the seller of shares is not liable to the buyer under Art. 197 *et seq.* CO for any "defects" (*i.e.,* for its economic value) of the company but only for defects of the share itself as a deed. If the parties would not agree on specific representation and warranties that would warrant particular property "behind the share", the seller would not be responsible for the economic value of the shares. Therefore, if the buyer wishes to protect its interest over the monetary value of the target company, it must ask the seller to provide specific warranties for the mere existence of the shares.[91]

Hence, a liability of the seller under Art. 197 *et seq.* CO can only exist if and to the extent that (1) the seller has issued a specific warranty to the buyer, (2) the warranted attribute is missing, (3) the buyer did not already know at the moment the share purchase agreement was concluded that the warranted attribute of the company is missing and (4) the buyer for his part complies with all the statutory provisions of Art. 197 *et seq.* CO (*i.e.,* the requirement of inspection of notification) and (5) the

[86] Esin (2015), p. 278.

[87] Sessler and Leimert (2004), p. 151.

[88] Frey and Müller (2018), p. 1124.

[89] Esin (2015), p. 278.

[90] Art. 197 *et seq.* CO.

[91] Honsell (2015), Art. 197, para. 1; BGE 107 II 419, para. 1.

claim is not time-barred (Art. 210 CO).[92] The buyer has the burden of proof for all prerequisites of a seller's liability under Art. 197 ff. CO.

At this point, it is noted that this is no different from Bosnian law. If the buyer, under Bosnian law, wants to cover the seller's various liabilities for a number of issues, it shall not be able to rely on the legal regime. The legal regime by itself will cover only the seller's responsibility for the existence of the share and its ownership over the share, but not, *e.g.*, unrecorded obligations of the company, *etc.* To the extent that the buyer wants to be protected from economic-related issues, it must carefully draft the contractual warranties in the SPA.

10 Case Law

Unfortunately, the Bosnian case law is not very helpful in dealing with these issues. This may be due to two main reasons: Firstly, advanced contractual regulation is often imposed by the buyer, who is typically a foreign company with more experience in M&A transactions. Consequently, this usually leads to agreeing on foreign applicable law and arbitration for dispute resolution. As a result, due to the privacy of arbitral proceedings, we are unaware of the positions taken in the arbitral cases. Secondly, the modern capitalist market in Bosnia and Herzegovina has a relatively short duration. It will likely take more time for the case law on M&A transactions to develop.

However, based on limited insight, the case law might support the positions taken in this chapter. The case law considers that share-purchase agreements are voidable if one party misled the other party about the company's financial affairs, which are the subject of the agreement.[93] In practical terms, this means that the legal regime of the defects warranties under LOO does not cover the target company's unfavorable financial situation. Therefore, the buyer shall not be entitled to require, *e.g.*, price reduction or indemnification unless the seller agrees to the specific warranties. The buyer's remedy in such a situation shall only ask for the agreement to be voided; for that purpose, it must prove that the seller misled it over the financial situation of the target company. Relying on the legal regime brings another risk: the buyer shall be protected only if it acted with due diligence. This means that the buyer must perform thorough due diligence, and only if such does not raise any red flags over the company's financial situation will it be able to ask for the agreement to be voided.[94] This is not a situation that can be compared with the situation where the buyer asked for a specific representation and warranties, where the buyer is only under the burden of showing the breach of the warranty, which will trigger the remedies for the buyer. Although due diligence usually occurs, unlike under the legal regime, with the

[92] Honsell (2015), Art. 197, para. 2.

[93] Supreme Court of Serbia Prev-374/01.

[94] Art. 61 LOO.

safeguard of a specific contractual warranty, it is not a prerequisite for the buyer's rights.

The other notable mention of the interplay between the general contractual regime and the share-purchase agreement refers to the application of the LOO rules regarding the nullity of the contract, which are likewise applicable to the share-purchase agreements.[95] Consequently, share-purchase agreements are subject to the court's scrutiny as any other agreement in case they contradict imperative rules.[96] However, the specific contractual warranties are also under scrutiny, and the parties must thoroughly check whether their particular regulation of the warranties does not violate the imperative rules.

11 Conclusion

Bosnian law, particularly the Law on Obligations, provides a flexible framework for representations and warranties in M&A transactions. Despite the limited case law and scholarly attention, Bosnian law is receptive to the contractual tools commonly used in M&A deals. The legal regime allows parties to adapt or exclude statutory rules, enabling the creation of custom-tailored contracts that reflect the specific needs and expectations of the buyer and seller.

This is the case primarily because Bosnian law's dispositive nature mirrors the Swiss approach, ensuring that material defects and liabilities in M&A transactions can be effectively managed through contract. Warranties for both material and legal defects can be incorporated to safeguard buyers from potential risks. Importantly, the parties are free to define the scope of these warranties, set inspection periods, and determine the consequences of breaches.

This provides a solid foundation for navigating M&A transactions with Bosnian law as applicable law. However, caution is necessary, particularly when combining Bosnian law with the jurisdiction of the local Bosnian courts. Given the lack of case law on the pertaining issues, it might be advisable to agree on arbitration instead of the local courts.

[95] Supreme Court of FB&H No. Rev-940/04; Constitutional Court of B&H No. AP-1730/11 – however, in this decision, the Constitutional Court took a completely wrong position on the disposal of the shares in the company that form marital property. Namely, it was found that the SPA without consent of the spouse whose shares are not recorded in the company's register is null and void. Irrespective of the fact that such a decision was wrong on so many levels, the parties are advised to mitigate such a risk by carefully investigating the marital status of the seller (in the case of private persons) and ensuring the consent of the unrecorded spouse. This case also shows why the parties in business transactions are often advised to agree on the arbitration in a more business-friendly setting where experienced and highly specialized arbitrators shall resolve their disputes.

[96] Art. 103 LOO.

References

Barbić J (2008) Pravo društava. Knjiga I, Opći dio
Barbić J (2013) Pravo društava, Knjiga II, Društva kapitala, Svezak II, Društvo sa ograničenom odgovornošću
Bikić A, Bikić E (2011) Obligaciono pravo – Posebni dio, drugo izmijenjeno i dopunjeno izdanje
Bikić E, Gagula A (2019) Pravo privrednih društava, Zenica
Blagojević-Krulj (1980) Komentar Zakona o obligacionim odnosima
Džidić M (2010) Gospodarska društva – Pravni položaj gospodarskih društava
Esin G (2015) Ismail, Chapter 10: Arbitrating M&A Disputes. In: Yesilirmak A, Esin IG (eds) Arbitration in Turkey
Fišer-Šobot S (2009) Odgovornost prodavca za isporuku robe u međunarodnom i domaćem pravu, doktorska disertacija. Univerzitet u Novom Sadu, Pravni fakultet, Novi Sad
Frey H, Müller D (2018) Chapter 8: Arbitrating M&A disputes, arbitration in Switzerland: the practitioner's guide, 2nd edn (© Kluwer Law International; Kluwer Law International)
Gorenc V et al. (2014) Komentar zakona o obveznim odnosima
Hiber D (2022) Prinudni propisi u novijoj domaćoj sudskoj i ugovornoj praksi. Anali Pravnog fakulteta u Beogradu, vol. 70
Honsell H (2015) Basler Kommentar Obligationenrecht I
Klarić P, Vedriš M (2009) Građansko pravo – Opći dio, stvarno pravo, obvezno i nasljedno pravo, XII. neizmijenjeno izdanje, Zagreb
Perović S (1995) Komentar Zakona o obligacionim odnosima Knjiga II, Beograd
Petrić S (2006) Odgovornost za materijalne nedostatke stvari prema novom zakonu o obveznim odnosima. Zbornik Pravnog fakulteta Sveučilišta u Rijeci 27(1)
Sessler A, Leimert C (2004) The role of expert determination in mergers and acquisitions under German law
Slakoper Z (2007) Odgovornost za pravne nedostatke u Zakonu o obveznim odnosima i izabranim pravnim porecima. Zbornik Pravnog fakulteta Sveučilišta u Rijeci 28(1)
Trifković M et al (2004) Poslovno pravo – Ugovori, vrijednosni papiri i pravo konkurencije. Ekonomski fakultet u Sarajevu, Sarajevo
Vujisić D (2009) Poslovno pravo – Trgovinsko pravo. Banja Luka
Walter S (2019) Die vertragliche Allokation rechtlicher Vollzugsrisiken bei privaten Aktienkäufen

DSA and CDSMD: Friends or Foes: Bridging or Exacerbating the Gaps Within Article 17 of the CDSMD?

Adna Škamo

1 Introduction

The digital age opens the door to rapid and cost-effective access to the copyright protected content, sparking a vibrant surge of creativity and the celebration of cultural diversity. Nonetheless, this dynamic landscape has also enabled the swift and unrestricted illegal circulation of the copyright protected content through the intermediary service providers (hereinafter: ISPs). Hence, the key issue was ISPs' liability for user-uploaded copyright protected content without rightsholders' authorisation.

In the previous period in the European Union (hereinafter: EU), three legal acts were of relevance for the ISPs' liability regime: Directive (EU) 2000/31/EC[1] (hereinafter: ECD), Directive 2001/29/EC[2] (hereinafter: InfoSoc Directive) and Directive 2004/48/EC[3] (hereinafter: Enforcement Directive). However, the ECD regulated the issue of ISPs' liability for illegal content in general. The InfoSoc Directive was a turning point for copyright regime in the online environment, still it did not

[1]Directive 2000/31/EC of the European Parliament and of the Council of 8 June 2000 on certain legal aspects of information society services, in particular electronic commerce, in the Internal Market, OJ L 178, 17 July 2000, pp. 1–16.

[2]Directive 2001/29/EC of the European Parliament and of the Council of 22 May 2001 on the harmonisation of certain aspects of copyright and related rights in the information society, OJ L 167, 22 June 2001, pp. 10–19.

[3]Directive 2004/48/EC of the European Parliament and of the Council of 29 April 2004 on the enforcement of intellectual property rights (OJ L 157, 30.4.2004), OJ L 195, 2 June 2004, pp. 16–25 (2004).

A. Škamo (✉)
University of Sarajevo, Faculty of Law, Sarajevo, Bosnia and Herzegovina
e-mail: a.skamo@pfsa.unsa.ba

Z. Meskić et al. (eds.), *Balkan Yearbook of European and International Law 2024*,
Balkan Yearbook of European and International Law 2024,
https://doi.org/10.1007/978-3-031-89952-2_7

specifically regulate ISPs' liability regime. The Enforcement Directive solely introduced the provisional and precautionary measures and injunctions in relation to ISPs.[4]

As it is evident the liability regime of the ISPs regarding copyright infringement lacked comprehensive regulation, necessitating protection for copyright holders, the need for the new legislation became apparent. In pursuit of achieving this aim, CDSMD[5] was adopted, introducing two novelties in Art. 17: (a) the new category of the ISP—"online content-sharing service providers" (hereinafter: OCSSPs), and (b) the new liability regime for OCSSPs. Nevertheless, shortly after the adoption of CDSMD the Digital Service Act (hereinafter: DSA)[6] was adopted in 2022, aiming to create a safer digital environment for users by revising the ECD with regard to ISPs' liability.

Accordingly, two separate pieces of legislation (the DSA and the CDSMD) with different legal effect (regulation v. directive[7]), were adopted in a very short period—both governing ISPs' liability regime. Hence, two copyright-related questions are raised; first, whether these two pieces of legislation regulate the same category of ISP; second, if they do regulate the same ISP categories, is there an intersection between them. Addressing these questions, the chapter will initially scrutinise OCSSP as a category of ISPs, then present the relevant shortcomings of Art. 17 of the CDSMD, focusing on liability exemption regime, and general monitoring problem. After that, the chapter will scrutinise the DSA provisions that intersect with Art. 17 of the CDSMD, analysing the potential impact and legal consequences of the DSA on Art. 17 of the CDSMD. Special interest will be dedicated to the possibility of the collective management organisations (hereinafter: CMOs) taking the role and being a relevant player in the application of the "trusted flagger" as a new legal category.

2 The Evolutionary Journey of the CDSMD

The roots of the creation of the CDSMD date back to 2013, when the Public Consultation on the Review of EU Copyright Rules[8] were held with the primary goal of revising and modernising the EU copyright regime for the digital single

[4]Ferri (2020), pp. 4–5.

[5]Directive (EU) 2019/790 of the European Parliament and of the Council of 17 April 2019 on copyright and related rights in the Digital Single Market and amending Directives 96/9/EC and 2001/29/EC, OJ L 130, 17 May 2019, Recital 3 and 61.

[6]Regulation (EU) 2022/2065 of the European Parliament and of the Council of 19 October 2022 on a Single Market For Digital Services and amending Directive 2000/31/EC, OJ L 277, 27 October 2022, pp. 1–102.

[7]See more: De Witte (2008), pp. 79–108.

[8]European Commission (2013).

market.[9] The Consultation resulted in the Commission's Report,[10] which was followed by the Commission's "white paper"[11] and the Communication "Towards a modern, more European copyright framework".[12] The proposal for a CDSMD was published in September 2016.[13] Three years later, in 2019, the official version of the CDSMD was approved by the Council.[14]

The CDSMD's primary aim lies in harmonising the EU law applicable to copyright and related rights, with the central focus on "digital and cross-border uses of protected content".[15] The secondary aim is to impose rules on exceptions and limitations to the copyright regime in order to ensure an efficient digital market.[16] Although the CDSMD introduced numerous changes to the existing EU copyright regime (e.g., text and data mining for the purposes of scientific research, collective management of out-of-commerce works, press publishers' right, etc.) which also deserve attention, the aim of this chapter is addressing Art. 17 of the CDSMD and its implications on OCSSPs liability regime.

3 General Shortcomings of Art. 17 of the CDSMD

The CDSMD introduced a new category of ISPs, the OCSSP, and a new liability regime for them in Art. 17 ("Use of protected content by online content-sharing service providers"). According to Art. 17, para. 1, OCSSPs can be directly liable for acts of communication or making available to the public when they give access to copyright protected works or other subject matter uploaded by their users, if there is no authorisation of the rightsholder.[17] This authorisation could be obtained through license agreements,[18] which shall extend to OCSSPs' users as long as they do not operate on a commercial basis.[19]

---

[9] Quintais (2019), p. 2.

[10] European Commission, Directorate General Internal Market and Services (2014).

[11] European Commission (2014).

[12] European Commission, Directorate-General for Communications Networks, Content and Technology (2015), Towards a modern, more European copyright framework, 9 December 2015, COM (2015) 626 final p. 10.

[13] European Commission, Directorate-General for Communications Networks, Content and Technology (2016), Proposal for a Directive of the European Parliament and of the Council on copyright in the Digital Single Market, 14 September 2016, COM(2016) 593 final, p. 10.

[14] European Commission (2019).

[15] CDSMD, Art. 1, para. 1.

[16] Ibid.

[17] CDSMD, Art. 17, para. 1.

[18] Ibid.

[19] Ibid., para. 2.

On the other side, OCSSPs are explicitly excluded from hosting "safe harbour"[20] under Art. 14 of the ECD[21], when the primary liability for OCSSPs is established. In this sense, Art. 17 of the CDSMD becomes *lex specialis* to the ECD.[22] Simultaneously, the provision imposes a complex set of cumulative rules in order to establish a liability exemption mechanism,[23] consisting of "best effort obligations" as preventive measures and the notice-and-stay-down and notice-and-take-down procedures,[24] analysed in detail in Section 5 of this chapter.

Furthermore, Art. 17 of the CDSMD encompasses various mitigation measures and safeguards. Following this, it mandates a proportionality assessment and the identification of relevant factors for adhering to OCSSPs' obligations.[25] A special regime for the newly established and minor OCSSPs is established.[26] Additionally, a set of mandatory exceptions mirroring user rights or freedoms is also outlined.[27] Then, there is a clarification that Art. 17 does not involve general monitoring, aligning with Art. 15 of the ECD.[28] Afterwards, it establishes a series of procedural safeguards, comprising an in-platform complaint and redress mechanism and regulations on out-of-court redress mechanisms.[29] Finally, it imposes an obligation to the European Commission (hereinafter: EC) to organise dialogues to discuss best practices for cooperation between OCSSPs and rightsholders.[30] These dialogues have resulted in the publication of an EC Guidance on the interpretation of Art. 17 of the CDSMD (hereinafter: Guidance on Art. 17 CDSMD).[31]

However, the above-mentioned Art. 17 suffers from several general deficiencies. Firstly, it introduces numerous obligations for OCSSPs and EU Member States. The issue is evident in the concentration of those complex and novel obligations within a single article, containing multiple paragraphs, without distinctness or subheadings to provide clarity and a systematic overview of the imposed obligations. Secondly, it lacks clear definitions of new legal categories, such as "best effort," "relevant and necessary information," and "sufficiently substantiated notice", leading to potential

[20] The principle of safe harbors provides immunity to ISPs for unlawful activities committed by users of their services, rather than for the ISPs' own actions, as long as the ISPs do not play an active role in those activities. See more: Madiega (2020), pp. 1–2; Rosati (2023), pp. 5–7.

[21] Ibid., para. 3.

[22] Quintais and Schwemer (2022), p. 196.

[23] CDSMD, Art. 17, para. 4.

[24] Geiger and Jütte (2021a), p. 523.

[25] CDSMD, Art. 17, para. 5.

[26] Ibid., para. 6.

[27] Ibid., para 7.

[28] Ibid., para 8.

[29] Ibid., para. 9.

[30] Ibid., para. 10.

[31] European Commission, Directorate-General for Communications Networks, Content and Technology (2021); Quintais et al. (2023a), p. 9.

differences in interpretation across EU Member States.[32] One may argue that vagueness is intentionally designed to create a framework within which regulated entities can develop their own effective regulatory solutions tailored to their specific services, acknowledging that no single standard can effectively address the diverse range of ISPs. However, it should not be overlooked that EU directives and regulations aim not only to harmonize EU law and judicial practice but also to prevent ISPs from independently establishing their own rules without state supervision.

Thirdly, there are no clear guidelines for the implementation of the new liability regime for OCSSPs, resulting in a wide margin of appreciation and thus undermining the aim of EU copyright harmonisation.[33] Finally, the provision's openness and lack of regulation may yield OCSSPs' self-regulation without state supervision. All of the above can have a negative impact on copyright holders, as well as end users.

Given that Section 5 is dedicated to the general monitoring problem and liability exemption mechanism under Art. 17, paras. 1–4 of the CDSMD, key points of Art. 17, paras. 7 and 9 of the CDSMD will be briefly referred in this part aiming to achieve a comprehensive understanding of ISP's liability regime and the problem of general monitoring.

In this context, it is essential to highlight that Art. 17, para. 7 of the CDSMD features both a general[34] and a specific[35] provision regarding exceptions and limitations to copyright. The general provision stipulates that the obligations outlined in para. 4, points b and c of Art. 17 should not impede user-uploaded content from being accessible, if such uploads do not violate copyright, including exceptions.[36] The specific provision imposes that users of OCSSPs shall be able to rely on the exceptions or limitations for (a) quotation, criticism, review, and (b) the use for the purpose of caricature, parody or pastiche.[37] Highlighting only these exceptions as an obligation, out of all others included in Art. 5, paras. 2 and 3 of the InfoSoc Directive, one could consider that these two specific sets of exceptions are of the greatest importance.[38] This is a concrete example of a wide margin of appreciation, which might undermine EU copyright harmonisation aim.

On the other side, this legal ambiguity and differing national legislations pose significant challenges for OCSSPs in adhering to the obligations outlined in Art. 17 of the CDSMD. Copyright is a territorial right, but internet does not recognise territorial borders. Consistently, the European Commission imposed that OCSSPs

[32] Quintais et al. (2023a), p. 8.

[33] Ibid., p. 3.

[34] First sub-paragraph of the Art. 17, para. 7 of the CDSMD.

[35] Second sub-paragraph of the Art. 17, para. 7 of the CDSMD.

[36] CDSMD, Art. 17, para. 7.

[37] Ibid.

[38] Geiger and Jütte (2021a), p. 533.

have to implement *ex ante* safeguards[39] to avoid over-blocking legal content.[40] Hence, the pressing question emerges, how can a single OCSSP adapt to diverse national legislations while safeguarding copyrights but also protecting rights of users. The possible solution might lie in implementing general monitoring for the OCSSPs' protection.

Nevertheless, when the removal of content occurs or access has been disabled, users of OCSSPs must have access to effective and expeditious complaint and redress mechanisms.[41] However, Art. 17, para. 9 of the CDSMD does not outline the specific design of these mechanisms, which is another example of a wide margin of appreciation in decision-making contributing to uncertainty in protecting users' rights. It is crucial to note that the absence of explicit guidelines regarding the content of the "statement of reasons" for removal or blocking, and timing of communication for those actions, may result in OCSSPs internal regulation without state oversight. While at first glance the link between this paragraph and the issue of general monitoring may not be apparent, it is important to bear in mind that exactly the amount of filtered content through monitoring ultimately influences the number of complaints directed towards OCSSPs. Anyway, this obstacle may be resolved through the DSA.[42]

4 The Flaws of the Central Player: OCSSP

Although the aim of this chapter is not to criticise the definition of the OCSSP, it is inevitable to refer to the central player in Art. 17 of the CDSMD.

The definition of the OCSSP at first glance introduces the new category of the ISP.[43] Despite this, the general category of the ISP is not new in the EU law. According to the ECD,[44] the ISP falls under the "information society service provider" term,[45] as an umbrella concept for different types of intermediaries based on their internet functions. Conversely, the InfoSoc Directive lacks the precise

[39] *Opinion Advocate General Saugmandsgaard Øe*, Court of Justice of European Union, Case C-401/19, 15 July 2021, ECLI:EU:C:2021:613; *Republic of Poland v European Parliament and Council of the European Union,* Court of Justice of European Union, Case C-401/19, 26 April 2022, ECLI:EU:C:2022:297, paras. 84–89.

[40] Quintais et al. (2023b), p. 8.

[41] CDSMD, Art. 17, para. 9.

[42] Digital Service Act, Arts. 20 and 21. See more: 7.1. Unveiling potential impact on the partially regulated segments in Art. 17 of the CDSMD.

[43] "The first subparagraph of this paragraph shall not affect the possible application of Article 14(1) of Directive 2000/31/EC to those service providers for purposes falling outside the scope of this Directive" (CDSMD, Art. 17, para. 3).

[44] ECD, Arts. 12, 13 and 15.

[45] Kunda (2021), p. 259.

definition of ISP within its provisions.[46] With the enthronement of the CDSMD, OCSSP is defined under Art. 2, para. 1, point 6,[47] with further interpretation guidance provided in Recitals 62 and 63 to the CDSMD. Essentially, OCSSPs constitute a subset of ISPs encompassed by hosting services, previously governed by the ECD, the InfoSoc Directive and the Enforcement Directive.[48]

The OCSSP is an ISP whose primary or one of the main purposes is storing, uploading, sharing, and providing public access to a large amount of copyright protected content directed to, directly or indirectly, generating profit.[49] Indubitably, the definition includes a number of undefined legal standards as "(one of) main purpose(s)", "large amount", "profit-making purpose", which are going to require a case-by-case assessment,[50] resulting in meaningful borderline cases that could affect larger, medium and small-sized platforms.[51] The above implies possible uneven jurisprudence when assessing which ISP meets the conditions to be categorised as an OCSSP.

Furthermore, Recital 62 highlights that the CDSMD should focus only on online services that "play an important role on the market" by competing with other services for the same audiences.[52] While Recitals are non-binding, each country has discretion in incorporating the Directive into national law, illustrating another potential inconsistency in defining OCSSPs. The syntagm "important role on the market" is unclear and vague. Clearly, the provider's market influence will be assessed based on the amount of protected content files it offers access to, and by the audience size.[53] This ambiguity could result in excluding medium and small ISPs from the OCSSP classification or narrowing its definition, potentially leaving rightsholders unprotected. Imposing the competition rule for the same audience could lead to the question of whether OCSSP can be determined throughout the category of copyright works.[54] All of the above leaves open questions.

---

46 Only mentioned in Recital 56 and Art. 8, para 1 of the InfoSoc Directive exclusively with regulation of the possibility of issuing injunctions towards ISP as an "intermediary who carries a third party's infringement of a protected work or other subject-matter in a network.

47 "Means a provider of an information society service of which the main or one of the main purposes is to store and give the public access to a large amount of copyright-protected works or other protected subject matter uploaded by its users, which it organises and promotes for profit-making purposes" (CDSMD, Art. 2, para 1, point 6).

48 ECD, Art. 14, para. 1; InfoSoc Directive, Recital 16 in connection with 59; Enforcement Directive, Art. 9, para. 1 and art. 11; Quintais and Schwemer (2022), p. 195.

49 This is achieved through organising, categorising, and promoting the content, including targeted promotion (CDSMD, Recital 62).

50 Quintais et al. (2023b), p. 12.

51 Quintais et al. (2024), pp. 160–161.

52 Ibid., Recital 62.

53 Ibid., Art. 17, para. 5 and Recital 63.

54 Leistner (2020), p. 145.

Alternatively, some of ISPs should be excluded from the scope of Art. 17 of the CDSMD.[55] The exclusions cover ISPs the main characteristics of which do not encompass enabling users to upload a large amount of copyright-protected works with the aim to obtain profit.[56] Given that these are recommendations prefaced with "should be", the manner of implementation remains up to each country to decide.

5 The General Monitoring Problem and the New Liability Regime Under Art. 17 of the CDSMD

There is a systematic link between paras. 1 and 4 of Art. 17 of the CDSMD. While the former establishes primary liability shared by OCSSP and its users, the latter would transform to secondary liability for OCSSP, if it failed to obtain authorisation from rightsholders.

Nevertheless, it is important to emphasize that there is problem of recognizing the difference between the primary and secondary liability between the EU member states.[57] Namely, the latest examples of misunderstanding the difference between the primary and secondary liability are decisions of Rome Court of First Instance in cases *RTI v Vimeo*[58] and *RTI v Kontakte*[59], deciding that any activity of OCSSPs such as filtering, selecting, indexing, organizing ect. excludes liability. Such a general conclusion is not in accordance with CJEU practice, especially the *YouTube and Cyando* case, where it was clearly established that these activities are taken into account only when it comes to illegal content -not just any content- and when these actions aim to reliably and effectively countering its presence.[60] In particular, it should be noted that the *YouTube and Cyando* case relates to primary liability.[61]

5.1 Primary Liability of OCSSPs

Considering the obligation to obtain the rightsholder's authorisation to avoid primary liability, the foremost challenge that arises for OCSSPs is how to qualify which user-uploaded content on their platform is copyright (un)protected. This

[55] CDSMD, Recital 62; see more: Husovec and Quintais (2021), p. 331.

[56] CDSMD, Recital 62.

[57] Rosati (2024b).

[58] *RTI v Vimeo,* Rome Court of First Instance Republic of Italy, Case 5700/2023, 7 April 2023.

[59] *RTI v Kontakte*, Rome Court of First Instance Republic of Italy, Case 14531/2023, 12 October 2023.

[60] *YouTube and Cyando*, Court of Justice of European Union, Joined Cases C-682/18 and C-683/18, 22 June 2021, ECLI:EU:C:2021:503, paras. 102 and 113.

[61] See more in: Rosati (2024b).

undoubtedly might lead to the conclusion that OCSSP will need to establish tools (e.g. automated filters) to monitor all circulating content on the platform, potentially resulting in general monitoring. In that case, a new issue arises—the development of these tools to identify copyright-protected content should not be solely entrusted to OCSSPs' self-regulation, due to the lack of transparency and any oversight from public authorities.[62] All of the above result in a new challenge for OCSSPs which could further result in a potential problem for users. Namely, automated filters carry the risk of generating "false positives",[63] struggling to discern contextual nuances, crucial for distinguishing *prima facie* infringements from exceptions discussed previously,[64] necessitating human judgment as *ex post* safeguard.[65] Hence, automated filtering may risk curtailing artistic freedom by potentially over-blocking legal content.[66] This is especially noticeable, since the research indicates a high percentage of "self-censorship" among user-creators as a result of algorithmic filtering.[67] On the other hand, this implies that OCSSPs may need to recruit copyright law experts for *ex post* checking, placing a significant burden on them.

Therefore, bearing in mind the general monitoring issue, it is not only about blocking of legal copyright-related content that comes to the fore, but these actions can also violate other human rights that are not exclusively related to copyright, such as the right to conduct business, the right to freedom of expression,[68] the right to information.[69] It is important to emphasize that a special problem is the lack of a legal definition of general monitoring, both in ECD and DSA, and in CDSMD. The key question is whether "general monitoring" in Art. 15, para. 1 of ECD has the same meaning as in Art. 17, para. 8 of CDSMD. This issue is crucial, given the CJEU's link between the prohibition of general monitoring and human rights protection.[70]

In order to facilitate the position of OCSSPs and enable more efficient implementation, the Guidance on Art. 17 CDSMD made two suggestions. First, the "manifestly infringing" standard should be applied, along with several optional criteria,[71] to clarify when platforms' algorithmic enforcement aligns with users'

[62] *Opinion Advocate General Saugmandsgaard Øe*, Court of Justice of European Union, Case C-401/19, 15 July 2021, ECLI:EU:C:2021:613, para. 212.

[63] Labelling content as copyright infringing even it is lawful.

[64] See more: Section 3. General shortcomings of the Art. 17 of the CDSMD.

[65] Ibid.; Geiger and Jütte (2021a), p. 533.

[66] Geiger and Jütte (2021a), p. 533; Keller (2020).

[67] Quintais et al. (2024), p. 171.

[68] *Delfi AS v Estonia*, European Court of Human Rights, App no. 64569/09, 16 June 2015, para. 67.

[69] See more: Senftleben and Angelopoulos (2020) p. 7; Golunova (2022) p. 62; Keller (2021) pp. 4–6.

[70] Senftleben and Angelopoulos (2020) p. 7.

[71] Involving the size of the identified content used in the upload, the proportion of matching content relative to the entire upload (e.g., whether the matched content is used alone or with other content), and the degree of modification to the work (e.g., whether the upload partially matches identified

ability to upload legal content or utilise exceptions and limitations.[72] An initial observation indicates that a particular type of *ex ante* automated filtering will be introduced. Additionally, while the EC deems the "manifestly infringing" standard as "reasonable" and "practical", the term lacks a clear legal definitions or interpretation.[73] The same issue is notable within Art. 14, para. 1 of ECD where definition of "illegal activity or information" is lacking, as well as in DSA in Arts. 6 and 8.

Moreover, this new "manifestly infringing" standard extends beyond the text of the CDSMD, potentially leading to subjective interpretations and further ambiguity. Nonetheless, the Court asserts that filtering or blocking systems are permissible only if they can differentiate between lawful and unlawful content without needing independent evaluation by OCSSPs,[74] which could be problematic bearing in mind limitations of the algorithmic system, especially taking into account the different national solutions in whose areas OCSSPs services are available for users.

In order to avoid primary liability, the process of gaining authorisation should be implemented through collective licensing by concluding contracts with CMOs as a minimum requirement.[75] However, this obligation also depends on the impact and size of OCSSPs. Namely, larger OCSSPs are required not only to proactively engage with CMOs and "easily identifiable" rightsholders, but to reach out to other rightsholders.[76] In any case, the meaning of "easily identifiable rightsholder" is not defined. Furthermore, OCSSPs do not have to obtain a separate authorisation when rightsholders have already explicitly authorised users to upload content.[77] However, the CDSMD also indicates that no presumption applies in favour of OCSSPs that users have, in all cases, obtained all the necessary authorisations for the content they upload,[78] which imposes again a significant burden on OCSSPs.

Despite the possibility of going unnoticed, Art. 17, para. 2 of the CDSMD introduces an intriguing provision. Namely, it imposes that if OCSSPs' user is operating on a commercial basis or its activity generates a substantial income, the authorisation from CMOs or rightsholders do not extend from OCSSPs to the user.[79] While this may seem initially straightforward, the challenge for OCSSPs emerges in determining whether each user engages in commercial activity and to what extent. The latter implicates that in order to determine this fact and to be exempted from

---

content due to user modifications). See more: European Commission, Directorate-General for Communications Networks, Content and Technology (2021), p. 21.

[72] CDSMD, Art. 17, para. 7; Geiger and Mangal (2022), p. 933.

[73] Geiger and Jütte (2021b), p. 630.

[74] Quintais et al. (2024), p. 161.

[75] European Commission, Directorate-General for Communications Networks, Content and Technology (2021), p. 9; Geiger and Mangal (2022), p. 22.

[76] European Commission, Directorate-General for Communications Networks, Content and Technology (2021), p. 9.

[77] Geiger and Mangal (2022), p. 7.

[78] CDSMD, Recital 67.

[79] Ibid., Art. 17, para. 2.

primary liability, the solution may lie in general monitoring. Even further potentially arising the privacy and personal data protection problem, considering that OCSSPs will have to collect, filter and store personal data of every user, including especially data on business activities, clients and their income. The situation is getting complicated, given that the Guidance on Art. 17 CDSMD stipulates that the concept of "substantial economic income" of OCSSPs' user cannot be determined quantitatively but must be resolved in a case-by-case approach,[80] bearing in mind that the question of balancing between copyright, right to privacy and the right to conduct business comes clearly to the fore and may lead to an imbalance.

5.2 *Secondary Liability of OCSSPs (Notice-and-Take-Down, Notice-and-Stay-Down)*

The liability regime established under Art. 17, para. 4 only applies in the absence of the authorisation from Art. 17, para. 1 of the CDSMD.[81] Hence, OCSSPs can be exempted from liability under three cumulative conditions: (a) they have made "best efforts" to obtain authorisation; (b) they have made them "in accordance with high industry standards of professional diligence, to ensure the unavailability of copyright-protected content for which the rightsholders have provided the relevant and necessary information"; and (c) in any event, took prompt action upon receipt of a "sufficiently substantiated notice" from the rightsholders to either block access to or remove the notified content from their platforms and exerted utmost efforts to prevent their future uploads.[82]

Analysing the first cumulative condition, there are a few remarks. The term "best efforts" is undefined and vague, resulting in a lack of foreseeability and illustrating a wide margin of appreciation in decision-making, sparking concerns that disparate transpositions may undermine harmonisation, which was already proved in practice.[83] However, "best efforts" are measured through the engagement of OCSSPs towards CMOs and other rightsholder—a shortcoming discussed above.[84]

If "best efforts" to obtain authorisations resulted unsuccessfully, OCSSPs incur the other two cumulative obligations: (a) to remove unauthorised content upon notice, (b) and prevent their future uploads. Analysing the above, this request should not lead to general monitoring, given that actions are taken when a notice is obtained. The obligation to remove content becomes problematic when it is combined with the

[80] European Commission, Directorate-General for Communications Networks, Content and Technology (2021), p. 7.

[81] Ibid., p. 8.

[82] CDSMD, Art. 17, para. 4.

[83] Larroyed (2020); Hümmer (2022).

[84] See more: 5.1. Primary Liability of OCSSPs

obligation to prevent future uploads of content that has been removed.[85] This obligation could lead again to the possibility of general monitoring.[86] In order to avoid this, the future unavailability cannot be extended *ad infinitum*, and the obligation to prevent uploads must be targeted.[87] In addition, the provision does not prescribe what defines "relevant and necessary information"[88] and "sufficiently substantiated notice",[89] which are further examples of shortcomings.

The CDSMD makes it very clear that new obligations should not lead to the duty to install general filtering systems that would monitor all uploads.[90] This view is supported by the Court of Justice of the European Union (hereinafter: "CJEU") in cases *Scarlet Extended*[91] and *Netlog*,[92] which argued that general monitoring imposed on ISPs by way of an injunction would conflict with various fundamental rights.[93] In another case, the CJEU concluded differently—if monitoring is "limited in terms of the subject and duration of the monitoring", an injunction is lawfully ordered.[94] Equivalent standard is notable in Glawischnig-Piesczek, as it likely demands a stricter interpretation for filtering audio-visual content on OCSSPs compared to textual defamatory posts on a social network.[95] On the other hand, the CDSMD requires in Art. 17, para. 8 that OCSSPs shall provide rightsholders with: (1) adequate information on the functioning of tools that they apply to ensure the unavailability of unauthorised content; and (2) an information when licensing agreements are concluded between ISPs and CMOs or rightsholders on the use of their content covered by the agreements,[96] obligations which are again undefined in the terms of implementation, vague, and ambiguous.[97]

[85] Geiger and Jütte (2021a), p. 538.

[86] *Scarlet Extended SA v Société belge des auteurs, compositeurs et éditeurs SCRL (SABAM),* Court of Justice of European Union, C 70/10, 24 November 2011, ECLI:EU:C:2011:771, paras. 36 and 40.

[87] Ibid.

[88] CDSMD, Art. 17, para. 4, point b.

[89] Ibid., point c.

[90] Ibid., Art. 17, para. 8.

[91] *Scarlet Extended SA v Société belge des auteurs, compositeurs et éditeurs SCRL (SABAM),* Court of Justice of European Union, C 70/10, 24 November 2011, ECLI:EU:C:2011:771, para. 36.

[92] *SABAM v Netlog*, Court of Justice of European Union, Case C-360/10, 16 February 2012, ECLI: EU:C:2012:85, para. 34.

[93] E.g. freedom of expression, right to receive or impart information, the right to protection of personal data and the freedom to conduct a business. See more: Gosztonyi (2020), pp. 133–144. Gosztonyi (2019), pp. 121–133.; Quintais (2022).

[94] *Tobias Mc Fadden v Sony Music Entertainment Germany GmbH, Court of Justice of European Union*, C-484/14, 15 September 2016, ECLI:EU:C:2016:689, para. 132; *L'Oréal and Others Case,* Court of Justice of European Union, C-324/09, 12 July 2011, EU:C:2010:757, para. 182.

[95] *Eva Glawischnig-Piesczek v Facebook Ireland Limited,* Court of Justice of European Union, Case C-18/18, 3 October 2019, ECLI:EU:C:2019:821.

[96] European Commission, Directorate-General for Communications Networks, Content and Technology (2021), p. 25.

[97] Peukert et al. (2022), p. 363.

However, considering all the obligations from Art. 17, para. 4 especially in relation to para. 7 of the CDSMD, everything indicates that OCSSPs might need to monitor all user-uploads to evade primary or secondary liability,[98] which was also approved in practice.[99] Even the European Copyright Society argues that this requirement would effectively amount to a general monitoring obligation.[100] The ISP aims to minimise its technical and legal engagement in user-copyright holder relationships to maximise its economic impact. If the ISP is required to monitor all the circulating content on its platform, its business model would be jeopardized.[101]

6 New Decade, New Rules: The DSA Enters the Stage

After 20 years of the ECD reign in the digital world, the EU, for the first time, adopted a Regulation imposing unified rules for ISPs. The ultimate goal of the DSA is to create a safer and trusted online environment that fosters innovation and protects fundamental rights in the EU.[102] A colossus of a regulation, the DSA consists of 156 Recitals and 93 Articles and shall apply as of 17 February 2024.[103] A bifurcated approach to regulation is applied.[104] On the one hand, Chapter II sets out a regime for the liability of ISPs revising the ECD.[105] The main difference from the previous legal regulation is the "Good Samaritan" rule,[106] the provision on orders to act against illegal content[107] and the provision to provide information.[108] On the other hand, Chapter III imposes "horizontal" due diligence obligations for a transparent and safe online environment, distinguishing obligations between different categories of providers.[109] Hence, the DSA introduces four categories of information society services providers: (1) intermediary services; (2) hosting services;

[98] Quintais et al. (2022).

[99] YouTube"s copyright transparency report revealed a significant disparity in copyright content moderation compared to other content types. In the first half of 2021, the platform received over 730 million unique claims or requests for copyright removal through its ContentID system, See more: YouTube (2022), p. 5; Dergacheva and Katzenbach (2024).

[100] Even the European Copyright Society (2020).

[101] Kunda (2021), p. 265; See more: Gosztonyi (2020), pp. 121–133.

[102] DSA, Art. 1, para. 1.

[103] Ibid., Art. 93, para. 2.

[104] Quintais and Schwemer (2022), p. 204.

[105] DSA, Art. 89, paras. 1 and 2.

[106] Ibid., Art. 7; Kuczerawy (2021).

[107] DSA, Art. 9.

[108] Ibid., Art. 10.

[109] Quintais and Schwemer (2022), p. 205.

(3) online platforms; and (4) very large online platforms or very large online search engines.[110]

This improvement in the regulation of the online environment would not be of concern if it were not for the fact that ISPs' obligations and responsibilities are simultaneously governed by legal acts of differing legal effect (regulation v. directive). Namely, both the CDSMD in Art. 17 and the DSA impose obligations on ISPs in relation to the illegal content uploaded by the users. Indeed, Art. 17 of the CDSMD is focused only on copyright protected content, while the DSA is focusing on illegal content in general but including copyright protected content.[111] It is notable that the CDSMD and the ECD, now DSA, take different regulatory approaches when addressing the liability of OCSSPs. Specifically, the CDSMD establishes a positive norm, defining the circumstances under which OCSSPs are liable for copyright infringements. In contrast, the ECD and DSA set forth a negative norm, specifying the service providers and situations in which they are exempt from liability for copyright violations.

One could argue that there is no intersection between the DSA and the CDSMD since *lex specialis derogat legi generalis*. Yet, the situation is more intricate due to the fact that the DSA complements Art. 17 of the CDSMD and places new additional obligations on ISPs qualifying as OCSSPs,[112] as will be further addressed.

7 DSA and CDSM: Friends or Foes?

The key question for consideration is whether the DSA is applicable at all to OCSSPs. Suppose the answer to this question is affirmative, then two more key questions arise: (1) Does the DSA only regulate subject matter unregulated by Art. 17 of the CDSMD, or (2) Does it regulate even those parts that are left to Member States' margin of appreciation.[113] If the answers are affirmative, the subsequent quandary is whether the DSA will rectify the shortcomings in Art. 17 of the CDSMD or further exacerbate the system's complexity.

Answering the first question, one should bear in mind that Art. 17, para. 3, subpara. 2 of the CDSMD excludes the application of Art. 14 of the ECD (now Art. 6 of the DSA). This was confirmed by the CJEU in the case *YouTube and Cyando*,[114] concluding that YouTube could be at the same time and for some services (copyright-related content) categorised as an OCSSP and for others

[110] Ibid.

[111] DSA, Recital 12.

[112] Quintais and Schwemer (2022), p. 193.

[113] Ibid., pp. 191–193.

[114] *YouTube and Cyando*, Court of Justice of European Union, Joined Cases C-682/18 and C-683/18, 22 June 2021, ECLI:EU:C:2021:503, paras. 137 and 138.

(information or child abuse-related content) as a VLOP now in relation to the DSA.[115] This interpretation is in line with Art. 2, para. 3, point c of the DSA stipulating that the DSA does not call into question the already established EU copyright regime. Furthermore, Recital 11 to the DSA explains that the EU copyright regime and specific rules and procedures "should remain unaffected".

However, Recital 9, which precedes the earlier ones, provides guidance by setting out that the DSA should, in fact, complement but not affect the rules from other EU acts governing specific aspects of ISP's provision.[116] Hence, if one begins with the chronological examination of the DSA and Recital 9, the answer to the first question is positive in the end. In that case, the rules of the DSA may apply to subject matter that is not addressed by other EU acts (e.g., the CDSMD), as well as to issues where Member States have a margin of appreciation.[117] Therefore, a positive answer to the first question could result in a positive answer to the other two questions.

It is not deemed consequent that the EU legislator intended to completely exclude the application of the DSA in relation to Art. 17 of the CDSMD since these two legal acts are complementary. This conclusion could be further supported by applying the analogy with the YouTube case example. If that is not the case, then Member States could freely establish, for example, a national redress mechanism or nationally define terms such as "sufficiently substantiated notice" for copyright-related content. Meanwhile, for other types of content, they would adhere to the fully structured system outlined in the DSA. This approach would not only undermine the ultimate goal of the DSA,[118] but also place a significant burden on ISPs, forcing them to have different procedures depending on the content category and territory where they provide services. This may also create legal uncertainty for users. Nonetheless, if the answers to the above-mentioned questions are positive, it remains to address whether the DSA will rectify the shortcomings in Art. 17 of the CDSMD or further exacerbate the system's complexity.

7.1 *Unveiling the Potential Impact on Unregulated Segments in Art. 17 of the CDSMD*

As clarified above, the DSA will not fully replace Art. 17 of the CDSM but potentially complement unregulated segments in Art. 17 of the CDSMD. In regard to this, general monitoring ban or active fact-finding defined in Art. 8 of the DSA could be fully applied.[119] Based on the above, the rules on orders against illegal

[115] Quintais and Schwemer (2022), p. 202.

[116] Peukert et al. (2022), p. 361.

[117] Ibid.; Quintais and Schwemer (2022), p. 204; Rosati (2021), p. 67.

[118] "harmonised rules"—Art. 1 of the DSA.

[119] Art. 17, para. 8 of the CDSMD merely states that "the application of this Article shall not lead to any general monitoring obligation". It does not set aside the application of Art. 15 of the ECD.

content and orders to provide information in Arts. 9 and 10 of the DSA could also apply to OCSSPs.[120] These provisions introduce new obligations for ISPs' regarding court or administrative orders, which are not found in Art. 17 of the CDSMD. Precisely, given the nature of the provision and the aim to create a safer digital space, this could also be one of the reasons why the DSA should complement Art. 17 of the CDSMD.

Subsequent to the preceding conclusions, provisions under Section I of Chapter III ("Provisions applicable to all providers of intermediary services"), such as points of contact, legal representatives, terms and conditions, and especially transparency reporting obligations, with amplification in Arts. 24 and 42 of the DSA could as well apply to OCSSPs.[121]

However, a different situation applies to the "Good Samaritan" rule of Art. 7 of the DSA,[122] since it empowers actions to detect, identify, and remove illegal content or to take measures to comply with EU law requirements.[123] As discussed previously within OCSSPs" secondary liability, the CDSMD has already established preventative measures for addressing copyright infringement, leaving no space for applying the new "Good Samaritan" rule.[124] It is interesting that the rule "Good Samaritan" originates from the common law system, which was ultimately implemented in EU law through the DSA.[125]

7.2 Special Case of Trusted Flaggers

A noteworthy novelty is the obligation for providers of online platforms to collaborate with trusted flaggers in Art. 22 of the DSA. A trusted flagger is a legal entity that has proved to have particular expertise for detecting, identifying and notifying illegal content.[126]

Considering that the DSA complements the CDSMD, trusted flaggers may have a pivotal role for the OCCSPs in detecting the copyright protected content.[127] According to Recital 61 to the DSA, the status of a trusted flagger could be awarded to industry associations representing their members' interests. This potentially implies an opportunity to involve CMOs as potential trusted flaggers. On one side, CMOs represent the interests of numerous authors for a specific territory, containing databases for their entire repertoire with regard to a certain copyright works. On

[120] Quintais and Schwemer (2022), pp. 208–210.
[121] Ibid.
[122] Ibid., p. 207.
[123] DSA, Art. 7.
[124] Quintais and Schwemer (2022), pp. 208–210.
[125] Kosseff (2019), pp. 27–28 and 30; La Rosa and Mazzilli (2022).
[126] DSA, Recital 61 and Art. 22, para. 2.
[127] See more: Rosati (2024a), pp. 87–91; Goldman and Schwemer (2024), pp. 36–37.

another side, CMOs employ staff who possess specialized expertise in copyright matters.

Hence, this could ease OCSSP's obligations when detecting copyright protected content on platform mitigating liability and minimising the risk of over-blocking legal content. However, Art. 22, para. 1 of the DSA imposes that flagging should be realised through the notice-and-action mechanism of Art. 16 of the DSA.[128] This means that the applicability of Art. 19 in the context of OCSSPs depends on the answer to the question of whether the notice-and-action mechanism applies to OCSSPs. However, a corresponding category for end users or users-creator, such as a 'trusted user' or 'rusted user-creator' who experience negative effects of over-blocking, is lacking.[129] Furthermore, the DSA does not establish equal protection for all stakeholders involved. Whereas ISPs are protected whether individually or collectively, copyright holders can act individually or via trusted flaggers and through representative entities, end users such as readers are more limited since they can act only collectively.[130]

7.3 *Unveiling the Potential Impact on Partially Regulated Segments in Art. 17 of the CDSMD*

The question of the DSA application to the categories, such as notice-and-take-down and notice-and-stay-down mechanism,[131] that are nevertheless regulated by Art. 17 of the CDSMD but left to margin of appreciation of the Member States regarding implementation, is more ticklish due to overlapping of two EU acts with different legal forces.

The concrete problem of vagueness and lack of definitions is recognised even by the EC in Guidance on Art. 17 CDSMD, which, for example, recommends the content of "sufficiently substantiated notice" should follow the content of notice exposed in the Recommendation on Measures to Effectively Tackle Illegal Content Online.[132] This supports the argument that the DSA may complement Art. 17 of the CDSMD[133] since Art. 16 of the DSA (notice-and-action mechanism) specifies the elements of the user-notice for uploaded illegal content in detail. Taking into consideration the aim of the uniform rules relating to the ISP's liability

---

[128] Ibid., Art. 22, para 1.

[129] Quintais et al. (2022), pp. 371–372; Rosati (2024a), pp. 90–91.

[130] See more: Quintais et al. (2022), pp. 371–173.

[131] See more: 5.2. Secondary liability of OCSSPs (notice-and-take-down, notice-and-stay-down).

[132] European Commission, Directorate-General for Communications Networks, Content and Technology (2021), p. 16.

[133] Peukert et al. (2022), p. 362.

exemption,[134] everything suggests the potential application of the DSA rules to OCSSPs.[135]

Regarding transparency and utilisation of tools used to block or remove copyright-infringing content,[136] the ambiguous provision and the fact that users are informed about reasons of the removal only through a complaint and redress mechanism could as well indicate the DSA application. The DSA in Art. 17 (statement of reasons) outlines specific details regarding the content of explanations provided by ISPs when they restrict access to or ban users' content on a platform.[137] Further, the obligation of transparency regarding content moderation system and used tools are regulated in more detail by Art. 14 (Terms and Conditions), Art. 15 (Transparency reporting obligations for providers of intermediary services) and Art. 24 (Transparency reporting obligations for providers of online platforms) of the DSA. However, one should bear in mind that private legal entities become "executors" of obligations imposed through the DSA, which they will probably implement in internal acts.[138]

Comprehensive internal complaint mechanisms and out-of-court dispute resolution processes are set in Arts. 19 and 20 of the DSA. Such mechanisms for OCSSPs are regulated in Art. 17, para. 9 of the CDSMD, albeit in less detail. Both the DSA and Art. 17 of the CDSMD specify that these internal complaint mechanisms must be effective, processed promptly, and involve human review.[139] However, the DSA provides more detailed requirements, including user-friendliness and a six-month window for filing complaints following takedown decisions.[140] Therefore, the DSA may complement the deficiencies of Art. 17, para. 9 of the CDSMD, otherwise all of the above would make the position of OCSSPs more difficult, as already described in the YouTube case example. Practically, platforms would need to broaden their reporting systems to encompass copyright infringement, alongside other forms of illegal content,[141] which could also affect users' rights.

8 Conclusion

Following a decade-long absence of uniform rules concerning liability regime for copyright infringement by ISPs, two pivotal legal documents emerged within just three years. On the one hand, Art. 17 of the CDSMD came to the stage of

[134] DSA, Art. 1, para. 2, point b.

[135] Quintais and Schwemer (2022), p. 210.

[136] DSA, Art. 14; see more in: Quintais et al. (2022), pp. 12–14.

[137] DSA, Art. 17, para. 3.

[138] Peukert (2021), pp. 22–28.

[139] CDSMD, Art. 17, para. 9 in connection to the DSA, Arts. 20 and 21.

[140] DSA, Arts. 20 and 21.

[141] Quintais and Schwemer (2022), p. 210.

establishing a new liability regime for copyright infringement by "new" category of ISPs. However, it is inevitable to note that Art. 17 of the CDSMD contains several shortcomings, which have promptly stirred turbulences among various stakeholders and led to court ruling. On the other hand, the EU legislator introduced the new Regulation, the DSA, establishing a liability regime for four categories of ISPs regarding the upload of illegal content in general, including content protected by copyright.

As a result, there are two pieces of legislation governing ISPs' liability regime concerning copyright protected content. Although the chapter advocated for the opinion that the DSA could have a complementary effect, given that it is *lex generalis*. However, the application of the DSA started only on 17 February 2024. Hence, a clear position has not yet been taken as to whether it can indeed complement Art. 17 of the CDSMD. If one takes into account the purposive interpretation of the DSA, it should not lead to the exclusion of the DSA's complementary effect on Art. 17 of the CDSMD, especially taking into consideration Recital 9 of the DSA.

Nevertheless, the DSA does leave unaffected the established liability regime from Art. 17 of the CDSMD (liability exemption mechanism). While the DSA has provided definitions for some previously undefined terms, other shortcomings such as the potential issue of general monitoring are still unresolved. Essentially, the DSA could address some of the weaknesses of Art. 17 of the CDSMD, or potentially provide better protection of users' rights and copyright holders through the introduction of the "trusted flaggers". The outcome is an elevated responsibility for OCSSPs, marked by increased liability and obligations concerning the content they host and the services they provide, alongside a heightened emphasis on ensurance rights of copyright holders. However, the end users and user-creators are still not fully protected, due to lack of category such as "trusted user" and equal possibilities of protection. The rights of users affected by over-blocking, as well as the rights of readers, are frequently treated as secondary. This approach is unjustifiable, especially given that the DSA is intended to create a secure digital environment where the fundamental rights of all users are upheld, creating the necessity for improved protection regulation.

Both the DSA and the CDSMD are new and highly complex legal documents, imposing a multitude of obligations on OCSSPs and EU Member States. However, there is still significant grey area which affect many of ISPs hard to legally categorize as OCCSPs, urging clearer guidelines for OCSSPs definition. This multi-layered legal framework that overlaps and its complexity is likely to exacerbate the existing liability system for OCSSPs, especially bearing in mind different national implementation of legal acts. Furthermore, one should not forget that the functioning of OCSSPs includes the processing of personal data, as well as the use of algorithms, which further includes the possible application of the General Data Protection Regulation and Artificial Intelligence Act, further complicating the application of legal rules. Clarity may only emerge over time, through the adoption and implementation, particularly with the guidance of court rulings addressing uncertainties. One thing is certain—the development of the online world and the scope of the legal issues that encompass represents "timeless poetry of working land"[142] for all of us, always bringing new challenges and battles to cope with.

Legal Documents

European Commission (2013) Copyright – Commission launches public consultation https://ec.europa.eu/commission/presscorner/detail/en/IP_13_1213

European Commission (2019) Copyright Reform Clears Final Hurdle: Commission Welcomes Approval of Modernised Rules Fit for Digital Age, 19 April 2019. https://ec.europa.eu/commission/presscorner/detail/en/IP_19_2151

European Commission (2014) White Paper A Copyright Policy For Creativity And Innovation In The European Union. https://www.editionmultimedia.fr/wp-content/uploads/2014/09/Draft-du-Copyright-White-Paper-CE-Barnier-June-2014.pdf

European Commission, Directorate General Internal Market and Services (2014) Report on the responses to the Public Consultation on the Review of the EU Copyright Rules. https://digital-strategy.ec.europa.eu/en/library/modernisation-eu-copyright-rules-useful-documents

European Commission, Directorate-General for Communications Networks, Content and Technology (2021) Guidance on Article 17 of Directive 2019/790 on Copyright in the Digital Single Market European Parliament and European Council, 6 June 2021. https://eur-lex.europa.eu/legal-content/EN/TXT/PDF/?uri=CELEX:52021DC0288

European Commission, Directorate-General for Communications Networks, Content and Technology (2016) Proposal for a Directive of the European Parliament and of the Council on copyright in the Digital Single Market, 14 September 2016, COM(2016) 593 final

European Commission, Directorate-General for Communications Networks, Content and Technology (2015) Towards a modern, more European copyright framework, 9 December 2015, COM (2015) 626 final

Directive (EU) 2000/31/EC of the European Parliament and of the Council of 8 June 2000 on certain legal aspects of information society services, in particular electronic commerce, in the Internal Market, OJ L 178, 17 July 2000, p. 1–16

Directive (EU) 2001/29/EC of the European Parliament and of the Council of 22 May 2001 on the harmonisation of certain aspects of copyright and related rights in the information society, OJ L 167, 22 June 2001, p. 10–19

Directive (EU) 2004/48/EC of the European Parliament and of the Council of 29 April 2004 on the enforcement of intellectual property rights (OJ L 157, 30.4.2004), OJ L 195, 2 June 2004, p. 16–25 (2004).

[142] Millet (1857).

Directive (EU) 2019/790 of the European Parliament and of the Council of 17 April 2019 on copyright and related rights in the Digital Single Market and amending Directives 96/9/EC and 2001/29/EC, OJ L 130, 17 May 2019, p. 92–125

Regulation (EU) 2022/2065 of the European Parliament and of the Council of 19 October 2022 on a Single Market For Digital Services and amending Directive 2000/31/EC, OJ L 277, 27 October 2022, p. 1–102

Case Law

L'Oréal and Others Case, Court of Justice of European Union, Case C-324/09, 12 July 2011, EU:C:2010:757

Delfi AS v Estonia, European Court of Human Rights, App no. 64569/09, 16 June 2015

Eva Glawischnig-Piesczek v Facebook Ireland Limited, Court of Justice of European Union, Case C-18/18, 3 October 2019, ECLI:EU:C:2019:821

Opinion Advocate General Saugmandsgaard Øe, Court of Justice of European Union, Case C-401/19, 15 July 2021, ECLI:EU:C:2021:613

Republic of Poland v European Parliament and Council of the European Union Case, Court of Justice of European Union, Case C-401/19, 26 April 2022, ECLI: EU:C:2022:297

RTI v Kontakte, Rome Court of First Instance Republic of Italy, Case 14531/2023, 12 October 2023

RTI v Vimeo, Rome Court of First Instance Republic of Italy, Case 5700/2023, 7 April 2023

SABAM v Netlog, Court of Justice of European Union, C-360/10, 16 February 2012, ECLI:EU:C:2012:85

Scarlet Extended SA v Société belge des auteurs, compositeurs et éditeurs SCRL (SABAM), Court of Justice of European Union C 70/10, 24 November 2011, ECLI:EU:C:2011:771

Tobias Mc Fadden v Sony Music Entertainment Germany GmbH, Court of Justice of European Union, C-484/14, 15 September 2016, ECLI:EU:C:2016:689

YouTube and Cyando, Court of Justice of European Union, Joined Cases C-682/18 and C-683/18, 22 June 2021, ECLI:EU:C:2021:503

References

Literature

De Witte B (2008) Legal instruments and law-making in the Lisbon Treaty. In: Griller S, Ziller J (eds) The Lisbon Treaty. Schriftenreihe der Österreichischen Gesellschaft für Europaforschung

(ECSA Austria)/European Community Studies Association of Austria Publication Series. Springer, Vienna, pp 79–108

Dergacheva D, Katzenbach C (2024) Copyright Moderation on YouTube following the implementation of Article 17 CDSMD. Kluwer Copyright Blog. 15 August 2024 https://copyrightblog.kluweriplaw.com/2024/08/14/copyright-moderation-on-youtube-following-the-implementation-of-article-17-cdsmd/

Ferri F (2020) The Dark Side(S) of the EU Directive on Copyright and related rights in the digital single market. China-EU Law J 7(1–4):21–38. https://doi.org/10.1007/s12689-020-00089-5

European Commission (2013) Copyright – Commission launches public consultation. https://ec.europa.eu/commission/presscorner/detail/en/IP_13_1213

European Commission (2019) Copyright Reform Clears Final Hurdle: Commission Welcomes Approval of Modernised Rules Fit for Digital Age, 19 April 2019. https://ec.europa.eu/commission/presscorner/detail/en/IP_19_2151 Accessed 16 Feb 2014

European Commission (2014) White Paper A Copyright Policy For Creativity And Innovation In The European Union. https://ec.europa.eu/commission/presscorner/detail/en/IP_19_2151 Accessed 5 Feb 2024

Geiger C, Jütte BJ (2021a) Platform liability under Article 17 of the copyright in the digital single market directive, automated filtering and fundamental rights: an impossible match. GRUR Int 70(6):517–543. https://doi.org/10.1093/grurint/ikab037

Geiger C, Jütte BJ (2021b) Towards a virtuous legal framework for content moderation by digital platforms in the EU? The Commission's Guidance on Article 17 CDSM Directive in the Light of the YouTube/Cyando Judgement and the AG's Opinion in C-401/19. Eur Intell Prop Rev 43(10):625–635

Geiger C, Mangal N (2022) Regulating creativity online: proposal for an EU copyright institution. GRUR Int J Eur Int IP Law 71(10):933–951. (SSRN 1-34)

Goldman E, Schwemer S (2024) How the DMCA anticipated the DSA's due process obligations. In: Quintais JP (ed) From the DMCA to the DSA A transatlantic dialogue on online platform regulation and copyright. Verfassungsbooks, Berlin, pp 35–42

Golunova V (2022) In tech we trust? Fixing the evolutionary interpretation by the Court of Justice of the prohibition of general monitoring in the era of automated content moderation. In: de la Sierra S (ed) Digital media governance and supranational courts: selected issues and insights from the European Judiciary Psychogiopoulou E. Edward Elgar Publishing, Cheltenham, pp 53–71

Gosztonyi G (2019) How the European Court of Human Rights contributed to understanding liability issues of internet service providers. In: Annales Universitatis Scientiarum Budapestinensis de Rolando Eötvös Nominatae – Sectio Iuridica, Tomus LVIII Annus, pp 121–133

Gosztonyi G (2020) The contribution of the Court of Justice of the European Union to a better understanding the liability and monitoring issues regarding intermediary service providers. In: Annales Universitatis Scientiarum Budapestinensis de Rolando Eötvös Nominatae – Sectio Iuridica, Tomus LIX Annus, pp 133–144

Hümmer F (2022) Implications From C-401/19 for National Transpositions in the Light of Freedom of Expression. Kluwer Copyright Blog, 1 November 2022. https://copyrightblog.kluweriplaw.com/2022/11/01/implications-from-c-401-19-for-national-transpositions-in-the-light-of-freedom-of-expression/

Husovec M, Quintais JP (2021) How to license Article 17? Exploring the implementation options for the new EU rules on content-sharing platforms under the copyright in the digital single market directive. GRUR Int 70(4):325–348. https://doi.org/10.1093/grurint/ikaa200

Keller D (2020) Empirical evidence of over-removal by internet companies under intermediary liability laws: an updated list. 8 February 2021. https://cyberlaw.stanford.edu/blog/2021/02/empirical-evidence-over-removal-internet-companies-under-intermediary-liability-laws/

Keller D (2021) Written evidence submitted by Daphne Keller, Director of Program on Platform Regulation (OSB0057), 20 September 2021. https://committees.parliament.uk/writtenevidence/39173/pdf/

Kosseff J (2019) The 26 words that created the internet. Cornell University Press, New York

Kuczerawy, A (2021) The good Samaritan that wasn't: voluntary monitoring under the (draft) digital services act. Verfassungsblog: On Matters Constitutional, 12 January 2021. https://doi.org/10.17176/20210112-181758-0

Kunda I (2021) Međunarodni privatnopravni odnosi. In: Mišćenić E (ed) Evropsko privatno pravo. Školska knjiga, Zagreb, pp 228–285

La Rosa A, Mazzilli MG (2022) DSA: the European 'good samaritan' rule and the 'safe harbour' regime, 24 March 2022. https://www.lexology.com/library/detail.aspx?g=889e875c-9f43-477d-8b3b-7d17fa0e3499

Larroyed AA (2020) When Translations Shape Legal Systems: How Misguided Translations Impact Users and Lead to Inaccurate Transposition – the Case of 'Best Efforts' Under Article 17 DCDSM. Social Science Research Network, 1 January 2020. https://doi.org/10.2139/ssrn.3740066

Leistner M (2020) European copyright licensing and infringement liability under Art. 17 DSM-Directive. Zeitschrift Für Geistiges Eigentum 12(2):126–212. https://doi.org/10.1628/zge-2020-0008

Madiega T (2020) Reform of the EU liability regime for online intermediaries. Background on the forthcoming Digital Services Act. European Parliamentary Research Service, pp 1–20. https://www.europarl.europa.eu/RegData/etudes/IDAN/2020/649404/EPRS_IDA(2020)649404_EN.pdf

Millet J-F (1857) The gleaners. Musée d'Orsay, Paris

Peukert A (2021) Five reasons to be skeptical about the DSA. In: Richter H, Straub M, Tuchtfeld E (eds) To break up or regulate big tech? Avenues to constrain private power in the DSA/DMA Package, no. 21–25. Max Planck Institute for Innovation & Competition, Munich, pp 1–112

Peukert A et al (2022) European copyright society – comment on copyright and the digital services act proposal. IIC - Int Rev Intell Prop Compet Law 53(3):358–376. https://doi.org/10.1007/s40319-022-01154-1

Quintais JP (2019) The new copyright in the digital single market directive: a critical look. Soc Sci Res Netw, 1 January 2019

Quintais JP (2022) Article 17 survives, but freedom of expression safeguards are key: C-401/19 – Poland V Parliament and Council. Kluwer Copyright Blog, 26 April 2022. https://copyrightblog.kluweriplaw.com/2022/04/26/article-17-survives-but-freedom-of-expression-safeguards-are-key-c-401-19-poland-v-parliament-and-council/

Quintais JP, Schwemer SF (2022) The interplay between the digital services act and sector regulation: how special is copyright? Eur J Risk Regul 13(2):191–217. https://doi.org/10.1017/err.2022.1

Quintais JP, Appelman N, Fahy R (2022) Using terms and conditions to apply fundamental rights to content moderation. Soc Sci Res Netw, 1 January 2022. https://doi.org/10.2139/ssrn.4286147

Quintais JP, De Gregorio G, Magalhães JC (2023a) How platforms govern users' copyright-protected content: exploring the power of private ordering and its implications. Comput Law Secur Rev 48:1–25. https://doi.org/10.1016/j.clsr.2023.105792

Quintais JP et al (2023b) Copyright content moderation in the EU: conclusions and policy recommendations (D6.4). Zenodo (CERN European Organization for Nuclear Research), ReCreating Europe. https://doi.org/10.5281/zenodo.7774112

Quintais JP et al (2024) Copyright content moderation in the European Union: state of the art, ways forward and policy recommendations. IIC- Int Rev Intell Prop Compet Law 55:157–177. https://doi.org/10.1007/s40319-023-01409-5

Rosati E (2021) The digital services act and copyright enforcement: the case of Article 17 of the DSM Directive. In: Cappello M (ed) Unravelling the digital services act package. European Audiovisual Observatory, Strasbourg, pp 59–74. http://su.diva-portal.org/smash/record.jsf?

pid=diva2%3A1605131&c=60&searchType=LIST_LATEST&language=no&af=%5B%5D&aqe=%5B%5D

Rosati E (2023) Role, responsibility and liability of online intermediaries under EU IP law. In: Forthcoming ER, Calboli I (eds) Handbook of fashion law. Faculty of Law, Stockholm University Research Paper No 128, pp 1–23

Rosati E (2024a) The DSA's trusted flaggers: revolution, evolution, or mere Gattopardismo? In: Quintais JP (ed) From the DMCA to the DSA A transatlantic dialogue on online platform regulation and copyright. Verfassungsbooks, Berlin, pp 85–91

Rosati E (2024b) When in Rome, do as the Romans do? Rome court 'misinterprets' CJEU YouTube judgment and reduces criteria for primary liability of platform operators to checklist. The IPKat Blog, 5 March 2024. https://ipkitten.blogspot.com/2024/03/when-in-rome-do-as-romans-do-rome-court.html

Senftleben M, Angelopoulos C (2020) The Odyssey of the prohibition on general monitoring obligations on the way to the digital services act: between Article 15 of the E-Commerce Directive and Article 17 of the Directive on Copyright in the Digital Single Market. University of Amsterdam – University of Cambridge, pp 1–34

The European Copyright Society (2020) Comment of the European Copyright Society Selected Aspects of Implementing Article 17 of the Directive on Copyright in the Digital Single Market Into National Law. JIPITEC – J Intell Prop Inf Technol E-Commer Law 11(2):115–131. https://www.jipitec.eu/issues/jipitec-11-2-2020/5104/#recommended_citation

YouTube (2022) YouTube Copyright Transparency Report. https://www.digitalmusicnews.com/wp-content/uploads/2023/07/youtube-transparency-report-H2-2022.pdf Accessed 16 Feb 2024

MIX
Papier aus verantwortungsvollen Quellen
Paper from responsible sources
FSC® C105338

If you have any concerns about our products,
you can contact us on
ProductSafety@springernature.com

In case Publisher is established outside the EU,
the EU authorized representative is:
Springer Nature Customer Service Center GmbH
Europaplatz 3, 69115 Heidelberg, Germany

Printed by Libri Plureos GmbH
in Hamburg, Germany